The Theory of the Divine Right of Kings

THE THEORY

OF THE

DIVINE RIGHT OF KINGS.

London: C. J. CLAY AND SONS,
CAMBRIDGE UNIVERSITY PRESS WAREHOUSE,
AVE MARIA LANE.
Glasgow: 263, ARGYLE STREET.

Leipzig: F. A. BROCKHAUS.
New York: MACMILLAN AND CO.

Cambridge Historical Essays. No. ix.

THE THEORY

OF THE

DIVINE RIGHT OF KINGS

BY

J. NEVILLE FIGGIS, M.A.

LECTURER ON HISTORY IN S. CATHARINE'S COLLEGE, CAMBRIDGE.

PRINCE CONSORT DISSERTATION, 1892.

Cambridge:
AT THE UNIVERSITY PRESS.
1896

Cambridge:
PRINTED BY J. AND C. F. CLAY,
AT THE UNIVERSITY PRESS.

TO

THE MEMORY

OF

EDWARD HENRY MOULE.

EXTRACT FROM THE REGULATIONS FOR THE PRINCE CONSORT PRIZE.

"There shall be established in the University a prize, called the 'Prince Consort Prize,' to be awarded for dissertations involving original historical research."

"The Prize shall be open to members of the University who, at the time when their dissertations are sent in, have been admitted to a degree, and are of not more than four years' standing from admission to their first degree."

"Those dissertations which the adjudicators declare to be deserving of publication shall be published by the University, singly or in combination, in an uniform series, at the expense of the fund, under such conditions as the Syndics of the University Press shall from time to time determine."

PREFACE.

I HAVE to thank the Adjudicators of the Prince
Consort Prize for their kindness in permitting
me very much to expand, and entirely to rewrite, my
dissertation of four years ago. To the late Professor
Seeley in particular was due the suggestion, that I
should investigate French political theories in the
sixteenth century and endeavour to discover their
bearing on English thought. Even so, I am sensible
of the extreme inadequacy of this sketch. Within
any reasonable time it would be impossible to arrive
at a complete account of a doctrine, which has relation
to every political theory from mediæval to modern
times. At some future date, it may be within my
power to attempt a fuller account of the develop-
ments which political theory has undergone since
the later Middle Ages. This little essay is at most
a preliminary survey of the ground, and can lay
claim to neither finality nor completeness. With
the view of fixing attention, so far as possible, on
the main subject, I have avoided discussing in any

detail the origin and development of the rival
theories, such as the original compact and popular
sovereignty. On the other hand I have endeavoured
in many cases to give the means of verification of
statements as to the true nature and purpose of the
doctrines discussed, by putting into footnotes a few
of the more striking utterances of all parties. Lest
however the notes should be unduly heavy, I have
collected into an Appendix a small number of
passages illustrating the points which Chapters
VIII. and IX. are intended to elucidate.

To Mr R. A. Nicholson of Trinity College, for
his kindness in going through the whole book and
drawing up the list of Errata, and to other friends,
for help and suggestions, while the sheets were
passing the press, I tender my grateful thanks.

LIST OF AUTHORITIES CITED.

Allen, William, Cardinal, *Defence of the English Catholics*, 103.
Apologia Catholica, 109, 123.
Aquinas, S. Thomas,*De Regimine Principum*, 46, 48, 52, 59,148.
Barclay, William, *De Regno* (1600), 49, 119, 273.
       De Potestate Papae, see Goldasti.
Barnes, Robert, *Supplication to the most gracious Prince Henry VIII.*, 94.
       Men's constitutions bind not the conscience, 94.
Barrow, Isaac, *A Treatise of the Pope's Supremacy*, 201, 286.
Beaumont and Fletcher, *The Maid's Tragedy*, 10, 104.
Bellarminus, *De Romano Pontifice*, 161, 179, 184, 248.
       De Excusatione Barclaii, 179.
       De Translatione Imperii, 184.
       De Verbo Dei, 184.
Berkeley (Bishop George), *Discourse of Passive Obedience*, 171.
Bilson (Bishop Thomas), *The True Difference between Christian Subjection and Unchristian Rebellion*, 97.
Blackwood, William, *Apologia Pro Regibus* (1588), 10, 132–4.
       De Vinculo Religionis et Imperii, 11, 130, 131.
Bodin, Jean, *De la République* (1593), 121–8, 245.
Bolingbroke, Henry St John, Viscount, *Works*, 168.
Bracton, *De Legibus Angliæ*, 25, 34, 35.
Bramhall (Bishop), *A Warning to the Church of England*, 188, 280–2.
Britton (ed. Nichols), 34, 36.
Bullinger, *Bullæ Papisticæ Refutatio*, 99.
Butler, Bishop Joseph, *Sermons*, 172.
Calderwood, *History of the Kirk of Scotland*, 192–6
Cardwell, *Synodalia*, 140.

Jewel, Bishop, *Apology for the Church of England* (Parker Society's Edition), 43, 96, 182.

John of Salisbury, *Polycraticus*, 51.

Johnson (Rev. Samuel), Works, 140, 5, 220, 3, 240.

Knyghton (in Twysden's *Decem Scriptores*), 75.

Knox (John), *Works*, 192, 4.

Latimer (Bishop), *Sermons*, 96.

Laud (Archbishop), *Sermons*, 237, 263 (Library of Anglo-Catholic Theology).

Leslie, Charles, *Cassandra*, 290, 1, 3, 4.

          The New Association, 284, 7, 293.

          The Good Old Cause, 20, 238.

          The Rehearsal, 171, 5, 287, 292, 6, 7.

          The Finishing Stroke, 288.

          The Sham Sermon Dissected, 289, 290, 93.

          A Battle Royal, 277, 289.

          The Best Answer, 171, 175, 292, 5, 6.

          Best of All, 238, 295.

          The Wolf stripped of His Shepherd's Clothing, 277.

          Obedience to Civil Government clearly stated, 289, 294, 5.

Locke, John, *Two Treatises on Civil Government*, 154, 224, 239.

Mainwaring, Roger, *Religion and Allegiance*, 148.

Majestas Intemerata, 27, 9, 33, 84, 227, 246.

Masson (Matharellus), *Responsio in Franco-Galliam*, 119.

Matthew Paris, *Chronica Majora* (Rolls Series), 25.

Mariana, *Del Rey y de la Institucion Real*, 180, 3, 4, 217, 221, 248.

Migne, *Patrologia*, 51.

Mirror of Justices, ed. by W. J. Whittaker, 42.

John Malvern in Appendix to Higden, 74, 5.

Milton, *The Tenure of Kings and Magistrates*, 224, 241, 2.

Nalson (Robert), *The Common Interest of King and People*, 161, 187, 277, 8, 283, 290.

Newman (John Henry, Cardinal), *Letter to the Duke of Norfolk*, 253, 259.

Overall's Convocation Book, 137, 236.

Pithou, *Les Libertez de l'Église Gallicane*, 120, 205.

Prothero, *Statutes and Constitutional Documents*, 33, 89, 138, 269.

Armstrong, E., *The French Wars of Religion*, 110, 18.

Balfour, A. J., *The Foundations of Belief*, 2.

Bryce, J., *The Holy Roman Empire*, 40, 4.

Creighton (Mandell, Bishop of Peterborough), *Persecution and Tolerance*, 41.

        History of the Papacy, 110.

Cunningham (William), *History of English Industry and Commerce*, 3.

Dicey, A. V., *Law of the Constitution*, 201.

Dictionary of National Biography, 129.

English Historical Review, 84, 5, 118.

Frazer, J. G., *The Golden Bough*, 17.

Freeman, E. A., *The Norman Conquest*, 20, 42.

Gairdner and Spedding, *Studies in English History*, 1, 15.

Gairdner (James), *Life and Reign of Richard III.*, 84.

        Preface to *Letters and Papers illustrative of the Reign of Henry VII.*

Gardiner, Samuel Rawson, *History of England*, 39, 89, 139, 201, 230.

        History of the Commonwealth and Protectorate, 182.

Kitchin (G. W.), *History of France*, 110.

Lecky (W. H.), *History of England*, 170.

Maine (Sir H. S.), *Ancient Law*, 22.

        Early History of Institutions, 14, 31, 230.

Maitland (Professor F. W.), *Select Pleas of Manorial Courts*, 31, see Pollock.

Mill (J. S.), *On Liberty*, 213.

Nineteenth Century, 104.

Pollock and Maitland, *History of English Law*, 13, 21–5, 33.

Pollock (Sir Frederick), *History of the Science of Politics*, 17.

        Oxford Lectures, 21.

Poole (R. L.), *Illustrations of the History of Mediæval Right*, 47, 61, 70.

        Wycliffe and Movements of Reform, 61, 70.

Round, J. H., *Geoffrey de Mandeville*, 20.

Stubbs (William, Bishop of Oxford), *Constitutional History of England*, 21, 2, 7.

        Lectures on Mediæval and Modern History, 85, 90.

CONTENTS.

ERRATA.

CHAPTER I.

INTRODUCTORY.

A MODERN essayist has said with truth, that "never has there been a doctrine better written against than the Divine Right of Kings[1]." But those, who have exhausted their powers of satire in pouring scorn upon the theory, have commonly been at little pains to understand it. That the doctrine is absurd, when judged from the standpoint of modern political thought, is a statement that requires neither proof nor exposition. But the modern standpoint is not the only one, and the absurdity of the doctrine in our eyes is the least interesting or important fact about it, except as driving us to seek further for its real meaning and value. Nor is "The Divine Right of Kings" differentiated by reason of its absurdity from other political theories of the seventeenth century. The rival doctrine of an original compact was no whit less ridiculous in theory, and (if we consider its

The Theory of the Divine Right of Kings commonly condemned as absurd.

But other theories of the time also absurd.

[1] Gairdner and Spedding, *Studies in English History*, 245. Cf. also Mr Gairdner's remarks in the preface to *Letters and Papers Illustrative of the Reigns of Richard III. and Henry VII.* xi—xiii.

1

influence upon Rousseau) infinitely more pernicious in practice than the notions of Indefeasible Right and Passive Obedience. It is noteworthy, that, while Macaulay has nothing but contempt for the supporters of Divine Right, he does not find it needful to mention that its opponents would make no better *The causes of the prevalence of the doctrine more important than the reasons against its validity.* figure among political thinkers of to-day. Instead of stating a fact, which is common to all obsolete doctrines, it were surely better to enquire into the notions of those, to whom the doctrine seemed natural, and to set it in relation to the conditions which produced it. Large numbers of men may embrace a belief without good reason, but assuredly they will not do so without adequate cause. And it is commonly of far greater importance towards the right understanding of a doctrine to know the causes, which lead to its prevalence or decay, than it is to be able to criticize the reasoning, by which men think to support it, while it is popular or to demolish it, as it grows obsolete[1].

Its import probably different from what it appears. Further, although the theory may seem absurd, when framed into a set of bald propositions, it is not wise therefore to infer that it had no other meaning to its supporters, than that which it bears to us. It may prove to have been in the main a counter-theory to some other notion of Divine Right, more ridiculous and less useful. Judged in relation to the circumstances which produced it, and to the rival

---

[1] Mr Balfour takes these two theories as offering the most salient illustration of the fact that the causes of belief are widely different from the reasons for it, *Foundations of Belief*, 216–17.

doctrines it was formed to extirpate, the theory of
the Divine Right of Kings may prove to be necessary and even sensible. The import of the battle-
cries of " Passive Obedience " and " Ius Divinum " to
those, who were fighting the battle, must have been
very different from what it seems to those, who can
see no meaning in the cries, because they have forgotten that there was a battle. The method of
Whig historians is apparently to isolate the phenomenon, and to observe it *in vacuo*. Considered
in this way any theory of government must appear
ridiculous, so soon as it has ceased to influence
practice. It is not so that the true import and
value of 'forsaken beliefs' is to be gauged. It
has been shewn that the earlier free-traders were
at fault in treating the believers in the Mercantile
theory as conscious knaves or incurable fools. They
erred in supposing, that since a theory has become
obsolete, it therefore had never anything to recommend it, save the self-interest of the few and the
stupidity of the many[1]. May not the same thing
be true of some of those, who have poured out upon
the believers in the Divine Right of Kings ridicule,
that certainly has the merit of being obvious ?

. Nor again can the doctrine be dismissed as the *The
doctrine
not*
work of an isolated thinker with a turn for paradox.
It was essentially a popular theory, proclaimed in *academic
but
popular.*
the pulpit, published in the market-place, witnessed
on the battle-field. The names, which have come
down to us, as especially connected with it stand out

[1] Cunningham, *History of English Industry and Commerce*,
Part II. §§ 307, 357. .

rather by lapse of time, than through any eminence
of their own. Filmer is not to be regarded as a
prophet or thinker, followed as a master by a crowd
of inferior men. He was only slightly more able
and far more notorious, than a host of other writers,
whose names and works have faded from the general
The   recollection. A belief so widespread was surely
outcome   the product far more of practical necessity than of
of actual   intellectual activity. No enthusiasm for a scheme
needs.   of ideal politics, no quasi-scientific delight in discus-
sions upon the nature of government could generate
so passionate a faith. The pressure of circumstances
could alone produce it. Nor as a matter of fact
is the doctrine much regarded by the makers of
Ideal Commonwealths in the sixteenth and seventeenth centuries. It might seem that no scheme
of politics could be more purely ideal than one which
asserts Divine authority for its basis. Yet there is
no trace of propagandism in the works of royalist
writers, whether in France or England. Some indeed
are at pains to assert that they have no quarrel with
other forms of government, when once established,
whether elective monarchies or republics[1]. There
is no desire to establish universal Kingship, akin
to the passionate enthusiasm of French Revolution-
aries for abolishing it. For the most part, the
horizon of the politico-theological writers of the
sixteenth and seventeenth centuries is bounded by
a particular country in a definite stage of development. A Frenchman will indeed find in the
Davidic kingdom the model of a state governed by

[1] E.g. Hickes in *Jovian.*

the Salic law. An Englishman will see in it the
Divine justification for the English law of succession. But, except for the purpose of finding God's
authority for a given polity, neither really looks
beyond his own country. The theory is the outcome of facts far more than it is of thinking. From
the consideration of the popular acceptance and
practical object of the doctrine, some obvious conclusions may be drawn. First, it seems clear that *The*
so general and enthusiastic a faith must have been *doctrine must have*
the expression of deep-seated instincts; secondly, *satisfied*
that a doctrine so fully elaborated and yet so *deep in-stincts*
eminently the product of a definite epoch must *and*
have been the result of a long chain of historical *fulfilled a function.*
causes, and that it must have been formed to meet
real needs. If so, it had a definite function to fulfil
in the development of society. It is the purpose
of this essay to enquire how far this was the case.

The theory of the Divine Right of Kings in its *Statement*
completest form involves the following propositions:— *of the theory.*

(1) *Monarchy is a divinely ordained institution.*

(2) *Hereditary right is indefeasible.* The succession to monarchy is regulated by the law of
primogeniture. The right acquired by birth cannot be forfeited through any acts of usurpation, of
however long continuance, by any incapacity in the
heir, or by any act of deposition. So long as the
heir lives, he is king by hereditary right, even
though the usurping dynasty has reigned for a
thousand years.

(3) *Kings are accountable to God alone.* Monarchy is pure, the sovereignty being entirely vested

in the king, whose power is incapable of legal limitation. All law is a mere concession of his will, and all constitutional forms and assemblies exist entirely at his pleasure. He cannot limit or divide or alienate the sovereignty, so as in any way to prejudice the right of his successor to its complete exercise. A mixed or limited monarchy is a contradiction in terms.

(4) *Non-resistance and passive obedience are enjoined by God.* Under any circumstances resistance to a king is a sin, and ensures damnation. Whenever the king issues a command directly contrary to God's law, God is to be obeyed rather than man, but the example of the primitive Christians is to be followed and all penalties attached to the breach of the law are to be patiently endured.

Illustrative quotations. The following passages set the doctrine forth in the language of the time :—

"We will still believe and maintain that our Kings derive not their title from the people but from God; that to him only they are accountable; that it belongs not to subjects, either to create or censure, but to honour and obey their sovereign, who comes to be so by a fundamental hereditary right of succession, which no religion, no law, no fault or forfeiture can alter or diminish[1]." "Obedience we must pay, either Active or Passive; the Active in the case of all lawful commands; that is whenever the Magistrate commands something which is not

[1] From an address of the University of Cambridge to King Charles II. in 1681, printed in the *History of Passive Obedience*, p. 108.

contrary to some command of God, we are then
bound to act according to that command of the
Magistrate, to do the thing he requires. But when
he enjoins anything contrary to what God hath
commanded, we are not then to pay him this Active
Obedience; we may, nay we must refuse thus to
act, (yet here we must be very well assured that
the thing is so contrary, and not pretend conscience
for a cloak of stubbornness), we are in that case *to
obey God rather than man*. But even this is a
season for the passive obedience; we must patiently
suffer what he inflicts on us for such refusal, and
not, to secure ourselves, rise up against him[1]."

"If Adam himself were still living and now
ready to die it is certain there is one man, and but
one in the world who is next heir, although the know-
ledge who should be that one man be quite lost[2]."

The theory is commonly supported by a number
of Biblical illustrations and texts, of which some of
the most important may be mentioned:—Samuel's
description of a king, on the Jewish nation demanding one[3]; David's refusal to touch "the Lord's
anointed"; the text "By me kings reign and
princes decree justice[4]"; the passage describing
the vision of Nebuchadnezzar, asserting that "the

Common arguments in favour of the theory.

[1] *Whole Duty of Man*, Sunday xiv. § 5. The passage is quoted
by Hobbes as giving the best expression of "the doctrine of the
King's party." (*Behemoth*, Part i. p. 80.)

[2] Filmer's *Patriarcha*. Chap. i. § 9.

[3] 1 Sam. vii. 10—18. There is much controversy as to
whether Samuel intended to describe a good king exercising his
sovereign rights, or a tyrant.

[4] Prov. viii. 15.

Most High ruleth in the kingdom of men, and giveth it to whomsoever he will, and setteth up over it the basest of men[1]"; the command to "render unto Cæsar the things that are Cæsar's[2]"; Christ's words to Pilate " thou couldest have no power at all against me except it were given thee from above[3]"; the behaviour of the primitive Christians; and above all the direct enjoining by both S. Peter and S. Paul of obedience to constituted authority, "The powers that be are ordained of God. Whoso- ever therefore resisteth the power, resisteth the ordinance of God. And they that resist shall re- ceive to themselves damnation." " Ye must needs be subject, not only for wrath, but for conscience' sake[4]." " Submit yourselves to every ordinance of man for the Lord's sake—whether it be to the king as supreme, &c.[5]"

The Pa-triarchal form of the theory not essential to it. The Patriarchal theory, the most unqualified form of which Filmer and others profess to find in Genesis, forms the basis of the most symmetrical form of the doctrine of Divine Right, but it is far from universal and there is no reason for regarding it as of the essence of the theory.

No im-portance Nor, again, does the sacramental character of unction play much part in the exposition of the

---

[1] Daniel iv.   [2] S. Luke xx. 25.   [3] S. John xix. 11.
[4] Rom. xiii. 1—7. It was held of great importance to maintain that κρίσις meant damnation in the strict sense. There is a lengthy dissertation of Hammond to prove this single point.
[5] 1 Pet. ii. 13—17. A favourite argument to prove that kings are accountable to God alone is the text "Against thee only have I sinned" (Ps. li. 4). It is quoted by a French writer as having the authority of Otto of Freising, and is used by Leslie among others.

divine authority of kings. Richard II. undoubtedly *attached to unction.*
believed that unction conferred an indelible mark,
and the notion of the sacredness of royal power,
as compared with all other constituted authority,
was certainly strengthened by this ancient ceremony[1]. But it plays, in the controversies of the
sixteenth and seventeenth centuries, a quite different part. In France the supporters of the League
are found arguing, that unction is necessary to
make a king, and that Henry IV., who as a
heretic cannot be anointed by the Archbishop of
Rheims, can therefore never be truly king. In
England, the writers on the popular side are continually pointing to the coronation oath as evidence
of the theory of compact, and as limiting the royal
authority. Hence both in France and England, the
counter-assertion is common that unction is of no
importance, and confers no special grace; that the
king is king before his coronation as fully as he is
after; and that resistance to an 'uncrowned' king is
verily damnable. The phrase, "the Lord's Anointed,"
is merely common form for the sacred person of the

---

[1] Shakespeare expresses the sentiment rather of Richard II.
himself than of the believers in the Divine Right of Kings, in the
famous lines:—

> "Not all the water in the rude rough sea
> Can wash the balm from an anointed king."

There can be no doubt that the notion of the sacred character
conferred by unction was held by Richard, and that it long remained
an element in popular feeling. But the exigencies of their position
drove the supporters of the theory of Indefeasible Right to minimize the effect of unction. Any stress laid upon it tended to
make the king a mere official, and to support the doctrine of
the originally elective character of kingship.

King and is used by writers who are far from attri-
buting any sacramental character to the ceremony.
Undoubtedly the ordinary view is that of a royalist
divine, who declares in set terms that "Royal
Unction confers no grace, but declares a just title
only." Indeed no other view was really compatible
with the notion of indefeasible hereditary right[1].

[1] *The Royal Charter granted unto Kings*, Chap. III. *What is
meant by the anointing of Kings.* "*Unxit in regem* includes
nothing but a due title, excludes nothing but usurpations; gives
him the administration to govern, not the gift to govern well; the
right of ruling, not of ruling right." "Anointing is a sacred
signature betokening sovereignty, obedience to the throne, allegiance
to the Crown." Usher after quoting David's sentence on the Ama-
lekite for slaying the Lord's anointed goes on: "And this indeed
must be the main foundation not only of the observance but also
of all the other branches of that allegiance, which we do owe unto
our Prince; that with the right which he hath obtained by Election
or Succession here below *we be careful to conjoin that unction
which he hath received from above.*" (*Power of the Prince*, p. 125.)
Clearly unction is regarded, as equivalent to God's institution
of kings, not as a grace conferred by the sacrament of anointing.
Cf. Coke on Calvin's Case. "Coronation is but a *royal ornament*
and solemnization of the royal descent, but no part of the title."
He goes on to quote the case of two seminary priests, who claimed
that before his coronation it was not high treason to seize and
imprison King James. This doctrine was of course condemned by
the judges, who declared him to be as full king before coronation as after (7 *Reports*, 10 b). It is significant, that neither
The Maid's Tragedy nor *The Royal King and Loyal Subject*,
although each asserts most emphatically the sacred character
of Kingship, contains the slightest hint that this character is
acquired through unction. In France again, Servin writing on
behalf of Henry IV. distinctly denies that unction has any
significance, or is more than a pious ceremony. Blackwood
indeed appears to take a different view: "An non quemadmodum
sacerdotes sic et reges cum inaugurantur oleo id est divina quadam
virtute inunguntur? Nam oleum, illud quo reges olim sacerdotes

Now a theory, such as that described, has plainly *The theory belongs to an age, when politics and theology were closely connected.* as much relation to theology as to politics, and cannot be judged from the standpoint of an age, when the two are sharply divided. Although something is heard at times of the importance of religious considerations in regulating international politics or state-inter-ference, yet no one now claims that politics is a branch of theology. Men may appeal with more or less of sincerity to Christian sentiment as a factor in political controversy, but they have ceased to regard political theory as a part of Christian doctrine. The theory of the Divine Right of Kings belongs to an age in which not only religion but theology and politics were inextricably mingled, when even for utilitarian sentiments a religious basis must be found if they were to obtain acceptance. All men demanded *The same methods are em-ployed by opponents of the theory.* some form of Divine authority for any theory of government. There is hardly a hint that those who disbelieved in the Divine Right of Kings had any quarrel with the methods of their opponents. Until towards the close of the seventeenth century, the atmosphere of the supporters of popular rights is as theological as that of the upholders of the Divine Right of Kings.

John Hall[1] indeed brushes aside the Biblical illustrations and authorities of the royalists; but most are content to argue on just the same lines as their

et prophetae perfundebantur, divinitatis symbolum erat ac *veluti sacramentum*" (*Apologia pro Regibus*, p. 15, cf. also *De Vinculo Religionis et Imperii*, pp. 282, 314). But this view is far less common than that given in the text.

[1] *The Grounds and Reasons of Monarchy* prefixed to *Harring-ton's Works*, p. 8.

opponents. They point out that Scripture has been misunderstood, that texts have been ignored which inculcate the right and duty of resistance, that the early Christians exhibited the virtue of Passive obedience merely because they could not help themselves. Even the original compact finds its biblical model in the 'law of the kingdom' laid down by Samuel. Towards the end of the seventeenth century, with Locke and Sidney and even the more able of the royalists, politics begin to pass into a more modern stage. But most writers, of whom Johnson the author of *Julian the Apostate* is a fair specimen, have hardly a notion, that political theory can be framed except on a theological basis, or proved save by the authority of the Bible. Writers on behalf either of unlimited obedience or popular rights, though they are undoubtedly impelled by a pressing sense of the utility of resistance or *vice versâ*, yet seek by appealing to Scripture to establish their theory upon an immutable basis, and to base it upon transcendental grounds, of which no fresh view of what was merely expedient should ever destroy the force. To judge aright the political theories of the sixteenth and seventeenth centuries, we must not consider them from the standpoint of an age in which all political theory is confessedly utilitarian[1]; their true relations are to a time when theology and politics were closely united both in theory and practice. It is useless to demonstrate, what nobody doubts, that the theory of the Divine Right of Kings has

---

[1] Professor Sidgwick (*Elements of Politics* 34) bears witness to the exclusively utilitarian character of modern politics.

no affinity with the creed of any modern political party. Rather we must seek to find what political theories of ecclesiastical power met their countervailing influence in this theological theory of politics.

Again, the theory assumes the fact of " sove- *The* reignty." When it is borne in mind, that the idea of *theory involves* sovereignty in the Austinian sense was unknown in *the notion* any single nation in the middle ages, it will at once *of sove-reignty.* become a matter for enquiry how far the uncompromising absolutism of the royalist writers may have been merely the expression of a thought, which came to them with all the force of a discovery. While the fact that the notion appears in the claims to universal supremacy of both Popes and Emperors, may point to the possibility of similar causes operating in the struggles on the part of the national states for independence of Papal control. It is not, perhaps, easy for a writer like Austin to see, how a theory of the state can ever be formed without the recognition, that there must be in it some ultimate authority, which because it can make laws is above law. Yet it is certain that this notion is modern, and that the idea of the complete supremacy of one body or person in the state did not enter the heads of those who wrote of the English polity in the middle ages. Bracton knows of no sovereign in the Austinian sense, and distinctly denies to the royal authority the attribute of being 'incapable of legal limitation[1].' How indeed could it have been

---

[1] Cf. Pollock and Maitland, *History of English Law*, I. 160. " That the king is below the law is a doctrine which even a royal

otherwise under the conditions of feudalism, however modified, and in the face of the admitted claims of the Papacy and the canon law[1]? In addition, then, to setting the theory of the Divine Right of Kings in relation to contemporary conflicts of politics and theology, it will be needful to enquire how far the doctrine is the expression of a dawning idea of sovereignty, whether or no this idea was realised by the opponents of Divine Right, and what are the true relations of the latter doctrine to the more systematic theory of sovereignty, expounded by Hobbes.

Origin of the theory to be sought in the conflicts of the Papacy and Empire.

The fact, that Imperialist writers in the middle ages, endeavouring to refute the claims of the Papacy, develope for themselves the essential notion of sovereignty, points, as was said, to the conflict with Rome as the true source of the theory of Divine Right. While the necessarily theological character of politics, so long as the Pope's claims to supreme political authority were a main factor in the situation, makes it yet more plain, that the history of the theory must be largely concerned with the political side of the Reformation struggle. But in order to learn how the weapons were forged, which were to be used in the seventeenth century, it will be needful to study the earlier conflicts of Pope and Emperor.

justice may fearlessly proclaim. The theory that in every state there must be some man or definite body of men above the law, some 'sovereign' without duties and without rights would have been rejected." See also p. 208, and Bk. II. Ch. II. § 13, The King and the Crown.

[1] Cf. Maine, *Early History of Institutions*, Lectures XII. and XIII. in which is shewn the practical inapplicability of Austin's theory to primitive societies and half developed states.

In these the Papalist writers first will be found developing a theory of sovereignty for their Lord the Pope, while this is met by the counter contention of the Imperialists that not the Pope but the Emperor is truly sovereign, and that he is so by God's direct appointment. Here clearly are the main elements of the later doctrine.

That to the Reformation was in some sort due the prevalence of the notion of the Divine Right of Kings is generally admitted[1]. If then it should prove that the doctrine was an essential element of success in the struggle against the political claims of the Papacy, it will be vain to condemn its supporters for trying to set back the clock of time. If the theory was needful, it did good work, and the fact that the work is done is no reason for pouring ridicule on those who took part in it. The value of a doctrine is to be gauged, not from its having given place to a better, but from its having superseded one which was either pernicious or had become obsolete.

If the doctrine was needful to effect the Reformation, it did good service.

The interest of the subject is great. It marks the transition from mediæval to modern modes of thought. In studying it we see the links of connection between thinkers like Dante and Ockham on the one hand, and Locke and Rousseau on the other. While despite the notion of natural rights, Locke and Sidney with their strong vein of utilitarian sentiment are plainly the forerunners of Bentham and Mill. But not only does the history

History of the theory of interest, as marking the change from mediæval to modern thought, as proving the dependence of theory

[1] See especially Mr Gairdner's valuable essay on the subject. Gairdner and Spedding, *Studies in English History*, 245 sqq.

upon practice.

of the doctrine serve to bridge the gulf between mediæval and modern thought. It also illustrates the inevitable dependence of theory upon circumstances. That facts are the parents of theories far more than theories of facts, that political thought is inevitably relative to political development, men are all too prone to forget. But no one who studies the origin and history of the theory of the Divine Right of Kings is likely to do so. On the other hand it is unquestionably true, that a doctrine produced by the pressure of circumstances may have a great practical work to perform. It gives expression to real needs, and strengthens men in their determination to make a stand, for what they instinctively feel to be of vital importance. No belief could be more the child of circumstance than that in the Divine Right of Kings; while it played no despicable part in giving the nation some sort of intellectual and doctrinal basis for its claim to independence of ecclesiastical control. These points it will be the aim of the following essay to elucidate.

CHAPTER II.

EARLY IDEAS OF KINGSHIP.

THE developed doctrine of kingship of the seven- *Early sentiment as to sanctity of Kings.* teenth century has been described by Sir Frederick Pollock as "not rational, not ingenious, not even ancient[1]." Yet the instinct, which it satisfied, is as old as history. In some form the sanctity of kingship has been held from very early times. Although the theory of the seventeenth century was mainly the expression of immediate needs, it is not possible to deny some part in it to a sentiment of loyalty, which is as old as human society. Most primitive tribes seem to have thrown some sort of halo round the person of the chief. Either the mysterious supernatural power of the medicine-man was the basis of his dominion among races, who perhaps had not risen to any definite notions of a divinity; or else he was believed to have been *The King an Incarnation.* an actual incarnation of the deity. Mr Frazer in *The Golden Bough* has brought together a large number of instances of the prevalence of this notion. He shews also the intimate connection between kingship and priesthood. The maxim, *Rex est*

---

[1] *History of the Science of Politics*, 65.

mixta persona cum sacerdote is the expression of
what was once an actual fact; and to this is probably due much common sentiment as to the sanctity
of royalty.

*The King
of Divine
descent.*
With the lapse of time, the belief that a king was
a god gave way to the notion, that he was of divine
descent. As the Incas claimed to be the children
of the Sun, so the notion of divine parentage is the
first germ of the theory, which meets us upon the
threshold of English History. When the institution
of royalty was developed by the circumstances of the
Conquest among the communities that migrated to
Britain, all the petty monarchs of the early English
tribes found it well to strengthen their title by a
direct claim to descent from Wodin, thus investing
the new authority with something of a supernatural
sanction.

*Influence
of Chris-
tianity.*
With the introduction of Christianity a fresh and
more enduring source of strength was given to the
notion that obedience was a divine command. Suffering for conscience' sake became a duty. The
divine institution of the Davidic kingdom, the
mysterious character of Melchisedec the priest king,
and the very definite commands of S. Peter and
S. Paul could not be, and, as a matter of fact, were
not overlooked. The suffering of the early Christians were an example, which later apologists of
resistance might explain away, but they could not
well be forgotten. Without crystallizing into a
definite theory of the nature of government or of
the limits of obedience in extreme cases, there
subsisted throughout the middle ages a feeling that

kings and all in authority were the vicars of God, *Obedienc* and that resistance to their commands was, in general, *to Kings* *as vicars* a damnable sin. An aspiring Pope like Hildebrand *of God* might indeed declare later, that all secular govern- *regarded* *as a reli-* ments were of diabolic origin. But there remained *gious duty* *throughout* in the common consciousness some sense that the *the middle* king's power was of God, that obedience to him *ages.* was a religious duty, taught and practised by Christ himself and the Apostles. It was not a theory, but it afforded material out of which a theory might be formed, if at any' time circumstances should drive men to seek for one. As an instance may be taken the report of the legates George and Theophylact of their proceedings in England A.D. 787[1]. They appeal, as a nonjuror might have done, to the fourth of Daniel, to the thirteenth of Romans, to the words of S. Peter. They quote the prohibition against cursing the king even in thought, and speak of all who are accessory to regicide, as on a level with Judas. It is evident that the legates are using the common form of enjoining obedience to civil government. Clearly they put forward no abstract theory of indefeasible right or of absolute sovereignty or even of invariable non-resistance. It must be remembered, that later royalist writers were only following in the wake of centuries, when they quoted

[1] Stubbs and Haddan, *Councils* III. 458, Cap. XII., *De ordinatione et honore regum.* "Omnes generaliter admonuimus, ut consona voce et corde Dominum rogent, ut Qui eligit eum in regnum, Ipse ei tribuat regimen disciplinae sanctae Suae ad regendam plebem Suam.......In necem regis nemo communicare audeat, quia *christus Domini* est. Omnis quisquis tali sacrilegio consensat... aeterno anathematis vinculo interibit, et Judae traditori sociatus."

Scripture to prove the duty of obedience, or called the king the vicar of God, and employed far-fetched Biblical analogies and forced interpretations to support their contention[1]. All this was old enough. What was new, was the attempt to draw from it a consistent logical theory of the nature of government and of the mutual relations of sovereign and subject.

Early English Kingship. With regard to early English kingship, that it was not strictly hereditary by the law of primogeniture, is well known. But it must be borne in mind, that, although the right of election[2] and deposition rested with the Witan, they could only exercise their right within the limits of the royal family. The case of Earl Harold is quite exceptional, and it is at least not proved that his election was legal[3]. Although

[1] The non-juror Leslie is very angry with Burnet for declaring that the theory of Divine Right was the product of the Reformation. "None knows better than his Lordship, that the notion of Kings having their power from God, was long in the world before either the Reformation or Popery. All the ancient Fathers are full of it. And they took it from the Holy Scripture, where it is abundantly testified" (*The Good Old Cause*, § 2). As to the developed doctrine there is no doubt that Burnet was right and Leslie wrong; but Leslie is quite right as to the notions out of which it grew, as is shewn by the passage cited on page 19. That the Fathers would have been astounded could they have seen their phrases about obedience to the Emperor, taken as proof that they held the theory of the non-jurors, is true enough; that the non-jurors had the least notion that their theory was in any way different from the sentiment of antiquity, there is no reason to suppose.

[2] Hotman in the *Franco-Gallia* tries to prove a similar rule of election, but election within one family, as the ancient custom of the Franks.

[3] Mr Round is at issue with Mr Freeman on the point. *Geoffrey de Mandeville*, 8, 487, *Norman Conquest*, iii. App. C.

the power of the Crown was circumscribed within somewhat narrow bounds, yet in various ways the sanctity of the king was asserted; his peace was of a high nature, above that of other men[1]. In the rise of the law of treason under Alfred we see how important the protection of the king's person is becoming, although as yet it is only as part of the general law, differing merely in degree from treason to a lord, that we discern the germs of the later code of high treason[2].

With the Norman Conquest the royal power *Effect of the Norman Conquest.* received a vast accession of strength. But the doctrine of elective kingship gained additional force from the circumstances of William and his sons. The struggles of the reign of Stephen shew, on the one hand, that considerations of hereditary right are not yet regarded as decisive. On the other, the mere fact of the Empress obtaining a large measure of support indicates, that men are beginning to attach importance to succession by primogeniture.

If the theory of sovereignty had been recognised at this time, there could be no doubt that all theoretical limits upon the royal authority must have been done away; for the king was immeasurably the strongest power in the state; but no such theory was held, and forms of constitutional checks remained in theory, for a later age to use them in practice.

Again, the action of the Conqueror in compelling *1086.* all landowners to take the oath of fealty to him

---

[1] See Stubbs, *Constitutional Hist.* I. § 72; Pollock, *Oxford Lectures,* 65; and Pollock and Maitland, *Hist. of Engl. Law,* I. 22.

[2] *H. E. L.* p. 28, and Stubbs, *Select Charters,* p. 62.

against everyone[1], including their immediate lords, tended to widen the generality of the duty of obedience to the central authority, and to form a basis for a complete theory of allegiance. Its significance as guarding against the dangers of an infinitely subdivided sovereignty, the worst evil of feudalism, has often been pointed out.

It was perhaps in another way that the Conquest led most directly to the development of principles, that made up an important element in the theory of

Primogeniture. Succession to Crown assimilated to inheritance of fiefs.

the Divine Right of Kings. While withstanding the danger of introducing feudal principles of government, the Conqueror introduced, or, at least, crystallized into system all the influences that made for a complete recognition of feudal principles of land-tenure[2]. The king is now not only the national representative, but also supreme landowner; all land is held of him mediately or immediately. This, "the great generalization that governs the whole of Domesday[3]" led not only ultimately to the conception of territorial sovereignty[4], but assimilated the succession of the Crown to the developing law of the inheritance to fiefs. The Norman kings were far more than national monarchs. They were lords of a great estate. And the rules which were beginning to govern the

[1] Stubbs, *Select Charters*, pp. 81, 2.
[2] Stubbs, *Constitutional History*, i. § 94.
[3] Pollock and Maitland, *History of English Law*, vol. i. p. 46. Cf. also p. 210: "Every acre of English soil and every proprietary right therein have been brought within the compass of a single formula, which may be expressed thus:—*Z tenet terram illam* de... *domino rege.*
[4] Maine, *Ancient Law*, 106.

succession to fiefs, were held to apply to the Crown.
The elective character of kingship will begin to
fall into the background, and the influences, leading
to a rigid rule of primogeniture in the case of land,
will tend to the same result in regard to the succession. Hitherto the Crown has been partially
elective, and so far as it tends to become hereditary,
there are reasons for supposing that it might have
descended, as was so often the case in the earlier
mediæval monarchies, by being partitioned among
all the surviving sons of the deceased monarch[1].
But the rise of the rule of primogeniture, after the
kingdom has become the greatest of estates, will
ensure that succession shall be impartible. It is
only because the notions of public law and sovereignty
are·as yet undeveloped, that this is possible. Because
men cannot think of the king as other than a natural
person, or of the rules governing the succession save
as a part of the ordinary law of inheritance, they
must perforce assimilate the succession to the Crown
to the succession to a fief. The king is the landowner *par excellence;* his lands must descend by the
same rules as those of other men[2].

It has been recently shewn, that it was probably
the interest of the overlord, the desire to have one

---

[1] Pollock and Maitland, *History of English Law*, II. 260 sqq.

[2] *Ibid.* I. 497, 8. "The king is conceived to hold his lands by a
strictly hereditary right. Between his lands and the kingship it
would be hard to distinguish....The descent of the Crown was
not so unique a phenomenon then as it is now." Cf. also I. 209.
"The king, it is true, is a highly privileged as well as a very wealthy
person; still his rights are but private rights amplified and inten-
sified."

Causes of primogeniture. person responsible for the discharge of all the feudal incidents, that led to the developement of primogeniture. For not primogeniture, but equal division is the most natural mode of hereditary succession. But though the holder might well desire that his lands should be partitioned among his children, this would not suit the purpose of the Crown, which stepped in and decreed the rule of impartible succession. And it was owing to the fact, that the notion of hereditary kingship only superseded that of election, when this rule was becoming universal in regard to private lands, that the succession to the Crown, when it became hereditary, went by primogeniture and not by partition[1]. There are grounds for supposing that the Conqueror divided his dominions among his sons, on the same principle that actuated so many Frankish monarchs. And Richard Coeur de Lion refused homage to his brother Henry, because brothers were equal[2]. However, primogeniture triumphed and was applied to the Crown, as to other estates.

King John. The 'case of the king' so often cited by Bracton is a proof both of the incomplete acceptance, as yet, of the rule of primogeniture, and of the entire assimilation of the succession to the Crown with that to a fief. On the one hand, John's succession to the throne in defiance of the strict rule of primogeniture, and the exclusion of Arthur his elder brother's son, are evidence that the theory of representative primogeniture was not yet accepted.

---

[1] Pollock and Maitland, *History of English Law*, II. 260 sqq.
[2] *Ibid.* I. 505.

On the other hand, this case, until the death of
Arthur's sister in 1241 determined it, was held to
leave the question of right undecided[1], and to
protect seisin in cases of private lands, as between
an uncle and the son of an elder brother, who had
not himself held the land[2].

John's case is also noteworthy as containing in
the reported speeches of Archbishop Hubert[3], the
strongest possible assertion of the right of election,
and (afterwards at the coronation) of the binding
character of the oath.   On the other hand, the
territorial character of kingship is now coming into
prominence.   John is *Rex Angliae*, no longer *Rex
Anglorum.* While the recent assumption of the style
royal is an indication of a dawning notion of the
mystical and official personality of the king.

John's reign is further important on account
of the submission to the Pope. So long as the
position accepted by John was, with whatever reluc-
tance, recognised at all, and the suzerainty of the
Pope admitted by the payment of tribute, the statement that the king was under no one save God was
the expression of patriotic aspiration rather than of
actual fact.   But the final rejection of the Pope's
demands in 1366, and the protest against Papal claims
with which it was accompanied[3], formed the basis of
the later assertion that 'this realm of England is an
Empire' and contained the germ of that appeal to
the grace of God against the will of the Pope,

[1] Bracton, *De Legibus Angliae*, ff. 267 b, 282, 327 b.
[2] Matth. Paris, *Chronica Majora*, II. 454, 5.
[3] *Rot. Parl.* II. 290.

which was the *raison d'être* of the theory of Divine Right.

Further it is to be noted, that in this case as in others the Papacy, though willing to loosen the bonds of allegiance in order to compass its own ends, shewed no preference for constitutional government as such. The tyranny of both John and his son leant largely upon Papal support.

Magna Charta needs no mention, save for the well-known fact, that the sixty-first clause approaches more nearly than any other statute of English History to giving legal sanction to the right of resistance, and making government and obedience truly a matter of compact.

Edward I.'s reign dates from election, not coronation. The accession of Edward I. marks a further step in the development of hereditary kingship and in the removal of the significance and necessity of the coronation ceremony. The story is well known. Edward was absent upon the crusade at the time of his father's death; the barons, dreading the evils of a lengthy interregnum, elected him king four days after. He reigned from the date of his election, and was not crowned for nearly two years. The crown is claimed by hereditary right, and the will of the barons[1]. Thus coronation, as a necessary element in kingship, sinks into abeyance, and the notion, that though kings may die, the authority of the Crown remains undisturbed, begins to arise. Not yet will men assert that 'the king never dies'; but the germ of the notion is here, and those who in later ages argued that coronation was

[1] Rymer, *Foedera*, i. 497.

merely a ceremony, and that the heir to the throne was 'every inch a king' without it were right in claiming, that they were merely following the precedent of Edward's reign[1].

With the accession of Edward II. election itself *Election* falls into disuse, and he succeeds his father with no *disappears.* interregnum. Thus the pressure of circumstances and the influence of feudal land law have brought about the triumph of the notion, that the right of inheritance is the only essential element in making a king. The right to the Crown is no longer that of election or of coronation, but that of the next heir, whom God alone can make. If we have not yet come to the days when hereditary right is regarded as indefeasible, and no breach is admitted, however short, in the continuity of the succession, yet there are by the beginning of the fourteenth century all the elements of the theory. The Crown has become a birthright.

But the reign of Edward II. had a deeper signifi- *Growth of* cance. It has been pointed out[2], that the very *theory of royal pre-* development of a constitutional system led to a *rogative.* counter-attempt to exalt and liberate from control the royal prerogative. "For every assertion of national right there is a counter assertion of royal

---

[1] *Majestas Intemerata*, p. 45.

[2] Stubbs, *Const. Hist.* II. §§ 247, 273. "On the one side every advantage gained by the parliament is regarded as one of a very limited number of privileges; on the other every concession made by the crown is made out of an unlimited and unimpaired potentiality of sovereignty.......The theory of sovereignty held by Henry III. is far more definite than that of Henry II., and that of Richard II. than that of Edward I."

autocracy." The growth of Parliament, as the source of legislative activity, emphasized the distinction between the power of the Crown in Parliament and the personal power of the king. Kings now will insist upon their personal privileges, upon their right to issue ordinances, to misinterpret at their pleasure the petitions of Parliament, in transforming them into statutes. Thus the whole constitutional struggle of the fourteenth century rages round the vexed question of the royal prerogative. On the one hand popular rights have been crystallized into a definite system; on the other the kings exalt their personal position, and are tempted to regard it as a thing apart, above the constitutional machinery. Before Parliament became an essential element in the state, there was no reason for the king to claim extra-legal authority, save in taxation, for with trifling limitations he was the source of law. He was in his own person not only supreme landowner, but the fountain of justice, the executive authority, and the amender, if not the maker of law. But when Parliament gained the right to petition for new laws, and when in 1322 this right was made exclusive[1], it was natural for the king to distinguish between his rights in his own person and his authority in Parliament. The growth of Parliament, then, is the origin not only of the immediate struggle around royal prerogative and privilege, but also of the distinction

---

[1] 'Revocatio Novarum Ordinationum.' It is remarkable, that the Act was passed in defence of the king, not of the people. The object is to secure the king's freedom from any lords ordainers of the future. *Statutes of the Realm*, I, 189.

between the personal and political capacity of the king, of which a later age was to hear so much.

Nor was the matter a trifling one at the time. *Distinction appears* Even in the days of Edward II. it became a matter *between* of controversy. The distinction was apparently one *the* of the arguments for the banishment of Gaveston. *personal* The ordinances of 1311 accuse him of "encroaching *and* to himself royal power and royal dignity and lording *capacity* it over the state of the King and the People," terms *of the* which the Long Parliament might have applied to *King.* Strafford. Later on, however, in the trial of the De Spensers, the doctrine that there is any distinction between the king and the Crown was condemned[1]

---

[1] The following is the passage condemned :—*Statutes of the Realm*, i. 182. "Homage and the Oath of Allegiance is more by reason of the Crown than by reason of the Person of the King, and it bindeth itself more unto the Crown than unto the Person ; and this appears in that before the Estate of the Crown hath descended, no allegiance is belonging to the Person ; wherefore if the King by chance be not guided by Reason, in right of the Crown, his liege Subjects are bound by the Oath made to the Crown to guide the King and the Estate of the Crown back again by reason, or otherwise the Oath would not be kept. Now were it to be asked, how they ought to guide the King? Whether by Course of Law, or by Violence? By Course of Law a man will not be able to get Redress, for he will have no judges but such as are the King's, in which case, if the Will of the King be not according to Reason he certainly will have only Error maintained and confirmed ; Wherefore it behoveth, in order to save the Oath, that when the King will not redress the matter and remove that which is hurtful to the People at large, and prejudicial to the Crown, it is to be determined, that the thing be removed by Violence, for he is bound by his oath to govern the people and his Liege Subjects, and his Liege Subjects are bound to govern in aid of him and in his default." It will be seen that these ideas were exactly those of the Long Parliament. The author of *Majestas Intemerata* makes

and writers of the seventeenth century are able to
point to the statute exiling them, as affording a proof
of the iniquity of the notion, that it was lawful to
levy war against the king's person in defence of
his Crown.

No theory of sove-reignty in England during middle ages.   It was the glory of England, that it was subject
not to the 'written law,' but to the ancient customary
law of the race, although many modern ordinances,
such as the assizes of Henry II., have become a part
of it. This fact, perhaps, as much as the prevalence
of the theory of feudalism, prevented during the
middle ages the growth of any theory of sovereignty,
save in the Empire. The doctrine would indeed have
seemed ludicrous to an English lawyer of the twelfth
or thirteenth century. The feudal idea, despite all
the efforts of the central power, was still strong, and
Its forma-tion pre-vented by feudalism. there is perhaps no more essential element in feudal
theory, than the belief in the infinite divisibility of
sovereign power. Doubtless, by the fiction of dele-
gacy, it is possible to stretch even the feudal system
on the Procrustean bed of Austinian sovereignty.
Yet at least it will be admitted, that no country, in
which feudalism was at all a force, whether as form-
ing theory or influencing practice, could possibly
have suggested to the acutest mind the conception
of an omnipotent sovereign with neither rights nor
duties. The relations of the Duke of Normandy, or
later of Gascony to the King of France, the Scottish

much use of the fact that the distinction between the political and
personal capacity of the king is a part of "the Spensers' treason."
Coke, *Calvin's Case* (7 *Reports*, 11 a) calls it a "damnable and
damned opinion."

overlordship, the question of the franchises (which it required all the dexterity of the Crown lawyer to get recognised as merely delegations of royal power[1]) must have been fatal to any attempt towards the formation of a theory of sovereignty. Indeed the nature of the feudal tie was more likely to suggest the notion that government is based upon contract.

Nor again was such a theory needed. So long *The doc-* as custom is regarded as the main source of law and *trine un-* the province of legislation is restricted, the abstract *necessary.* truth of Austin's doctrine may remain, but its practical applicability is gone. For the idea of sovereignty to arise, there must be a developed state and a considerable measure of legislative activity. Both these conditions were unfulfilled at the time of Bracton. The only sources, from which such a theory might have been drawn, were the civil and the canon law. But, if any writer with a turn for the Roman jurisprudence should have directed his attention thereto, facts would have been too strong for him. The claims of the Pope, recognised and unrecognised, the existence of the canon law, the wide sphere of spiritual jurisdiction, and benefit of clergy would have been a sufficient bar to the formation of any such doctrine[2]. The theory of sovereignty is only of value, when applied to states which are organized; at this time the organization of national states was only in the making[3].

---

[1] See Maitland, *Introduction to Select Pleas in Manorial Courts;* also *History of English Law,* i. 559.　　[2] *Ibid.* i. 160, 1.

[3] See Maine, *Early History of Institutions,* Lectures xii, xiii.

Lawyers ascribe almost sovereign rights to the King, yet do not treat him as sovereign.

If, then, it be borne in mind that no theory of sovereignty was or could be held by Bracton, it will not be surprising to find him ascribing to the king rights, which apparently amount to little less than complete sovereignty, while in set terms the king is declared to be under the law. Many passages there are which to modern ears sound inconsistent, such as the statement, that the king is under no one but God, and yet is not above the law. Where then is the source of law? Whence is its sanction derived, if neither the King nor any other person or body of persons are above it? This inconsistency is apparent only to us, because we are unfamiliar with the notion that custom can be truly sovereign. The blunder which a modern reader might be tempted to make on first opening Bracton is that of either charging the author with contradicting himself or of understanding the law, under which the king is said to be, in some fanciful sense as equivalent to no more than moral or natural law. This mistake was actu-

Writers in seventeenth century misunderstood Bracton.

ally committed by the uncritical pamphleteers of the seventeenth century. Circumstances had generated in them the idea that in every state there must be some sovereign. Observing that Bracton and Britton ascribed to the king rights which seemed of the essence of sovereignty, they jumped to the conclusion that in the thirteenth century the power of the Crown was believed to be free from all legal limitations. Unless they were setting forth the moral and religious duties of the king, they ignored all that was said about his being subject to the law; and this without conscious dishonesty. They were wedded to the idea of sovereignty, and seeing that in Bracton's view the sovereignty, if not vested in the king, was nowhere to be found, they adopted, what seemed to them the only possible alternative, and inferred that the power of the Crown in the thirteenth century was legally unlimited. Once the fact is grasped, that the royalist writers of the seventeenth century were as deeply imbued with the idea of sovereignty as was Austin, and the course which they took, is seen to be natural. It has been said that "had it [the theory of sovereignty] been accepted in the thirteenth century, the English kingship must have become a tyranny, for nowhere else than in the person of the king could the requisite sovereignty have been found[1]." If this be so, it follows that those, who had no suspicion that the theory was not accepted in the thirteenth century, must have imagined that English kingship at that time was an absolute monarchy.

Hence it is not surprising, that royalist writers of the seventeenth century quote Bracton only less frequently than the Bible, and, although they must have read his distinct assertion to the contrary, regard him with evident *bona fides* as irrefragable testimony to the truth of their doctrine that England in the Middle Ages was an absolute monarchy, tempered only by (always iniquitous) revolutions[2].

They thought that Bracton regarded the King as absolute.

[1] Pollock and Maitland, *History of English Law*, i. 160.

[2] *Majestas Intemerata*, a pamphlet of 50 pages, is crowded with appeals to the authority of Bracton, Britton, &c. Cf. also *Jenkins Redivivus*. Cowell quotes Bracton's authority for his assertion that "the king is above the law by his absolute power" (Prothero, *Statutes and Constitutional Documents*, 409, and note).

They had plausible grounds for their view in many phrases of Bracton and Britton.

They found it declared repeatedly that the king is God's vicar[1]; that all persons in the realm are under him; that he is under none but God; that he has no peer: that if he break the law, it is enough that he await the vengeance of God, for none of his subjects may punish him[2]; that no judgment to make void an act or charter of the king is valid[3]; that our Lord the King has ordinary jurisdiction over all in the land; that all (save spiritual) rights are in his hand[4]; that he was created king to the end that he should do justice to all that the Lord should sit in him[5]; that a jury may be fined for deciding against the king[6]; that none may impose on him without his consent the necessity to amend an injury of his own doing, for necessity may not be imposed on him[7]. They found that Britton regards the whole common law as an emanation from the royal authority[8], that he declares his regality to be inalienable[9], and the king to be the sole interpreter of his will[10].

The passages in a contrary sense explained away.

It is not wonderful that writers of an uncritical age, imbued with the idea that there must be in the State some power above the law, should have sup-

[1] Bracton, f. 1 b.
[2] Ibid. ff. 5 b, 6, 369.
[3] Ibid. f. 34.
[4] Ibid. f. 55 b, 412.
[5] Ibid. f. 107.
[6] Ibid. f. 290 b.
[7] Ibid. ff. 368 b and 389 b.
[8] Britton, I. 1.
[9] Ibid. I. 221. "Rois aussi ne porrount rien aliener les dreitz de lour coroune ne de lour reauté, qe ne soit repellable par lour successours." This is on the same lines as the arguments of seventeenth century writers, to prove that all the rights of Parliament and people are but concessions, which may at any moment be recalled.
[10] Britton, I. 414.

posed that the lawyers of the thirteenth century regarded the king in that light. It was easy to ignore what was said about the king being subject to law[1], to treat it as a fine phrase, or to suppose that nothing more was intended than their own distinction between a king, who rules according to the law of nature, i.e. morality, and the tyrant who governs by caprice. The seventeenth century royalists were willing enough to admit the desirability of the sovereign governing by fixed rules; they only denied that he was legally incapable of altering them. They no more desired a king to govern without law, than a modern writer, asserting the omnipotence of Parliament and its power to abrogate all existing laws, would desire that each successive Parliament should repeal all the acts of its predecessors. They too wished the king, in obedience to Divine law, to govern according to the law of the land; in this sense they understood Bracton's assertion, that the king was under God and the law[2].

Another idea to be found in Bracton must have

[1] Bracton, ff. 5 b, 34. The lengthy passage, in which a king who rules without law is treated as the vicar not of God, but of the devil, would serve to strengthen the view of the royalists, that Bracton regarded moral law alone as superior to the Crown. They must have explained these passages as suggested; for it was impossible for any writer, however dishonest, to ignore the strong phrases about the supremacy of the law used in the very passages, which they quote as asserting the power of the Crown. Bracton was a book constantly in the hands of their opponents, and, without some such justification in their minds, they could not have faced them. See next note.

[2] The strongest evidence that this was the common view is the remarkable passage in which Filmer boldly grapples with the most

'*Only God* can make an heir.' contributed much towards generating the belief in the sacredness of primogeniture. The view of the lawyers of the thirteenth century, that *only God can make an heir*[1] although expressed with reference to private inheritance, must have tended to greatly strengthen the sentiment in favour of strict hereditary succession. It led men to regard this mode of the devolution of the Crown, as in some mysterious way superior to the merely human method of election. The birth of an heir is the judgment of God, and has the same sanctity attached to it, as the ordeal or the lot. Men, if they elect, may well make a bad choice; God, though we may not fathom His reasons, will not make an heir without good grounds.

Summary. To sum up, it appears that Kingship has ever been regarded as in some especial way protected by a Divine authority; that the influence of Christianity has in all ages been held to support this view; that English Kingship from being elective in a single family has become purely hereditary by the fourteenth century; that coronation has ceased to be regarded as necessary to the making of a king; and that in the

awkward of all Bracton's statements. He declares that the words asserting that the king has a superior in his court of Earls and Barons are to be explained of the king's own consent to this check, which has thus no real authority, for the king's consent may be withdrawn. After boldly sweeping aside this difficulty, he naturally enough declares, that, in saying the king was under the law, Bracton merely meant that he ought to govern by means of it, he is thus under the directive, but not the coactive power of the laws. (*Freeholders' Grand Inquest*, p. 12.) This method of escaping the dilemma is exactly that attributed above to the royalist writers.

[1] Bracton, f. 62 b.

systematic presentment of English law in the thirteenth century there are ample materials for men in a later age, devoid of the historical sense and imbued with the theory of sovereignty, to suppose that the English Kingship towards the close of the Middle Ages was strictly hereditary and unconditioned by constitutional restraints.

CHAPTER III.

THE HOLY ROMAN EMPIRE AND THE PAPACY.

The Holy Roman Empire embodies mediæval ideal of a state. THE mediæval notion of an ideal state is embodied in the theory of the Holy Roman Empire. The failure of events to give practical effect to the theory generated controversies, out of which was developed the root idea of the later doctrine of the Divine Right of Kings. The dream was a noble one, of a perfect state with two elected heads, one temporal and one spiritual, working in harmony for the maintenance of peace and for the ordered conduct of life among Christians, in a polity that should combine all that was of lasting value in the system of the *The theory unworkable.* Roman Empire with all that was essential to the realization of the City of God. But for the most part it remained but a dream, save for a few fitful intervals of brilliancy under Charles the Great or Otto III. or even Henry III. Yet the controversies of the seventeenth century took the shape they did, owing to the earlier struggles between Popes and Emperors. If there had been no Holy Roman Empire, or if there had been no failure to realize the ideal embodied in it, there would have been no theory of the Divine Right of Kings[1]. The whole standpoint of political thought during *Contro-* the period of the Reformation is only explicable, *versies about* by being referred to its counterpart in the ideas *Imperial claims* and the methods of the men, who wrote on *form ex-* behalf of the Papal or Imperial pretensions to *planation of theory* sovereignty. One, who has not entered into the *of Divine* feelings of the earlier age, can scarcely fail to *Right.* be hard put to it to comprehend those of the later. A study of the controversies that raged around the claims of Pope and Emperor, will reveal the genesis of most of the notions embodied in later theories; and will bring us into contact with the mental atmosphere, in which alone such theories could take shape.

The Holy Roman Empire, however shadowy *Connec-* its power, was, so long as men made it an aim *tion of theology* to work for, a testimony to the most important *and* characteristic of political thought till the close of *politics.* the seventeenth century—the belief in the intimate connection of politics and religion. The ideal of the Empire with Christ as its King and His two vice-gerents upon earth, was that of a theocracy. This is the explanation of the otherwise strange fact, that men should ever have believed in so unworkable a theory, as that of two equal heads of the State. Christ is the real head of the Empire, and Pope and Emperor are both conceived rather as executors armed from above with administrative powers than

[1] The claim to Divine Right......was first put forward by Imperialist and Royalist opponents of the Papacy. Gardiner, *History of England*, VIII. 182.

as themselves ultimate authorities[1]. There is no difficulty in having two superior officials independent of one another, if they are both regarded as essentially subordinate to a single supreme governor. It was the vividness with which men realized the position of Christ as Lord of the Christian commonwealth, that could alone render possible as an ideal, a state in which temporal and ecclesiastical jurisdiction existed side by side, and each claimed 'coactive' power.

That the ideal State is the kingdom of God upon earth, and that no other can be an object of veneration to a Christian, is the notion that lies at the root of the Holy Roman Empire. It is only as the immediate character of Christ's Kingship is lost sight of, and the two subordinate authorities begin to claim, each for itself, perfect independence and supremacy, that there is revealed the insoluble character of the problem involved in the recognised positions of the Pope and the Emperor. As this process continues, first the Pope, as most plainly the depositary of Divine Authority, afterwards the Emperor, as called to his office by God's election and appointment, claims to be the true and supreme head of the Christian commonwealth, by Divine Right Lord of the world. But the notion of an earthly polity has for neither party disengaged itself as yet

[1] "Opposition between two servants of the same king is inconceivable, each being bound to aid and foster the other : the cooperation of both being needed in all that concerns the welfare of Christendom at large." Bryce, *Holy Roman Empire*, p. 102 ; and the whole of Chap. VII.

from that of the heavenly kingdom. Both Emperor
and Pope are forced to claim Divine Right for their
pretensions, for each believes himself to be head
of something more than a temporal state founded
from motives of human convenience. They are not
merely the directors of an artificial contrivance for
satisfying ephemeral needs; they conceive themselves the chosen captains of the divine organization
revealed by Christ, as part of the eternal order of
the universe.

And thus, whatever claims of supremacy are
made for either Pope or Emperor, it remains that
the theory upon which they were based is essentially
religious. Neither side dreams for a moment of asserting, that the sphere of theology can be separated
from that of politics, or that the source of political
theory is to be found save in revelation. Neither
side imagines that the views of its opponents can be
discredited, unless their opinions as to religious duty
and the drift of Christ's teaching can be shewn to be
false. Those who deny the political supremacy of
the Pope are heretics, says Boniface VIII. Those
who affirm it are heretics, says Marsiglio of Padua.
Theology can in some way teach men the true
theory of government, the relations between various
powers in the State, and the mutual duties of
sovereign and subjects. No one doubts this, and it
remains, with whatever admixture of philosophical
and historical argument, the fundamental basis of
political controversy, not only throughout the Middle
Ages, but until the theory of Divine Right has
passed away, and men have abandoned the attempt

to defend or controvert a doctrine, which has disappeared.

Position of Emperor bars the way to theories of sovereignty in national States.

Further, the position of the Emperor as in theory, lord of the world, must have had an influence, however slight, in retarding the development of any clear notions of sovereignty in the national states. In England, with its belief in the Imperial position of English kings[1], this influence may have been small or virtually non-existent. Yet the fact that an ignorant writer in the fourteenth century can declare that a statute which he dislikes is invalid, because it has received no confirmation from the Emperor[2], is evidence not indeed of the truth of his statement, but of the existence in men's minds of some lingering belief, a relic from earlier times, in the Imperial claims to universal sovereignty. In regard to France the writings of William of Ockham are evidence of a belief equally untrue to actual fact, that the Emperor in the fourteenth century was still possessed of inalienable rights of sovereignty over the French kings[3].

[1] Cf. Freeman, *Norman Conquest*, i. 132, 3, and Appendix B, 552—556.

[2] *Mirror of Justices*, Lib. v. c. 5, p. 195: cf. also the passage: "Jurediccion est poer a dire droit. Cele poer dona deux a Moysen, e cel poer unt ceaux qi tenent ore son lu en terre, si com lapostoill e lempereur *e de souz eux tient ore le Roi cele poer en son royaume.*" (L. iv. c. 3, p. 123.)

[3] "Licet Imperator possit multas libertates concedere regi Franciae et aliis; tamen nullo modo potest regnum Franciae vel aliud totaliter ab Imperio separare, ut nullo modo subsit Imperio. Quia hoc esset destruere Imperium, quod non potest Imperator." (*Dialogus*, Pars iii. Tr. ii. Lib. ii. c. 7; Goldast, ii. 908.) In the ninth chapter Ockham declares all kings to be subject to

Moreover, in the notion that the Holy Roman *Possibility* Empire was but the continuation of the Empire of *of such a* *theory for* the Caesars, the Flavii, and of Justinian, there was *Emperor.* the material for a theory of sovereignty, which the nations did not as yet possess. But, if the action of any power should operate to lower the prestige of the Emperor and to place kings upon a level with him, so that an English, or French king can speak of himself as Emperor[1], it would be only natural for the pretensions asserted by the civilians on behalf of the Emperor to pass over to them, and to be regarded as of the essence of all kingship that is real, *i.e.* imperial[2]. The mere use in later times of the phrase imperial rights as equivalent to sovereignty ✓ is evidence of the source, from which the theory was derived[3].

the Emperor, even though he has not commanded it, and they are unaware of the fact.

[1] Richard II. in legitimating the Beauforts speaks of himself as "Entier Emperour de son Roialme." (*Rot. Parl.* III. 848.) Raoul of Praelles declares, "Un chacun Roy est chief de son royaume, et Empereur de son Empire." (Goldast, I. 51.)

[2] Bishop Jewel asserts that what was the Emperor's right "is now a common right to all princes, for so much as kings are now possessed in the several parts of the whole Empire." *Apology*. Works, III. 98.

[3] The Statute of Appeals in the well-known words of its preamble "this realm of England is an Empire" is an instance of this. Here it is plain that rights of empire are equivalent to rights of sovereignty.

Phrases of this sort can only be explained by the fact that there was a belief, that true sovereignty, *i.e.* independence and unquestioned authority, had been derived from an appropriation by each kingdom of rights originally confined to the Empire.

Papacy reduced Emperors to an equality with other Kings.

This work was performed by that power in the Empire, which overshadowed and eventually destroyed for all practical purposes that of its temporal head. It may indeed be doubted, whether the claims of the Emperor as lord of the world, to be universal sovereign and international arbiter[1] could ever have been brought into effect, as the new peoples awoke to the consciousness of national life. As a fact, however, it is certain that this was prevented by the action of the Papacy[2]. To establish their own claims-to supremacy, the Popes were driven to minimize the prerogatives of the Emperor, and to recognise in him less instead of more authority, than they did in the case of other kings. Thus all monarchies were free to appropriate such rags and trappings of his ancient majesty, as still belonged to the 'ever august increaser of the Empire' in the shape of theories of power that was never exercised and claims of sovereignty that was never effective. In the contest of the Popes with the Emperors was evolved a theory that was destined to play an important part in future antipapal conflicts, and to perform during the period of the Reformation, the work, that was too hard for it,

Origin of theory of Divine Right of Kings.

when Pope John XXII. crushed Lewis of Bavaria. This theory was *the divine right of secular governments to be free from Papal control.* It took shape

[1] See Bryce, *Holy Roman Empire*, Chap. xv. *The Empire as an International Power.*

[2] Wyclif distinctly declares the division of the Empire to be due to the claim of the clergy to secular power. *De Officio Regis,* 252.

in the fourteenth century as the Divine Right of the
Emperors. With various additions, of less importance
than is commonly supposed, it was to re-form itself
in the sixteenth and seventeenth centuries as the
Divine Right of Kings.

It is in the gradual rise of Papal claims to *Theory of* universal supremacy, that are first put forth those *Papal supremacy.* notions which form the basis of all theories of Divine Right; the conception of sovereignty, of the absolute freedom from positive laws of some power in an organized human society; the claim that this sovereignty is vested in a single person by God, and that resistance to the sovereign is the worst of sins. With two powers within the State in the relative positions of Pope and Emperor, it was inevitable that sooner or later there should arise between them a struggle for supremacy. The condition of coördinate *Need of* authority in two diverse but ill-defined spheres *unity in* *the state a* could not be one of lasting duration. Sooner or *source of* *conflict* later the desire of power, coupled with a sense *between* of the need of unity in the society, must bring *Popes and* *Emperors.* either temporal or spiritual head to claim for itself absolute supremacy. There could not fail to be awakened the sense, that the unity of the Christian commonwealth, whether as an earthly state or as a reflection of the Divine order, could only be secured by the recognition of the ultimate authority as vested in one or other of the two powers. Nor was it doubtful which of them had, as a fact, the best claim to superiority. At the best of times, the Emperor was hard put to it to maintain his position even as king of Germany, against the disintegrating

Emperor weak, Pope strong and possessed of universal authority. tendencies of feudalism; while his authority over other nations as lord of the world, was, save perhaps under Charles the Great, of the most shadowy kind. The Pope on the other hand could allege that with some limitations his jurisdiction was admitted by all western nations; and was effectively exercised. In every nation there was a large class of men subject to his tribunals, and exempt from the ordinary law, while in a number of matters only constructively ecclesiastical, such as testamentary and matrimonial cases, the Canon law regulated the lives of the laity, and drove numbers of them to the *curia* to buy justice. It is not surprising that there was developed against the Imperial claims a complete theory of Papal sovereignty. Later ages might dispute as to whether this sovereignty was direct or indirect, immediate or constructive. But, from the days of Hildebrand to those of Boniface VIII. and John XXII., the theory goes on developing and it is of course a theory of sovereignty by Divine Right. The doctrine of the '*plenitudo potestatis*' is an assertion of the Pope's claim to sovereign power, as a direct grant from God to S. Peter and his successors[1].

[1] The views of S. Thomas Aquinas on the subject are comparatively moderate. Yet he declares all kings to be subject to the Pope, and alleges the great authority of the Druids in secular politics as a proof of the natural superiority of sacerdotal power to royal. (*De Regimine Principum*, 1. 14.) The author, whoever he was, of the latter part of the treatise goes farther; he proclaims with emphasis the doctrine of the "plenitudo potestatis" as one of absolute monarchy, vested in the Pope, and quotes the stock instances of Papal jurisdiction over the Empire. S. Thomas, it is noticeable, carefully avoids all debateable ground in his com-

The canonist could allege the donation of Constantine *Arguments* as evidence of temporal dominion, and with good *for Papal claims.* show of justice point to the 'translation of the Empire' from east to west, as proof that from the time of Charles the Great, the Emperor's authority was derived from the Pope. In support of the Pope's claim to judge of the fitness of the Electors' choice, he could urge the fact that no Emperor was more than Emperor-elect, until he had received coronation at the hands of the Pope. He could find in Scripture many passages asserting the superior dignity of priestly power to royal; and could explain away, as he pleased, any which bear at first sight an opposite sense. The image was ready to hand of the greater and the lesser lights signifying (it was plain) the spiritual and the temporal power; the two swords which Christ declared to be "enough, not too much" in the hands of His disciples, would form an apt illustration of the Papal authority in temporal as well as spiritual matters. And so it is proclaimed that the Pope cannot be bound by the Emperor[1], that Imperial laws are void, if they conflict with the Canon law[2], although the Church may

---

mentary on Romans xiii.; but the position there taken up appears to differ widely from that afterwards assumed by Boniface VIII. (For a fuller account of the political theory of S. Thomas see Poole, *Illustrations of the History of Mediæval Thought*, Chap. VIII. *The Hierarchical Doctrine of the State.*)

[1] A saeculari Potestate Pontifex prorsus nec solvi nec ligari valet. *Decret.* Dist. xcvi. c. 7.

[2] *Decret.* Dist. x. c. 4. The usual method of argument is that of the next chapter, "Suscipitisne libertatem verbi? Libenter accipitis quod lex Christi sacerdotali vos subjicit

employ the laws of the Emperor to assist her[1], that
the Emperor as the son not the sovereign of the
Church is subject to the Pope[2], for did not Constantine give the Crown and all kingly dignity to
Pope Sylvester[3]? While the translation of the
Empire is a final proof of the Pope's supremacy
over the Emperor whom he had set up of his
own mere and proper motion[4]. Against the Latin
Emperor of Constantinople urging the command of
S. Peter to obey the secular prince, Innocent III.
can answer, that it only applies to those who hold
their temporalities from him, or else that obedience
is only enjoined for the Lord's sake and may therefore presumably be neglected, if the Lord speaking
through His vicar should order otherwise, or, thirdly,
that the command to obey him is not without
qualification. He can point to the commission of
the prophet, " I have set thee over the nations and
over the kingdoms to root out and to pull down, and
to destroy," and, after drawing edifying conclusions
from the lights in the firmament, finally crush his
imperial disputant with the commission to S. Peter[5].

potestati atque istis tribunalibus subdit? Dedit nam et nobis
potestatem, dedit et principatum multo perfectiorem princi-
patibus vestris. Aut numquid justum vobis videtur, si cedat
spiritus carni, si terrenis caelestia superentur, si divinis prae-
ferantur humana?"

[1] *Decret.* Dist. x. c. 7.

[2] *Ibid.* Dist. xcvi. c. 11, "Si Imperator Catholicus est, filius
non praesul ecclesiae."

[3] *Ibid.* c. 13.

[4] *Decret. Greg.* Lib. i. Tit. vi. c. 34.

[5] *Ibid.* Tit. xxxiii. c. 6. There is a delightful explanation of
obedience being ordered not to 'the king,' but merely 'the king as

It is well known, that the theory of Papal supremacy with the power of releasing subjects from their allegiance and deposing kings involves a claim to universal monarchy[1]. It is clear, that the doctrine of the *plenitudo potestatis* embodies the most important elements of the theory of sovereignty, the notion, that is, that unity in a state is only to be obtained by the unquestioned supremacy of some one authority, whose acts are subject to no legal criticism. Further, it asserts the Divine institution of monarchy, as a form of government. This was the position claimed by the Papacy; men were driven thus to formulate its pretensions by the sense of the need of unity in the commonwealth. They do so by asserting the unity of the Church and of the universe, the claims of the Pope to derive his power immediately from God alone, and to be subject to none other. This is expressed most clearly in the Bull *Unam Sanctam*. There Boniface VIII. after

A theory of sovereignty by Divine Right.

The Bull Unam Sanctam.

supreme,' "Nec pure sit subscriptum regi praecellenti, sed interpositum forsitan non sine causâ, tanquam."

[1] An instance of the habit of alleging the Papal sovereignty in proof of the superiority of monarchy to other forms of government is the following passage of Barclay:—"Deus enim in suo peculiari populo hunc gubernandi modum expressit, unum illis ducem judicemque praeficiens. Ejusdem sic et Christus typum nobis edidit, sacratissimam illam monarchiam in persona Petri instituens......Neue in tam augusto perfectôque imperio imperfectam regiminis formam post se sineret inolescere; unum omnium hierarcham esse voluit, quem tota vbique Ecclesia principem agnoscat pastorem. Quae res satis declarat, quanto caeteris gubernandi speciebus, gratior sit unius principatus, ad quem omnes fere nationes, quantumuis barbarae et feroces, occulta quadam naturae vi, et primorum parentum exemplis incitantur." (*De Regno*, 82.)

asserting emphatically the unity of the Church and of all government and speaking of the unrent coat of Christ, declares that a body politic with two heads is a monstrosity. He employs the illustration of the two swords, declaring that the material sword is to be used for, not by the Church; and goes on to proclaim that the temporal power must be subject to the spiritual, that derelictions on the part of the temporal power may be judged by the spiritual, but that the supreme spiritual power is accountable to God alone. He quotes the commission to Jeremiah as proof that he is invested immediately by God with sovereign authority; and closes with applying to himself the command, "Whoso resisteth the power, resisteth the ordinance of God[1]."

Same method as that of seventeenth century.

Now, here, it is to be noted, are the methods and arguments, which subsist until the close of the seventeenth century. The Pope proclaims for himself a theory of complete sovereignty; he is king, the one true king, accountable to God alone; he asserts that unity is the soul of government, and that every government must have some supreme head as the centre of its unity; that the Christian commonwealth is a monarchy with this supreme authority vested in himself: he denies that there can be two ultimate authorities in the commonwealth, one temporal, one ecclesiastical; one must be subject to the other. He claims that his power comes from God alone, and is derived from no earthly intermediary. He declares that, on no pretence whatsoever, is resistance allowable to this

[1] *Extrav. Commun.* Lib. I. Tit. VIII. c. 7.

divinely ordained sovereign; while, in order to prove his doctrine of non-resistance to Papal commands, he employs the very text, which a later age makes the bulwark of its defence against the Pope in the claim that resistance to the king as God's vicar is worthy of damnation.

Here then is a theory of government by Divine Right, the exact converse of the theory of the Divine Right of Kings. It will be strange if the latter doctrine is not found to have its *raison d'être* as a contradiction and a counter-theory to that of Papal supremacy.

Once more, it is to be remarked, that the theory described above is essentially one of obedience, and of obedience from motives based upon religion. It is needful to bear this fact in mind. In the pursuit of their own aims the Popes were frequently driven to dissolve the bonds of allegiance in communities. Their supporters will speak slightingly of the duties of subjects to their sovereign. In their zeal for Papal authority, they will be found developing that theory of an original compact, which lies at the root of all theories of popular rights in the seventeenth century. Yet this was but an accident of the Papal position. Of its essence was the claim to the implicit obedience of all men, based upon even stronger sanctions of eternal punishment, than was the Divine Right of Kings.

A theory of obedience, not of liberty.

Hildebrand indeed may argue that all secular government is of diabolic origin[1]. John of Salisbury may quaintly decide the question as to whether it be lawful to flatter a tyrant, by the suggestion that it is lawful to flatter a man whom it is lawful to kill[2].

[1] Migne, *Patrologia*, 148, 595.   [2] *Polycraticus*, iii. 15.

With evident leaning to the more lenient view, S.
Thomas Aquinas may debate the point as to whether
a nation acting in common may restrain the excesses
of a tyrant, and declare in an *obiter dictum* that
regal as distinct from political power is a consequence of the Fall[1]. Lastly, John XXII., who in
the Bull *Si fratrum* takes up a position of complete
sovereignty and claims that the Imperial authority
being merely a delegation from the Pope it reverts
to him during an interregnum[2], may seem to ascribe
to the Emperor the same merely official position as
delegate of another earthly power, as was attributed
to kings by Whig theorists. Yet all this is not
because these men believe government and obedience to be things of small importance with 'the
trail of the serpent over them all.' It is because
government is in their eyes a sacred thing, and
obedience an integral part of the Divine Law, that
they cannot conceive of secular government, as
possessing any beyond subordinate authority. All
power is of God; therefore the temporal power
is only secondary, and must be subject to the spiritual. Obedience to governors is a Divine injunction; therefore in the last resort all men must obey
the Pope, the depositary of Divine authority as
against King or Emperor, whose position is either,
as some say, of merely human origin, or, as in another
view, a grant from God through the mediation of the
Pope. Men must obey a king, although obedience

---

[1] *De Regimine Principum*, i. 6. He is quite clear that private
individuals are forbidden to resist the sovereign.

[2] *Extrav. Joh.* Tit. v. c. 1.

involves disloyalty to an immediate lord, the king's vassal; but the Emperor is God's vassal, therefore he may be deposed at the bidding of the Pope, whose word is the voice of God.   So far indeed were the Popes from claiming on behalf of subjects any general rights against their sovereign, that, as in the case of John or Henry III. in England or of the Spanish monarchy, they ever shewed themselves stern supporters of royal rights, where they felt sure of the king. . The very claim to release subjects from their oath of allegiance implies that the oath is binding without such release on the part of the Pope.   In essence the theory of Papal sovereignty is a doctrine of obedience, of the Divine institution of all government, 'simply and strictly so called,' and of perfect sovereignty vested in a single head.   It is merely an accident that the theory was accompanied by views of the rights of resistance against governors of the secondary order, whose authority is merely delegated.   Absolute monarchy deriving its title from God alone, and obedience as a Divine command, are the root ideas of Papal theories of dominion.

Now against these claims it was needful for the Imperialists to manufacture some weapon.   The materials were ready to hand.   The Pope had claimed entire sovereignty because the commonwealth was one, and two authorities in it are a monstrosity; the Imperialists must do the same. The Pope had claimed rights of jurisdiction over the Emperor as evidenced by the donation of Constantine, and the translation of the Empire;

A counter-theory needed for the Empire.

the Imperialists must argue that the donation of
Constantine if a fact, was invalid, and that the
translation of the Empire had been misinterpreted.
They could maintain that, since the Empire was
inalienable, Constantine could not have given lasting
authority to the Papacy, and that the Pope, far from
creating Charles the Great Emperor, had merely
assented to a *fait accompli*; that so far was the
Pope from possessing a right to review' the choice
of the electors of the Holy Roman Empire, that
the Emperor possessed the right of reviewing the
choice of the conclave, and of examining into the
fitness of a proposed occupant of the Papal chair;
and that, as a fact, this right had been exercised.
Lastly, the Pope had claimed Divine Right for his
sovereignty, the Emperor must claim it for his. He
must demonstrate that the Empire is held of God
immediately and not of the Pope; that, since the
Emperor is God's vicar, he cannot be the Pope's
vassal; that the passages of Scripture alleged in
support of the duty of unlimited obedience to the
Pope are, if rightly interpreted, evidences of the
unconditioned authority of the Emperor; that the
words "my kingdom is not of this world" shew the
falsity of the pretended Papal supremacy; that the
true heretic is not he who denies, but he who asserts
that supremacy; that the command to "Render
unto Cæsar the things that are Cæsar's," and the
words of Christ to Pilate, "Thou couldest have no
power at all against me, unless it were given thee
from above," prove at once that the Pope has no
universal sovereignty and that secular government

is of Divine appointment. In a word, to the Divine Right of the Pope must be opposed the Divine Right of the Emperor.

Divine Right of Emperor opposed to Divine Right of Pope.

Imperialist writers claim in the first place that "unity, the soul of government" is entirely lost, if there be two distinct powers with competing systems of law and jurisdiction claiming authority at the same time; for "every kingdom divided against itself cannot stand." This is the burden of a great part of the *Defensor Pacis* of Marsiglio[1] of Padua, of the great *Dialogus* of William of Ockham[2], and of

Unity needed in a commonwealth.

---

[1] *Defensor Pacis*, i. 17; the whole of the second part is taken up with a demolition of the Papal pretensions, the great cause of disturbance and discord in the Empire. Cf. Hobbes's *Leviathan*, Bk. iii., "The Kingdom of Darkness," where the Church of Rome is regarded in the same way as above all things the enemy of peace in a State.

[2] *E.g.* the following passage: "Non solum illa societas est propinqua desolationi et ruinae, quae est contra se divisa; sed etiam illa quae ex modo regendi est disposita ad divisionem et divisioni propinqua. Sed si communitas fidelium habeat duas partes quarum una habeat judicem summum, et alia alium; communitas illa est disposita ad divisionem et divisioni propinqua." Ockham is feeling his way to the notion of territorial sovereignty, though it was entirely alien from the early theory of the Empire. "Potestas non solum est impatiens consortis super eosdem subjectos; sed etiam impatiens est consortis in eodem loco; sicut enim judex aliquis nollet, quod subditi sui essent alterius subditi; ita nollet quod aliquis alius haberet potestatem in loco, ubi subditi sui morantur. Ergo non solum est periculosa societas fidelium, si sint plures judices super eosdem populos vel subditos; sed etiam periculosa est societas fidelium, si in eodem loco etiam super diversos subditos fideles fuerint plures summi judices constituti, et ita non expedit quod clerici habeant unum summum judicem ecclesiasticum, scilicet papam; et laici unum summum judicem scilicet imperatorem; cum clerici et laici in eisdem locis simul commaneant......Nulla communitas simul viventium vita

the *De Monarchia* of Dante[1]. A large section of the work of William of Ockham could have no more appropriate title than "the anarchy of a mixed monarchy."

Need of unity in the State an argument for monarchy. This passionate sense of the importance of unity in the State is the ground of much of the sentiment not only against the Pope, but also against those who propose any but a single person as head of the State. It cannot be denied that "unity, the soul of government," is theoretically more completely realised in a monarchy than in any other form of government. At least there is no danger of the sovereign power dividing from within and splitting into two hostile factions, as may be the case with government under a representative system. There could be no fear of a schism in Prince or Pope as there might be in Parliament or Council. If this be taken into account, and the reaction against Papal claims be admitted as a ground of the feeling that unity in the State must be secured at all costs, there will be less inclination to blame the men in the seventeenth

politica est optime ordinata, nisi sit civiliter una. Unde fideles sicut sunt unum corpus in Christo, (*ad Rom.* I. 2), ita etiam debent esse corpus seu collegium in vita civili: sed communitas illa quae habet diversos summos judices seu diversa capita sive rectores, non est civiliter una; sicut illi, qui non habent unum regem, non sunt unum regnum." (*Dialogus*, Pars III. Tr. II. L. III. c. 19.)

[1] Dante argues that God cannot will what is contrary to nature; apparently he means by this that God cannot approve of any competing jurisdiction within the Empire, or of any earthly authority claiming to restrain the acts of "the lord of the world." (*De Monarchia*, III.)

or the fourteenth century[1], who argued that not only must there be one sovereign and not two, but that the sovereign must be one person, or else unity cannot be secured. The noteworthy fact is that the arguments employed are precisely the same in the fourteenth as in the seventeenth century. Ockham's long argument to shew that the Emperor is "over all persons and all causes supreme[2]" is on exactly the same lines as those of later times on behalf of royal authority against Papal interference; save that Ockham treats the Pope as an authority within the State, while English writers regard him as a foreign sovereign.

Similarity of arguments in fourteenth and seventeenth centuries.

There appear other elements of the theory of the sovereignty. It is a maxim with anti-papal controversialists that sovereignty is *in* alienable. Thus Dante[3] and Ockham[4] are found arguing that the

Other elements of theory of sovereignty.

---

[1] Dante indeed carries the argument further and makes it the basis of his proof, of the need of a universal monarchy. *De Monarchia*, Lib. I.

[2] *Dialogus*, Pars III. Tr. II. Lib. III. cc. 16-23. What could express more completely the claim to be ‘supreme over all causes’ than the following passage? "Concluditur ergo, quod communitas fidelium non erit optime gubernata civiliter, *etiam quantum ad vitam politicam*, nisi tota et omnis pars ejus habeat unum judicem et rectorem supremum, de cujus jurisdictione immediata vel mediata in omni casu ab eo vel à judicibus inferioribus eo omnis alius pro quocunque delicto debeat judicari." (*Ibid.* c. 20). The words I have italicised shew that secular politics are not the primary consideration of the author. *Supra*, pp. 39-41.

[3] *De Monarchia*, III. 10.

[4] Ockham's argument is that the Empire not having been founded by the Pope could not afterwards have become subject to him; any action of the Emperor with that object is invalid, for it destroys the Empire. *Dialogus*, Pars III. Tr. II. Lib. I. c. 18.

Donation of Constantine must be invalid, for the Emperor may not destroy the Empire. Ockham declares that sovereignty can neither be divided, nor diminished, nor alienated[1]. Although his notions of obedience are not those of later times, he distinctly asserts, that an emperor or king is *solutus legibus*[2]. In the seventeenth century all these notions reappear. The king grants privileges to Parliament, but sovereignty is inalienable, therefore they may be revoked. He governs by the law, because he is virtuous, not because he is obliged by it. He cannot by diminishing his sovereignty prejudice the rights of his successors.

Contro-versy about corona-tion and unction, as in later times.

Even the special points, around which later controversy rages, are discussed. The importance of coronation is insisted upon by Papalists, as a means of proving that the Emperor holds his office from the Pope, exactly as in the later times it is held to be evidence of a compact between king and people. The author of the latter part of the *De Regimine Principum* regards the ceremony of unction, as evidence of the authority over kings vested in the Pope, the interpreter of the Divine Law; the king is the Lord's anointed; and therefore the Lord by means of His vicar may exercise authority over

---

[1] "Romanum imperium non potest minui nec dividi, saltem absque consensu tacito vel expresso communitatis mortalium." *Dialogus*, Pars III. Tr. II. Lib. I. c. 31.

[2] "Imperator in imperio mundi, et rex in regno suo solutus est legibus, nec tenetur de necessitate judicare secundum leges." *Ibid.* c. 15. Cf. also c. 16, "Imperator est super omnia jura positiva."

him[1]. Controversialists assert, on the other side, precisely as those of later times, that coronation has no necessary place in conferring royal or imperial power, which exists equally before it[2]. There are arguments, quite in the manner of Hickes, to prove that an infidel may be the lawful recipient of obedience; special stress is laid on the case of Julian the Apostate; just as French writers on behalf of Henry IV. and English opponents of the Exclusion Bill were to argue, that since the primitive Christians were loyal to Julian, the fact of the heir being a heretic could not bar his claim to the succession.

But this was not enough.   It was vain to demonstrate the necessity of unity in a stable commonwealth.   The Papalist was as ardent an enthusiast *More than this needed.* for unity as the Imperialist.   Indeed, had the dream of Papal sovereignty ever been entirely realised in practice, it would not have been of the lack of unity in the governing authority that men would have complained.   It was useless to prove the inconvenience of the Papal claims or the utility of the Imperial power.   What could avail considerations of expediency and theories of utility against an opponent, who claimed to exercise power derived by a direct grant from God?   The only effective method *Divine Right must be claimed for the Emperor.* of controverting the Papal pretensions was to elaborate a counter theory that the Emperor's rights came direct from God.

[1] *De Regimine Principum*, III. 16.
[2] "Omnem gladii potestatem et administrationem temporalem habent ante coronationem quam habent post." *Dialogus*, Pars III. Tr. I. L. I. c. 22.

Dante perceived this. The De Monarchia.
Dante perceived the necessity of this more clearly than some other Imperialist writers. This it is, which gives to the *De Monarchia* a value, as a controversial treatise, far above that of other works in many ways more interesting. Dante meets the Papal claim to a universal sovereignty by Divine Right with a direct counter-claim on behalf of the Empire. He shews that a universal monarchy is ordained by God, that the Roman Empire won its position through God's grant, and that the Emperor derives his authority not from the Church, but immediately from God. Since all power is of God, if the Emperor's power be lawful at all, the only question is whether it comes from God directly, or through the medium of the Church. Dante occupies himself with a careful demolition of the Papalist arguments, thus proving indirectly that the Emperor holds his crown immediately from God alone; he finally proves this directly. Even had Dante written no other work than the *De Monarchia*, it would be hard to refrain from admiration of the mind, which struck out with such force and lucidity the line of argument, which was to remain for centuries the one effectual answer to all claims of the right of Papal or clerical interference with the freedom of secular governments. By its intellectual grasp and breadth of treatment, the *De Monarchia*, despite its scholastic character, is raised far above the great majority of controversial treatises on the same subject.

Marsiglio of Padua, Defensor Pacis.
It is easy for us to admire the political philosophy of Marsiglio[1], to hail him as the earliest upholder of

[1] *Defensor Pacis*, I. 12, 13. For a further exposition of

religious toleration and to recognise his acuteness in
striking out the notion of representative democracy.
Yet it is impossible not to feel that this very fact,
the modern character of the *Defensor Pacis*, which
renders its interest so great, must have detracted
from its controversial value. As a counterblast to
the Papal claims, it is far less effective than Dante's
short work, and lacks the ring of enthusiasm which
vibrates through every page of the *De Monarchia*.

Moreover, both Marsiglio of Padua and William *Utili-*
of Ockham are largely though not exclusively, con- *tarian ar-*
guments of
cerned with utilitarian arguments, and utilitarian *Marsiglio*
arguments must ever appear beside the point to an *and*
Ockham.
opponent arguing on behalf of an authority which
he believes to be Divine. Again, both these authors
allow to subjects some right of resisting the sovereign[1]. Such an admission made immensely in favour
of the Papacy. For if resistance or coercion of the
prince be justified at all, clearly it must be so in defence of the Divine Law, and who is to interpret the
Divine Law save the vicar of Christ? Further, the
notion of Marsiglic that the true legislative authority
is the people may have the merit of anticipating

Marsiglio's philosophy and its relation to modern thought see
Poole, *Illustrations of the History of Mediæval Thought*, chap. 9,
The opposition to the temporal claims of the Papacy: also
Wycliffe and Movements of Reform, 28–42. On his teaching of
religious toleration, see Creighton, *Persecution and Tolerance*,
94–97.

[1] *Defensor Pacis*, i. c. 18. Ockham argues that monarchy is
the best form of government, because it is easier to restrain a
single head of the State. "Facilius sit populo emendare unum
rectorem (si taliter exorbitaverit), ut sit puniendus vel etiam
amovendus quam plures." *Dialogus*, Pars III. Tr. II. L. i. c. 18.

modern ideas[1]; but it weakened his position as a
controversialist. For it detracted from the dignity
and authority of the Emperor, the only power whom
it was possible to regard as upon a level with the
Pope. If, as Marsiglio claimed, the Emperor was to
have coercive authority over the Pope, he needed
every possible accession of dignity and prerogative.
It was absurd to lay claim to this position, for one
who is not conceived as truly sovereign, but is merely
an official executing the will of the true sovereign,
the people. So exalted a privilege as that of judging
the vicar of God, asserted on behalf of a merely
representative Emperor, must have appeared su-
premely ridiculous in the eyes of men, for whom
Canossa was the *terminus a quo* of Papal assumption,
while their theory of ecclesiastical dominion exceeded
the wildest dreams of Gregory VII. or Innocent III.

William of Ockham. Both William of Ockham and Marsiglio of Padua
assert, that the Emperor's power is from God. But
both of them regard the constitution of the Empire
and even its existence as of human institution[2]; if
in the future it should transgress the principle of
utility it may be abolished. For both of them it
arises by human, not Divine ordinance. Yet Marsiglio
regards the Emperor as God's vicar in a far fuller
and truer sense than is the Pope. With the rights
of the Electors still effectively exercised, it was
plainly impossible to assert any such claim of im-

[1] *Defensor Pacis*, i. 12, 18.

[2] *Defensor Pacis*, i. 18. *Dialogus*, Pars iii. Tr. ii. L. i. cc. 8,
29–81. Marsiglio expressly disclaims any inquiry into the Mosaic
polity, which was ordained directly by God; he is concerned only
with principalities set up by human law. (i. 9).

mediate investiture by God, as might be claimed
for hereditary monarchs. Although, however, Marsiglio[1] and William of Ockham are aware that some
Divine authority must be asserted on behalf of the
Imperial power, they are far too much governed by
the notion of utility to make this the kernel of their
work. Ockham indeed, in a passage that sounds to
modern ears like an echo of Hobbes, places the
origination of the Empire in the people[2]. The
account, as may be supposed, is far less historically
accurate, than is that of Dante. The latter is so
wedded to the notion that the Empire is held
immediately from God alone, that he regards the
electors, not as themselves choosing the Emperor,
but as merely announcing God's choice[3].

In asserting his claim to supremacy the Pope *Conflict of*
came into collision not merely with the decaying *the Papacy*
with
forces of the Empire, but with the rising nationalities *France.*
of Europe, which were growing stronger every year,
as feudalism gave way before the central power.
Perhaps the most dramatic achievement of the
middle ages, if the journey of Henry IV. to Canossa
be excepted, was the repudiation by Philip the Fair
of the claim of Boniface VIII. to a position of complete supremacy over all earthly potentates. In the
Bull *Unam Sanctam*[4] Boniface VIII. had carried
Papal assumption to its highest point; and the ruin,
that in consequence befell him, forms the starting-

---

[1] *Defensor Pacis,* II. 30. Marsiglio is at pains to expound the
true meaning of Rom. xiii., and to declare in strong terms the sin
of resisting the ordinance of God. (*Ibid.* II. 25).

[2] *Dialogus,* Pars III. Tr. II. L. I. c. 8.

[3] *De Monarchia,* III. 16.   [4] *Supra,* p. 49.

point of all later French argument against the political claims of the Papacy.

Theory of Divine Right in France.

From this time forth the freedom of France from Papal interference is the despairing admiration of Imperialist authors[1]. It is not then a matter for surprise, that writers in France begin to develope the same notions of the Divine Right of secular govern-

Raoul of Praelles, 1870.

ments, as are to be found in the Empire. One author in the fourteenth century asserts with emphasis, that the French king holds his kingdom immediately from God alone[2]. Another argues, that, all priesthood before Christ being merely typical, kingship is the

John of Paris, 1805.

older and therefore the superior of the two[3]. He declares, that the Papal authority cannot come im- mediately from God, for in that case the prince would be the servant of the Pope, as he is of Christ, and this would be to contradict the xiiith of Romans, where the king is spoken of as the vicar of God, not the Pope[4]; he goes on to argue in the usual manner from the words, "Touch not mine anointed" and other texts[5].

Summary.

Thus it appears that from the beginning of the middle ages politics are conceived as essentially a branch of theology; that the Popes were gradually driven by the exigencies of their position to claim for themselves a position of perfect sovereignty,

[1] Ockham repeatedly alleges the case of the King of France, who is admittedly free from Papal interference, as an argument on behalf of the Emperor.

[2] "Il tient et possede son Royaume de Dieu tant seulement sans aucun moyen en tele maniere, que il ne se tient de quelque homme, ne qu'il ne le tient du Vicaire de Jhesu Christ, ne en tant come homme, ne en tant com son Vicaire." (Goldast, i. 49.)

[3] *De Potestate Regia et Papali*, cc. 4, 5.

[4] *Ibid.* c. 11.   [5] *Ibid.* c. 14.

sovereignty by Divine Right, disobedience to which is a mortal sin; that, as against this doctrine, the supporters of the Emperor formulate a theory of sovereignty based upon the ground of the necessity of unity in the state; that they meet the Pope's pretensions to supremacy as God's vicar by asserting, all of them in some measure, Dante most clearly and completely, that the Emperor's authority exists by Divine Right and comes by grace of God not of the Pope; that they apply to him the scriptural injunctions to obedience, which Boniface VIII. made bold to wrest into a command of unlimited obedience to the Papacy; and, lastly, that this or a similar position is taken up by writers on behalf of the French king. The necessity of unity as the foundation of sovereignty, and the Divine Right of secular governments to be free from Papal interference are the root ideas of Imperialist writers. The Divine Right of the Emperor is asserted not for its own sake, but against a similar claim to Divine Right put forward by the Pope. Both sides recognise that power is of God, both are aware, that there must be in the state some supreme authority above the law. But in one view the Divine source of all authority is held to carry with it the supremacy of the spiritual power. These pretensions could only be met by the assertion, that secular government was not merely allowed but was actually ordained by God, and that the secular prince held immediately of Him with no intervening authority; or in the words of John of Jandun, *Potestas imperialis est immediate a Deo, non a Papa.*

F.   5

CHAPTER IV.

WYCLIFFE AND KING RICHARD II.

English claims of freedom from Papal control.

IN the middle ages thought and learning were international, and it would be strange, if the controversies which were seething on the Continent during the earlier part of the fourteenth century found no counterpart in England. Moreover William of Ockham was an Englishman and an Oxonian. England had claimed for long to be an Empire; freedom from Papal interference was more or less an aspiration of English statesmen from the times of the Conqueror and Henry II. Even at the period of completest subjection to the Papacy, the Barons could meet the attempt to assimilate the English law of inheritance to the rules of the Canon law with the emphatic negative "*nolumus leges Angliae mutari*[1]." From the time of Edward I., who outlawed the clergy rather than submit to the bull *clericis laicos*, there had been passed a series of statutes in restraint of Papal claims. All this might well induce a writer with an anticlerical bias or a monarch with high ideas of his own dignity, to claim complete 'freedom,'

[1] *Statute of Merton*, c. 9.

i.e. sovereignty for the English Crown, and to claim it as coming by Divine Right. This view finds expression in the writings of Wycliffe, and is also, so far as we can gather, the basis of the definite theory of kingship held by King Richard II.

I.

The *De Officio Regis* was written by Wycliffe *Wycliffe's* rather with the object of asserting the duty 'of the' *'De Officio Regis.'* sovereign to 'assist' the Church by disendowing the clergy of their temporalities[1] than with any direct purpose of exalting regal as against Papal authority. Yet the writer bases his practical exhortations upon a doctrine very similar to that proclaimed in the Empire and France[2]. The king is God's vicar in things *Royal* temporal, as is the priest in things spiritual. But *power superior to* the dignity of the king is superior to that of the *sacerdotal.* priest, for the king reflects the godhead of Christ, the priest only His manhood[3]. Thus the spiritual

[1] *De Officio Regis*, 216. The references are to the pages in the Wycliffe Society's Edition.

[2] *Ibid.* 73. "Non enim est jus humanum nisi de quanto fundatum fuerit in lege Dei divina." This is the fundamental basis on which all anti-papal writers ground their theory of Divine Right. There is no human right except by God's law. But there are real human rights. Therefore divine authority must be asserted for them. Starting from the same major premiss the Pope drew the conclusion that all human rights centred in him; and thereby would have ultimately dissolved them. Those who felt the importance of justifying secular governments, were forced to argue that they have true rights by Divine law independent of the Papal grant.

[3] *Ibid.* 12—14. "Ex quibus videtur, quod oportet vicarium Cristi sub racione qua Christus per vicarium Cristi sub racione qua deus capitaliter regulari."

power is inferior to the temporal in earthly dignity
and authority, although in true dignity the priest
excels the king. The famous decretal of Innocent
III. is explained away, and a theory extracted from
it of the complete sovereignty of the temporal power[1].
The author admits that of the two jurisdictions secular and ecclesiastical one must control the other.
But he argues that the more perfect state has not
always the higher authority; Christ's cleansing of
the temple is an imperial, His submitting to death a
sacerdotal act; hence royal authority is the higher[2].
There must be one supreme head in a state, else
there will be confusion; the temporal power is this
head, and it is not enough to have the king supreme
in temporals, he must be supreme in all causes[3].
Wycliffe is not certain, which of the two powers is

[1] *Supra* p. 48. *De Officio Regis*, 84—86. The argument is less
sophistical than might appear. For Innocent's letter was merely
about a question of precedence, and might be held to imply no
more, than would a claim to give the toast "Church and State."
Compare Cardinal Vaughan's explanation of his giving the toast
"The Pope and the Queen" at the Mansion House in 1898.

[2] *Ibid.* 137. "Unde Cristus quedam fecit ut Imperator, ut
ementes et vendentes in templo flagellando ejecit. i q. iii *Ex
Multis*, quedam ut sacerdos cum se ipsum in cruce obtulit. Cum
igitur prior potestas habet racionem agentis eciam in sacerdotes,
secunda vero potestas habet racionem pacientis eciam ab eisdem
sacerdotibus, videtur quod ex hoc naturali principio 'agens est pre-
stancius passo' potestas regalis sit prestancior potestate sacerdotali."

[3] *Ibid.* 138, 9, "Item vel oportet illas potestates ex equo haberi,
vel unam subordinari alteri. Si enim neutra subordinaretur
alteri secundum leges humanas vergeret ad confusionem ecclesie."
Note that the Church, not the State, is his object; politics are as
yet merely the handmaid of theology, the secular State is needful
for the sake of the Church.

truly greater, yet the Pope cannot be above the
Emperor in the sight either of God or man; for he
is his minister[1]. Besides (according to S. Augustine)
Adam was the first king, and Cain the first priest[2].
Priests should not refuse to be called the king's
priests[3]. The common arguments and illustrations
are employed. The Pope was the liegeman of the
Emperor before the donation of Constantine, and
he can never have ceased to be so since[4]. Emperors
have deposed Popes[5]. To understand Romans iii. or
1 Peter ii. of any but the secular power is sophistry[6].

Wycliffe will not allow that the king is subject *The King above the Law.*
to positive law. He should obey his own laws but
his obedience is voluntary, not by compulsion. For
the king is *solutus legibus*; and when law is spoken
of as governing him it is moral or Divine and not
positive law that is intended[7].

For him as for Ockham the necessity of unity in
the state is the main proof of the excellence of
monarchy[8].

---

[1] *De Officio Regis*, 143. "Unum audenter assero quod, nec
clamor cleri nostri nec scriptura faciunt quod papa iste sit majus
cesare vel quo ad seculum, vel quo ad deum. Nam ministrare
sacramenta non est opus auctoritatis, sed vicarie servitutis, sed
conducere et precipere taliter ministrare. Quod autem papa sit
sic magnus reputative quo ad mundum hoc habet a cesare."

[2] *Ibid.* 144.   [3] *Ibid.* 197.

[4] *Ibid.* 202.   [5] *Ibid.* 128.   [6] *Ibid.* 67.

[7] *Ibid.* 98 sqq. After defining the law of reason or nature
he goes on, "Lex contracta per civilitatem connotat supra
talem veritatem ordinacionem et promulgacionem humanam ad
civile dominium regulandum, et sic est rex principalis conditor
legis sue."

[8] *Ibid.* 246.

Similar theory to that of Imperialists. Here is a theory of sovereignty, vested in the king by Divine Right and in no way subject to the Pope. It can hardly be supposed, that so great a scholar as Wycliffe wrote his treatise in ignorance of the works of Ockham. Although its method is not quite the same, and the whole book is inferior in grasp and insight to that of the earlier author, yet the conclusions are the same, and it cannot be assuming too much to suppose, that the Imperialist theory influenced English thought in this way.

Inconsistency of notions upon obedience. It need scarcely be mentioned, that with Wycliffe's theory of dominion founded in grace, a bad king has no real dominion[1]. Yet in Wycliffe's system this would be no bar to a doctrine of unlimited obedience[2]. Throughout the greater portion of his work he appears to uphold a theory of this sort, arguing in favour of passive obedience and quoting with approval the examples of the Saviour, and the primitive Christians[3]. Yet in other places he contradicts this, first declaring that it is possible to obey by resisting[4] (by which he might mean no more than passive obedience), but going on to inculcate the duty of rebellion and even tyrannicide as possible modes of obedience[5]. It is impossible to acquit him of inconsistency in this respect. Indeed this same inconsistency is found in Marsiglio and

[1] *De Officio Regis*, 17. Tyrants have power but not dominion. "Realiter habent potestatem et dignitatem consequentem secundum quam regunt....Sed illa potestas non est dominium."

[2] For expositions of Wycliffe's theory of Lordship, see Poole, *Illustrations of the History of Mediæval Thought*, Ch. x. ; Wycliffe, *Movements of Reform*, Chap. vi.

[3] *De Officio Regis*, 6 sqq.   [4] *Ibid.* 82.   [5] *Ibid.* 201.

Ockham.   They both emphatically proclaim the
authority of the Scriptural prohibitions of resistance,
yet in certain cases they seem to approve *a* resistance.

Causes of this.

It is only natural that this should be the case.
The writers of the fourteenth century were en-
gaged in elaborating an anti-papal theory.   In a
doctrine, which is only in the making, it is vain to
look for the same harmony and consistency in all its
parts, as is to be found, for instance, in the developed
theory of the Divine Right of Kings.   Yet there is
no doubt, that this admission of a right of resistance,
however qualified, gives away the whole case against
the Papacy.   Once resistance under any circumstances be admitted, heresy is seen to be a plain
case for it, and the Pope on any view is the judge
of that.   Wycliffe condemns all who resist a tyrant,
save on behalf of God's law; he will have nothing to
do with utilitarian obedience[1].   Now this is to proclaim a doctrine of complete subjection, so far as
civil matters are concerned, while it by implication
grants to the Pope, as the interpreter of the Divine
Law, the right of interference in all states.   Wycliffe
takes away the independence of the prince without

---

[1] *De Officio Regis*, 8. " 'Vel illata est iniuria quo ad causam
propriam vel pure quo ad causam dei. In primo casu post exhorta-
cionem evangelicam paciencia est optima medicina. Si pure in causa
dei cristianus debet, post correpcionem evangelicam, preposito suo
usque ad mortem, si oportet, confidenter et obedienter resistere.
Et sic utrobique innitendum est paciencie, comittendo humiliter
deo judicium iniuriam vindicandi.' Et qui excedit hanc regulam
resistit dampnabiliter potestati et dei ordinacioni, ut faciunt hii
qui rebellant precipue, id est *affeccione comodi temporalis potestatis.*"
Mutatis mutandis, Wycliffe's view is that of Bellarmine.

establishing the liberty of the subject; and his theory, if practically carried out, would have been used to support both the tyranny of an orthodox[1] king, and the interference of a meddlesome Pope. It would have had all the disadvantages of the theory of the Divine Right of Kings combined with those of clerical supremacy and would have been without the advantages of either doctrine. But this was not foreseen by Wycliffe, and the main drift of his work is to inculcate the universal authority of the Crown and the religious duty of submission to it on the part of all classes. Until religious toleration should become an accepted maxim, or the claim of Pope or clergy to authority in spiritual things be disallowed, there was no completely effective method of meeting the Papal claim to political supremacy save by a theory of absolute non-resistance and Divine Right. The mediæval controversialists had arrived at the latter notion, and were gradually feeling their way towards the former. But they did not proclaim it with the same uncompromising firmness, as characterised the divines of a later day; and their doctrine failed to attain its object, whether in practice or theory.

II.

Possible influences upon Richard II.

Whether the speculations of Wycliffe exercised any influence over Richard II. may be doubted. Nor is there evidence that his theory of kingship

---

[1] 'Orthodox' here must be taken to mean orthodox in the view of the recognized spiritual authority, whether Pope or "poor priest." The theory really subjects the temporal power to the spiritual, and would justify all ecclesiastical theories of politics.

was in any way derived from the writings of the
Imperialist advocates. Yet at least it is certain
that men could not remain unaffected by the great
controversy between John XXII. and Lewis of
Bavaria, and that the ideas expressed by writers on
behalf of the Emperor would be peculiarly welcome
to Englishmen. Nor can it be denied that the
assertion about this time of the independence of
England from Papal interference might easily move
a man of Richard's narrowly logical type of mind to
claim for himself the position of an absolute monarch
by Divine Right. He was the last person to ignore
the significance of the preamble to the great Statute
of Praemunire, which asserts, that "this crown of
England hath been so free at all times that it hath
been in no earthly subjection in all things touching
the regality of the said crown[1]." If this were really *His*
so, he would take care to maintain intact the "right *position*
anti-
and liberty of the crown," and would see to it, that *papal.*
no Parliamentary or baronial combination should
drive him to abate it one jot or tittle. Although we
find him attacked for lowering his dignity before the
Pope[2], this is undoubtedly a case of collusion, in which
he sought to obtain the Pope's authority for the great
constitutional changes of the Parliament of Shrewsbury. When it is his interest, he is willing enough
that Archbishop Arundel should be translated to S.
Andrew's, by Papal authority; yet he complains to

[1] 16 Ric. II. c. 5, *Statutes of the Realm.*
[2] *Articles of Deposition*, c. 10. Cf. also Walsingham, II. 203;
the king and John of Gaunt are regarded as more inclined than
Parliament to yield to the Pope in regard to the repeal of the
Statute of Provisors.

the clergy of the abominable custom of Papal trans-
lations, which in the case of Archbishop Nevill had
been employed as a political weapon against himself;
and he offers his support, if they will make a stand
in the matter against the see of Rome[1].   He cannot
understand why the Pope should demand the repeal
of the "statutes" of *Praemunire* and *Quare Impedit*,
although he is glad to learn that his Holiness has no
desire to diminish the right and liberty of the Crown
of England[2].   When he is on the side of the Pope,
it is for reasons of immediate convenience; at heart
he is as anti-papal as Henry VIII.[3]   Indeed he is
accused of interfering with the ecclesiastical
courts[4].

Richard's theory of absolute monarchy.   But whether or no Richard was influenced by
the writings of Wycliffe and the Imperialist theory,
he certainly believed in the sacredness of his office,
and in the 'liberty' of his Crown more strongly than
any of his predecessors, and devoted all his energies
to the establishment of a despotism.   He is ever
nervously 'guarding' and 'saving' his Crown and
dignity.   In the shrill tones of the *doctrinaire* politician, he repeatedly declares that nothing he does

[1] Walsingham, II. 228.
[2] John Malverne in Appendix to Higden, IX. 256.
[3] Walsingham, II. 109; Higden, IX. 26.
[4] *Articles of Deposition*, c. 29.   In regard to a dispute as to an
election of the Abbot of S. Edmondsbury we are told, that "the seide
kynge sende embassiatours to the Pope commawndyng them to saye
to the pope, that his wylle schoeld not be flexible in this matter."
Appendix IV. to Higden's *Polychronicon*, VIII. 452; Walsingham,
II. 68.   Richard afterwards yielded, much to the disgust of Walsingham.   "Sicut Ecclesiae Anglicanae detrimentum, ita Papae et
curialibus magnam peperit materiam insolescendi." (*Ibid.* 97.)

shall prejudice his prerogative.   On the nobles
threatening him with deposition he gives way 'saving
the rights of the Crown[1].'   The commission of 1386
he sincerely regards as void, as being against the
liberty of the Crown[2].   He is the sole source of law,
not bound by custom[3]; king by God's grace and right
of birth[4], he will not endure that his liberty be
touched.

Nor did Richard confine himself to words. He *His*
tampered with the Rolls of Parliament[5]; he altered *practice.*
and nullified statutes agreed upon by both Houses
of Parliament[6].   He exercised a dispensing power
that was liberal beyond the custom of such a king
as Edward III. ; he in various ways shewed that he
regarded neither law nor custom as binding his
action.   But it is in the last years of his reign, that

---

[1] John Malverne, Appendix to Higden's *Polychronicon*, IX. 115.

[2] Richard appears to have felt that in assenting to the demands
of this commission he was virtually resigning the crown. Walsingham, II. 152. Cf. also *Rot. Parl.* III. 224, "Le roi en plein Parlement devant le fyn d'icell, fist overte Protestation par sa bouche
demesne Qe pur riens qu'estoit fait en le dit Parlement il ne vorroit
que prejudice avendroit a lui ne a sa corone; einz que sa Prerogatif
et la Libertees de sa dite Corone feussent sauvez et gardez."

[3] "Rex...dixit expresse vultu austero et protervo, quod leges
suae erant in ore suo, et aliquotiens in pectore suo, et quod ipse
solus possit mutare et condere leges regni sui." *Articles of Deposition*, c. 16.

[4] *Rot. Parl.* III. 839.

[5] Walsingham, II. 227; *Articles of Deposition*, c. 8.

[6] Walsingham, II. 48. "Sed quid juvant Statuta Parliamen-
torum, cum penitus expost nullum sortiantur effectum? Rex
nempe cum Privato Consilio cuncta vel mutare vel delere solebat,
quae in Parliamentis ante habitis tota regni non solum communitas, sed et ipsa nobilitas, statuebat." *Articles of Deposition*, c. 17.

Parlia-
ment of
1397-8.

✓

ᵥ·

his views found their fullest expression and came
near to being embodied in the constitution. In
the famous Parliament of 1397–8, he obtained the
repeal of the pardon of the Lords Appellant; he procured the ratification of the opinions of the judges
at Nottingham, which condemned the Commission
of Reform of 1386, declared the proposers of it guilty
of high treason, and gave the king power to arrange
the order of business in Parliament, a rule that would
have entirely prevented the growth of the maxim
Redress of grievances before supply; finally he persuaded the Parliament to delegate its authority to a
perpetual committee of eighteen[1].

His object
to create a
permanent
despotism.

There can be no question, that by these measures
Richard was attempting to create a written constitution, a *lex regia*, which should save the rights of
the English Crown for ever. It is made high treason
to attempt the repeal of the statutes; all solemnly
swear to keep them. For the future, tenants of fiefs,
whether barons or bishops, are to swear to maintain
the acts, before obtaining livery of seisin[2]. The
king writes to the Pope in order to obtain his confirmation of the measures, an unheard of thing, made
one of the grounds of his deposition[3]. Finally, in his
will Richard bequeaths his private treasure to his
successor, with the proviso that he shall ratify and
observe the statutes of the Parliament of Shrews-

---

[1] 21 Ric. II. cc. 1—20. *Statutes of Realm* II. 94—110.

[2] *Rot. Parl.* III. 852 sqq. Even this oath is taken "sauvant
au Roi sa Regalie et Liberté et le droit de sa corone."

[3] The articles of deposition are given in Knyghton (Twysden,
Decem Scriptores, 2746—2756); *Rot. Parl.* III. 417—427.

bury. Failing his requirement with the condition, the treasure is left to others, who are to labour even unto death to effect the ratification of the statutes[1].

The import of this is plain. Richard desired to found an absolute monarchy, and to relieve the Crown of all the limitations, with which custom had fenced it about. The principle which animates the king is clear and definite. He acts not from caprice or momentary lust of dominion; but with a settled purpose and resolute endeavour he asserts the rights of kingship and attempts to render them secure for future ages. The clearest insight into Richard's theory is given by the sermon preached by the Bishop of Exeter at the opening of this Parliament[2].

The text is *Rex unus est omnibus*[3], and the preacher argues that there must be one king, and one governor; otherwise no realm can be governed; in a word, "mixed monarchy" is anarchy. To this end of unity in the state three things are necessary; the king must be powerful, the laws must be kept, and subjects must be obedient. The Crown is possessed of certain privileges, which may not be alienated; any act attempting to do so is void. Parliament is therefore summoned to enquire, whether any such rights have been alienated in the past, that remedy may be taken, *non obstante* any ordinance to the contrary. For the king is the source of law and the judges

Sermon of Bishop of Exeter.

[1] Rymer, VIII. 75, *Articles of Deposition*, c. 81.
[2] *Rot. Parl.* III. 347.
[3] Ezek. xxxvii. 22.

are bound to maintain the rights of his Crown. The same idea comes out in the speech of the Chancellor at the re-assembling of Parliament at Shrewsbury; the object of meeting, he says, is to see that there be not several sovereigns in the kingdom, but one only[1]. All this is on exactly the same lines, as the anti-papal arguments of Ockham and others, to prove the omnipotence of the sovereign authority from the necessity of unity in the state.

It may be noticed, that in making Parliament the instrument of the destruction of its own liberties, Richard set the precedent, afterwards followed with better success by Henry VIII. The general pardon which he granted to his subjects[2], is an exact parallel to the famous pardon of the whole realm by Henry VIII. for its breach of the Statute of Praemunire. Richard appears also to have been the first king, who saw the advantage of manipulating Parliament; he is accused of packing the House with his own nominees and of bribing members[3].

Richard's views of sacredness of kingship and of unction. Walsingham tells us that after this act the sheriffs throughout the kingdom were compelled to take new and unaccustomed oaths, that they would obey the king's commands whether signified under the Great Seal, the Privy Seal, or even the Signet[4]. That Richard was standing up for what he believed

---

[1] *Rot. Parl.* III. 857.

[2] 21 Ric. II. c. 20: the Bishop of Exeter declares the granting of this pardon to be one of the chief grounds of the summoning of Parliament.

[3] *Articles of Deposition*, c. 19.

[4] Walsingham, II. 231; *Articles of Deposition*, c. 20.

to be a principle seems proved by his repeatedly
declaring during his troubles, that his wretched
condition was an outrage on all kings, and would
bring royalty into dishonour[1]. We know, that until
the day of his death he regarded himself as king
by virtue of unction, despite his deposition, that
he regarded this ceremony as conferring a sacramental grace[2], and that he directed in his will, that
he should receive a royal funeral. It seems clear,
then, that ideas, originally framed into a system of
defence against the Papacy, found expression in a
doctrine of absolute monarchy held by a self-willed
English king, and of the divine origin of kingship
as evidenced by the custom of hereditary succession
and by the indelible character of unction.

· For the position of Richard as king was itself a *His*
strong proof of the progress of the idea that in- *accession
a proof of*

[1]   "Ce sera pour lui [le roi de France] grant vitupere,
        Voire et pour tous les royz qui nez de mere
        Sont au jourduy;
        Veu loultrage et le tresgrant ennuy,
        La povrete et le point ou. je suy."
                    (*Histoire du Roy d'Angleterre Richard*: Archaeol.
                        Britann., xx. 339.)
There is much more in the same strain. In speaking of Bolingbroke Richard is made to say:
            "Tous ceulx seront ses ennemis
            Qui aymeront honneur, loyaute, pris
            Et vasselaige."
[2] Walsingham, II. 240. The king had wished to be a second
time anointed, with oil from the Holy Land. It was used for
Henry IV.; Richard speaks of himself as unworthy *tam nobile
sacramentum.* That he desired the ceremony of unction to be repeated is nothing against his regarding it as a sacrament, conferring
a grace.

advance of ideas of primogeniture. herent birthright is the chief title to the regal dignity. Like Arthur of Brittany, Richard was a boy when the throne became vacant; as in the case of Arthur, his father had not himself worn the Crown; while, in both cases, there was living an uncle ambitious and unscrupulous, and one of the most powerful men in the country. Yet while in the twelfth century, the uncle succeeded and the principle of an elective monarchy was affirmed; in the fourteenth, there is no question about the nephew's succession; the principle of representative primogeniture has triumphed.

Appearance of doctrine of legitimism. Lastly, the speech of the Bishop of Carlisle, which is familiar to us from Shakespeare's version[1], is evidence that the doctrines of unlimited obedience, and of legitimism are becoming popular, and that the new dynasty which bases itself on the rights of the nation and the choice of Parliament will have to encounter an opposition grounded upon the claims of hereditary right and upon the iniquity of rebellion[2].

---

[1] *King Richard II.* Act IV. Sc. I, ll. 114—149. Shakespeare, who changes the circumstances, took the speech from Holinshed, who got it from Hall. The latter apparently found it in *Lystoire de la traison et mort du roy Richart dengleterre.* (*English Historical Society's* Edition, pp. 70, 1.) Cf. also the speech of the Earl of Warwick in 1386. (Higden, IX. 110.)

[2] The proclamation of the French king against the usurper is further evidence of this. *Lystoire de la traison,* Appendix H.

CHAPTER V.

KINGSHIP IN ENGLAND FROM HENRY IV.
TO ELIZABETH.

THE claims of Richard II. to found a despotism *Constitu-* were repudiated by the nation. The Revolution of *tional Re-volution* 1399 is an assertion of the right of Englishmen to *of 1399.* constitutional government. The articles of deposition in which the charges against Richard are set forth, contain or imply a theory of constitutionalism as uncompromising as the absolutist doctrine of the king. Nor was this all. In elevating Henry of Bolingbroke to the throne the English nobles passed over the nearest heir, and asserted the right of Parliament to elect the fittest person from within the royal family. Yet the position is not quite clear. Henry paid homage to the principle of legitimism by his claim to be the nearest heir to Henry III. The fiction was transparent enough; no one believed *Henry's* Henry's ancestor Edmund Crouchback to have been *claim to hereditary* older than his brother Edward I. Yet the more *right* ridiculous the fable appears, the stronger is the *evidence of popular* evidence it affords of the hold upon the minds of *sentiment.* Englishmen of the principle of strict hereditary succession. Men will not bolster up a claim by a transparent falsehood, save to satisfy some really existing sentiment. ⌈However, constitutionalism triumphed for a time,⌋ and the theory of government propounded by an English lawyer[1] at the close of the period is as emphatic in its repudiation of despotism and preference for 'mixed monarchy,' as were the doctrines of Wycliffe and Richard II. upon the other side. Yet the new dynasty was a failure; strong government was needed, and the country "perishing for lack of it" called the legitimate line to its assistance[2]. It is as a reformer, not as a pretender, that Richard Duke of York first comes into prominence. Yet it was only owing to his position as the legitimate heir of Edward III. that he gained the leadership of the reforming party. From the position of popular leader clamouring for good government he quickly passes to that of the dispossessed heir demanding his rights. It is now that the notion of indefeasible hereditary right first appears in English history[3]. On no theory of the

Inde-feasible hereditary right a Yorkist doctrine.

[1] Fortescue, *De Laudibus Legum Angliae* (1468–70); *The Governance of England* (1471–6).

Accounts of Fortescue's theory are given by Mr Plummer in his introduction to the latter and by Dr Stubbs, *Constitutional History*, § 365.

[2] *Ibid.* § 372. Parliament thus sums up the grievances of the nation under the Lancastrian dynasty, "In whose [Henry's] time not plenty, peace, justice, good governance, policy, and virtuous conversation, but unrest, inward war and trouble, unrighteousness, shedding and effusion of innocent blood, abusion of the laws, partiality, riot, extortion, murder, rape and vicious living have been the guides and leaders of this noble realm of England." *Rot. Parl.* v. 464.

[3] It is an extension to the succession of the doctrine *Nullum tempus occurrit regi*. Some of the arguments employed are noticeable: The Duke of York answers the objection raised

State can a rightful heir be greatly blamed for heading a revolt against a usurper. But after the original usurper is dead, and his dynasty to all appearance established, the dispossessed line will not obtain any general support, unless there be prevalent a strong sentiment of legitimism, a widespread belief that, so long as the rightful heir is to be found, nothing can bar his claim. Thus the nominal occasion of the Wars of the Roses, however little it may have been their real cause, is a proof of the influence, which the principle of legitimism had gained by the middle of the fifteenth century. Men will not profess to take *The* up arms in support of a doctrine, that is not popular *principle trium-* and widespread. And the principle triumphed. Not *phant.*

against his claim, that allegiance had been sworn to Henry VI. with the assertion that no oaths are binding if they conflict with the law of God, i.e. hereditary right. He claims to be "right inheritor of the said crowns as it accordeth with God's law and all natural laws." (*Rot. Parl.* v. 377.) In the first year of the reign of Edward IV. Parliament condemns the treatment of Richard II. "king anointed, crowned, and consecrate," as "against God's law, man's legiance, and oath of fidelity." There is no act upon the Statute book granting the crown to Edward, as in the case of Henry VII. and even James I. Parliament merely declares that he took to him the right on the death of his father. It speaks of the Duke of York claiming the crown as "using the benefice of the law of nature, not having any Lord then above him but God." (*Ibid.* 464, 5.) It would be impossible to express more strongly the notion of inherent right, as the one title to the crown; questions with regard to the succession are already acquiring a mystical character, and lawyers refuse to meddle with the *arcana imperii.* The judges on being asked to discuss the validity of the Yorkist claim, declared that the "matter was so high and touched the king's high estate and regalie, which is above the law, and passed their learning, wherefore they durst not enter into any communication thereof." (*Ibid.* 876.)

only was Edward IV. able to oust those who were " Kings in deed and not in right[1]"; but his opponents themselves put forward pretensions to hereditary right. Abandoning the claim that Henry IV. was the nearest heir to Henry III., they advanced the plausible contention that the Yorkist line was barred by its descent from a woman. Thus in one way or another the validity of the hereditary test was admitted.

Nor are the breaches of the principle before the reign of Henry VIII. as important as might appear. Richard III. may have been a usurper, but at least he claimed to succeed by the best right. He alleged, that Edward V. was illegitimate, and that the young Earl of Warwick's claim was barred by the attainder of the Duke of Clarence. If this were so he was the undoubted heir of Edward IV. Anyhow the *titulus regius* said he was, and gave him the Crown for that reason[2].

Hereditary succession under the Tudors. Bosworth field put an end for a time to the claims of strict right, and the Crown was won by an adventurer, who probably had a better title to be regarded as heir of Welsh princes than of English. Yet even for the hereditary claim of Henry

[1] *Statutes of the Realm,* II. 380.
[2] *English Historical Review,* VI. 260 sqq., 453, and Gairdner, *Life and Reign of Richard III.* Chapter III.; Speed's *History,* 717-25. The author of *Majestas Intemerata* is well aware that "the first of Richard III. bastardizes Edward the Fourth's posterity to flatter a tyrant; but what historian since ever fixed a truth upon this act?" The Act professes merely to resolve the doubts by declaring the succession not granting the crown, to which the title of Richard III. is "just and lawful *as grounded upon the laws of God and nature* and also upon the ancient laws and customs of this said realm."

Tudor something might be said. The legitimation
of the Beauforts might be held to extend to the succession. It could be pretended that the titles of all
other claimants were barred; that of Elizabeth of
York as a woman, that of Richard III. as a usurper,
and that of Warwick as scion of an attainted house[1].
At least, by marrying Elizabeth Henry endeavoured
to secure for his dynasty the hereditary title, which he
must have felt flimsy in his own case[2]. Henry VIII.
reigned as the unquestioned heir of Edward III.
These facts shew that, if the principle of hereditary
right was not allowed to prevent title by conquest
or choice, it was at least felt desirable to pay to it
the decent respect of ingenious falsehood. On the
other hand, a curious contrast to the sentiment is
the statute, which gives protection to all supporters
of a *de facto* king[3], and even attempts to prohibit
future Parliaments from attempting its repeal.

The next reign exhibits the most startling breach
of the principle of hereditary succession. The peculiar matrimonial relations of Henry VIII. necessi-
tated continual changes in the succession, which can
hardly now be regarded as a sacred thing. When
Henry is empowered to choose his own successor,
absolutism has triumphed at the expense of legitimism[4]. Certainly a king, in whose hands are

---

[1] On the claim of Henry VII., see Stubbs, *Lectures on Mediæval and Modern History*, 392—4.

[2] For the pains, which Henry VII. took to destroy all evidences
of the early marriage of Edward IV. see *English Historical Review*,
vi. 265.

[3] 11 Henry VII. c. 1.

[4] 28 Hen. VIII. c. 7, and 35 Henry VIII. c. 1.

placed the control of the succession, is more completely sovereign in theory, than even Louis XIV. whose will might indeed be law, but he would never have been recognized as competent to alter the succession. Henry named his own children in the order which appeared to follow most closely the rule of primogenitary succession : in that order they succeeded. Doubtless it is true that Mary and Elizabeth could not both of them be lawful heirs; one of them must be illegitimate; yet at least the succession of Edward VI. and his sisters followed the natural order; if the dissolution of the marriage with Catharine of Aragon be regarded as merely a divorce, it is even possible to maintain, that the sentiment of hereditary right had not been violated.

Position of Elizabeth. Yet Elizabeth's case, which was the most doubtful of the three, certainly aroused controversy. It does not appear, that she was regarded upon the Continent as a legitimate sovereign. From the outset, Mary Queen of Scots claimed the Crown by hereditary right. This right she undoubtedly possessed, if the divorce of Catharine were invalid. Elizabeth's irritation at Mary's quartering of the arms of England, her vain attempts to obtain from Mary the ratification of the treaty of Edinburgh, in which her present and future claims to the throne were renounced, were the inevitable result of her own doubtful title. They shew how deeply Elizabeth was penetrated with a sense of the insecurity of her position, and testify to *Claims of Mary Stuart.* the strength of Mary's claim and of the sentiment in its favour. Doubtless other and more potent causes led to the insistence upon Mary's rights; yet these alone would not have been sufficient to render Mary a dangerous competitor, had not a defective hereditary title been felt to be a good handle against a sovereign, who was for other reasons objectionable. Upon no other grounds were Mary's claims formidable; for not only had Henry VIII. been at pains to exclude the Scotch line from the succession, but this disposition had been ratified by Parliament in the first year of Elizabeth's reign[1]. It appears, then that, as in later times, there was some popular sentiment that hereditary right was indefeasible, a 'fundamental law,' which no Act of Parliament could override.

Additional evidence of this is the statute 13 Eliz. cap. 1[2], which makes it high treason to question the right of Parliament to alter the succession. This Act is evidence both ways. In the first place it proves, what indeed is clear on other grounds, that neither Elizabeth nor her ministers regarded themselves as bound by the rules of primogenitary succession, and that they claimed for Parliament absolute freedom of choice; clearly, hereditary succession is no 'fundamental law' to them. On the other hand the doctrine of indefeasible hereditary right would not have been condemned, had it not been prevalent among a considerable section of the nation. Thus then in the theory of the Tudor period assertions of indefeasible hereditary right are not to be expected; actual facts are against it. Probably however the

Importance of the statute 13 Eliz. c. 1.

Popular sentiment as to hereditary right.

---

[1] 1 Eliz. c. 3. § 2.

[2] *Statutes of Realm*, IV. 52: also printed in Prothero's *Statutes and Constitutional Documents*, 89.

notion was widespread, but its utterance was unsafe. The sentiment must have been general, or the unanimity which welcomed James I. to the throne would have been impossible; for James had no title save that of inherent birth-right, and succeeded in spite of the two Acts of Parliament excluding his house. On the other hand the existence of these Statutes and that discussed above is alone proof that the Crown is far the most important power in the State, and that theories are prevalent which exempt it from all restraints in regard to the succession.

Nature of Tudor despotism implies theories of universal obedience.
The causes and character of the Tudor despotism need not be here discussed. Yet one point must be noted. The exaltation of the royal authority was due to the need of a strong government. The crime of the Lancasterian dynasty had been, not that it was capricious or self-seeking or oppressive, but that it was weak, that law and order were not maintained and private war was once again becoming prevalent. It is as 'saviours of society' that the Yorkists and afterwards the Tudors win their position. In the statutes of liveries and in the Star Chamber is to be found the *raison d'être* of Tudor despotism. Government must be effective, private oppression must be punished, great offenders must be forced to submit to the authority of the Crown. That is the general sentiment. In a word, obedience must be enforced. The very causes, which drove men to support the Tudors at all, drove them also to insist on the paramount importance of obedience, and to proclaim the iniquity of rebellion.

But, if the Tudor dynasty was essentially a

dynasty of rulers, the Reformation gave to them a *Result of the Reformation.* vast accession of power. One aspect alone is important here. In the series of statutes enacted in the years 1529—1534, culminating in that of the royal supremacy, another stage was reached in the long struggle, for centuries waged by the English kings against clerical immunities and the political claims of the Papacy. What had been little more than an aspiration under Henry II. or Edward III. or Richard II. was at last an accomplished fact. England was free from Papal interference, if only she could maintain her position. The battle was *The independence claimed by Henry VIII. has yet to be made good.* not won yet, and in this fact lies the justification of men's passionate faith in the Divine Right of Kings. We are too apt to think that from the time of Henry VIII. or at least of Elizabeth, the success of the English Reformation was assured. The persistent efforts of foreign powers to convert England, the dreams of so able a man as Gondomar[1], and the overtures to Charles I. and Laud[2], are alone sufficient proof to the contrary. If all danger of England's submitting to the Papal yoke were over, certainly the fact was unknown at the time either to English statesmen or to Papal diplomatists. England in the time of Henry VIII. asserted her claims to independence. A century of statesmanship and conflict was required before they were finally made good. Thus a theory was needful which should express the national aspirations. It was impossible to assert the

[1] Gardiner, *History of England*, II. 218, 19, 252—4.
[2] *Ibid.* VIII. ch. LXXIX.

A theory needed to justify the position taken up against the Pope. sovereignty of the English Crown and its independence of Papal control without some grounds being given. It was necessary to meet the Pope's claim to allegiance and his pretended right of deposing kings, with some counter claim. There is no need to investigate afresh the causes, which determined the nature of this counter claim. They were at work in the earlier struggles between the Empire and the Papacy. Clearly, the Pope's claim to a universal monarchy by Divine Right, and to implicit obedience on pain of damnation, must be met in similar fashion, whether in the sixteenth or the fourteenth century. The English State must assert a claim to Divine appointment. Obedience must be demanded as due by God's ordinance, and all resistance must be treated as sin.

Need of a single central authority. Now it is to the conception of a single supreme authority in the State, that men are inevitably driven in seeking to formulate an anti-papal theory. Wearied of quasi-feudal anarchy, and disgusted with ecclesiastical interference, Englishmen felt the need of relying upon one central power and of asserting its universal jurisdiction. Nor could it seem doubtful at that time, who was vested with the sovereignty.

The king naturally regarded as 'sovereign.' The king was immeasurably the most important element in the State; in the case of Henry VIII. especially after the Act of 1539, the idea of sove-

---

[1] 31 Henry VIII. c. 8. It is thus described by the Bishop of Oxford. "Here was a 'lex regia' indeed; a dictatorship, which with all conceivable limitations, left the 'king master and only master' in his own house." *Lectures on Mediæval and Modern History*, 303.

reignty was almost completely realised in his person. It is far easier to arrive at the notion of sovereignty, if it be seen to be vested in a single person, than if it belong to an assembly or to a body such as Parliament made up of more than one assembly. Only under the form of monarchy does the notion of sovereignty readily lend itself to popular exposition. Further, the Reformation had left upon the statute book an emphatic assertion of unfettered sovereignty vested in the king. And the supremacy of the Crown constituted a new prerogative, which, since Parliament could allege no precedent for controlling it, might be claimed as the personal right of the head of the State. Lastly, the king had the name of sovereign. *Act of Supremacy.*

That complete sovereignty is to be found in some person or body of persons in the State is a necessity of effective anti-papal argument. If during the Tudor period it was not to be found in the Crown, where was it? Sir Thomas Smith might indeed write of the power of Parliament[1], but if the directing will is the supreme power in the State, Elizabeth was sovereign far beyond any despotic Premier or 'uncrowned king' of our own day. If we take into account the powers of arbitrary jurisdiction exercised by the Privy Council, the infrequency with which Parliament sat, and its lack of independence when sitting, there can be no doubt that Elizabeth was the person 'habitually obeyed' by the majority of Englishmen throughout her reign. Whether based upon authority or influence, the

[1] *De Republica Anglorum*, II. 1.

supreme power could be more truly conceived as belonging to the queen alone than as shared with anyone else. Some theory of uncontrolled secular authority is needed to meet the Papal claims; some power must be called into play to overthrow them. The most natural theory of sovereignty is that of monarchy. The only authority which could for an instant match itself with the Pope was that of the Crown. For the purposes of theoretical consistency and practical efficiency alike, a doctrine of sovereignty vested by Divine Right in the king was the indispensable handmaid of a national Reformation.

Obedience to law the governing thought in the sixteenth century.

For a time, the thought will suffice of the universality of law and of its absolute claim on the conscience. Men must assert the power of the Crown and the duty of obedience to it, not so much because they have framed any general notions of its majesty and dignity, as because it is the one effective authority. Royal power must be exalted as against that of the Pope. If phrases slip in which grant to kings an unconditioned omnipotence, which few of them ever dreamed of exercising, that is rather because no one as yet is concerned to deny them, than because they are construed strictly or regarded as of much importance. Against the Papal supremacy the unlimited jurisdiction and authority of kings is asserted. That these positions were destructive of popular rights, which nobody claimed and nobody exercised, is not as yet seen. Monarchy will only come to be defended for its own sake when Bellarmine and Suarez have elaborated a theory of popular sovereignty as a weapon against recalcitrant monarchs, and when Knox and Goodman have proclaimed the lawfulness of resistance (when the Presbyterian clergy command it) and the duty of deposing 'idolatrous' kings. Meanwhile it is of kings and their appointment by God as necessitating obedience that men will talk. This is the position most easily proved from Scripture and forms the natural antithesis to the Papal monarchy. Unlimited authority must be claimed for the law or the king; as yet there seems no difference. The king is the source and interpreter of law; men have no fear that he will seek to change existing arrangements or to overstep the boundaries set by custom. The only authorities which claim unlimited allegiance are the king and the Pope; there is no question as yet between Crown and Parliament. Obedience is essential. To give it to the Pope dissolves 'the political union.' It must therefore be due to the king.

Divine authority of kings.

Thus it is obedience, rather than a theory of government, that writers in the sixteenth century insist upon. Nor did they repeat the error of Wycliffe and Ockham, and leave a loophole for Papal interference by admitting the possibility of resistance in extreme cases. While claiming, as the writers of the fourteenth century, Divine sanction for secular governments, they dwell further upon the absolute duty of non-resistance in all cases.

A theory of obedience not of the State. In the sixteenth century no case of resistance is admitted.

In Tyndall's work, *The Obedience of a Christian Man*, passive obedience is inculcated without any qualification. No terms could be stronger than those in which the writer enforces the duty of non-resist-

1528.

ance. Written to demonstrate the groundlessness
of the charge of anarchism levelled at the Reformers,
the book asserts that the Pope is the true anarchist,
and declares that under Papal dominion "kings are
but shadows, vain names and things idle, having
nothing to do in the world, but when as the holy
father needeth their help."[1]   Robert Barnes in his
1534. *Supplication to the most gracious prince Henry VIII.*
and *Men's Constitutions bind not the conscience*, declares most emphatically in favour of Passive Obedience.   Another work of 1534 carefully expounds
regal authority as against Papal, and claims God's
ordinance on behalf of kings[2].   Bishop Gardiner
1535. in his Oration *On True Obedience* developes completely the notions of absolute subjection to the
sovereign, of the King's power · being God's
ordinance, and of the sinfulness of resistance;
and infers from this the weakness of the Papal
claims[3].   More clearly than other contemporary
writers he sees, that the real question is not as to
the religious duty of obedience in general, but of
the limits of obedience in extreme cases[4].   For only
then does the Pope enjoin disobedience; but he
denies that any limits to obedience are to be found

[1] *The Obedience of a Christian Man*, 114.

[2] *Opus eximium de vera Differentia Regiae Potestatis et Ec-
clesiasticae.* Goldart, III. 22.

[3] The argument is as follows: "If he [the king] be the head
of the people, and that by the ordinance of God, as no man sayeth
nay," the Pope's claims to supremacy must fall to the ground (58).
I quote from the reprint of Heywood's translation of 1553.

[4] "It is certain that obedience is due, but how far the limits
of requiring obedience extend, that is the whole question that can
be demanded." Ibid. 59.

in Scripture[1]. Like Wycliffe he repudiates the
notion, that the thirteenth of Romans can refer
to the Pope. The distinction between the greater
and lesser lights is declared to be a "blind distinction and full of darkness."[2] He is at pains to assert,
that the royal supremacy is no new doctrine, but runs
through English history and implies no more than
that "the Prince is the whole prince of all the people
and not of part."[3] The central idea of the book is the
same as that of all effective anti-papal treatises; that
obedience is due to the king, as a divinely appointed
governor. Papal precedents of royal subjection are
brushed away by a development of the doctrine *nullum
tempus occurrit regi.* "Time may not prescribe
against God's truth," and kings can not alienate a
God-given right. His contention, that examples are
needless, for God's law is constant, and man's precepts
variable, implies the whole force of the sentiment, that
led men to frame a theory of the Divine Right of
Kings[4]. A stable bulwark was needed against the
Papal attack. Obedience must be absolute and immutable, or the Pope will find it possible to make
good some part of his claim. This can only be if the
power of the Crown be regarded as God's appointment and non-resistance as a Divine ordinance[5].

[1] "What manner of limits are those that you tell me of, seeing
that the Scripture hath none such?" Ibid.

[2] Ibid. 63.

[3] Ibid. 72. "It appeareth that the thing itself which was
expressed by the name was not only true but ancient."

[4] Ibid. 80, 81.

[5] Gardiner declares that his purpose in writing is "to move all
men to obedience, which only in the commandments of God and
for God's sake maketh us happy and blessed." (Ibid. 101.)

1548.   The *Necessary Erudition of a Christian Man* is another early work, which authoritatively asserts the Divine authority of Kings and the iniquity of all resistance[1]. In more than one of Latimer's Sermons[2] and in the two famous homilies, that of the reign of Edward VI. entitled *An Exhortation concerning Order and Obedience*, and that of Elizabeth's collection directed *Against Wilful Rebellion*, the religious basis of non-resistance is asserted. Doubtless it is true, as the popular party afterwards claimed, that it is non-resistance to law which is here set forth in general terms; and that no guidance is given by the Homilies for the case of a monarch, like James II., arbitrarily violating the laws.

In the reign of Elizabeth there are the strong assertions of Jewel that "obedience is due to princes and magistrates though they be very wicked,"[3] that the "Pope ought to acknowledge and call the Emperor Lord and Master," and that "we ought so to obey princes as men sent of God."[4]

Contro- versial im-   The arguments of Jewel's *Apology* are evidence

---

[1] *The Necessary Erudition of a Christian Man*, the Fifth Commandment. "Scripture taketh princes to be as it were fathers or nurses to their subjects." "By this commandment also subjects be bound not to withdraw their said fealty, truth, love and obedience towards their princes, for any cause whatsoever it be, ne for any cause they may conspire against his person, ne do anything towards the hindrance or hurt thereof." The terms of the following passage are significant. "And furthermore by this commandment they be bound to obey also, all the laws, *proclamations, precepts and commandments* made by their princes and governors except they be against the commandment of God."

[2] Latimer's *Sermons*, 148, 496.

[3] *Apology for the Church of England*. Jewel's *Works*, III. 74.

[4] Ibid. 76.

of the direct connection between the theory of the *portance* sixteenth and seventeenth centuries and the earlier *of early Imperial* Imperialist doctrine. Further evidence is the transla- *history.* tion of Marsiglio's great work which was published in 1535, the chapter on the modes of restraining a bad prince being significantly omitted as not "pertaining to this realm of England." Bilson's work, *The True* 1585. *Difference between Christian Subjection and un-Christian Rebellion* is important, as not merely containing a theory of non-resistance, but also as covering almost the whole ground of the historical argument against the Papal claims. The relations of Popes and Emperors form the subject of many a page of anti-papal argument, which must seem to modern readers pedantic and unimportant. But the independence of the Emperors was the necessary ground on which to rest the later claim to the independence of all states. Without this, it was impossible to prefer for national independence any claim founded on right as distinct from force. If the King was or had been supreme and free from Papal control, nothing of course could alter the fact. But it was no more than a fact. The Pope claimed a Divine Right for his position, and this could only be met by a counter claim not of fact, but of right. The historical question depended entirely upon the relations of Popes and Emperors, Eastern as well as Western. If it could be clearly proved, that in early times the Pope had submitted without a murmur to the authority of the Emperor, the fact would go far to justify the assertion that the political claims of the Papacy were of modern growth, and rooted in nothing better

F. 7

than the false decretals and acts of power. In the view of the defenders of the Act of Supremacy the position of the Pope was that of a usurper. The Protestant writers were maintaining the claims of the genuine heir. It is true that their contention could not be demonstrated by shewing that Papal interference was of recent growth; yet such a proof would raise a strong presumption in their favour. Thus the position of Constantine, the rights of Julian, the acts of Theodosius, the powers of Justinian, the claims of the mediæval Emperors were of vital importance in the controversy. Unless the Imperialist position were tenable, the Pope's claims were unassailable historically, and there would be small ground for the oft-repeated assertion of the freedom of the English monarchy. If the Pope had always claimed and exercised the powers he now pretended to, there was good reason for supposing them given of God. If on the other hand they were originally vested in the Emperor, his power must be of God, and the cause of secular governments in general was justified. Thus that Paul of Samosata or the Donatists appealed not to the Pope but to the Emperor is no mere academic point, but a necessary step in an argument of incalculable practical importance. This fact may account also for the leaning some shew in the direction of Erastianism. Bilson, for instance, appears thoroughly to approve the conduct of the Eastern Emperors in regard both to Popes and Patriarchs. His desire to demonstrate the political supremacy of the secular power carries him to extremes.

Bilson's book is further noteworthy, in that it *Bilson on* contains not merely the customary announcement *Heredi-* that the King's power is from God and subject *archy.* to him alone, but also a demonstration that God especially prefers hereditary monarchy. From the example of the Davidic kingdom the author infers that "succession in kingdoms hath not only the consent of all ages and nations; but the manifest subscription of God himself; that it is His special favour and blessing to continue the successions of godly princes[1]."

· The last instance of anti-papal argument that 1571. need be considered here is Bullinger's reply to the Bull of Pope Pius V. excommunicating Elizabeth. In this the anti-papal character of Tudor theories of obedience is fully exemplified. The author declares that the Pope usurps the rights granted to Kings by God, but regards (naturally enough) these rights as equally attributable to the supreme power in a republic[2], and equally granted by God in that case. With Mary Stuart still alive he is at pains to declare that the succession to the Crown goes by election[3]. One phrase of this book expresses the whole sentiment at the root of the theory of the Divine Right of Kings: *The bonds of political society are not dissolved, but strengthened by the word of God[4].*

It is the occasion of this treatise which marks most *Need of a* completely the necessity of a theory of the Divine *theory of* Right of Kings. So long as the Popes were content *Right of Kings.*

---

[1] *True Difference,* 515.   [2] *Bullae Papisticae Refutatio,* 44.
[3] *Ibid.* 69.
[4] "At politica vel civilis gubernatio confirmatur, non dissolvitur verbo Domini." *Ibid.* 71.

with a general claim, or dreamed of converting
Elizabeth, an uncompromising royalist doctrine was
scarcely needed. But, when it was attempted to put
the theory into practice, and all good Catholics were
bidden to become traitors on religious grounds, it
was necessary that a theory should appear of the
religious duty of obedience to the established
government. Loyal and patriotic feeling under
the circumstances must inevitably lead to the
exaltation of the dignity and authority of the
Crown. Its complete independence of the Pope, its
institution by God, and the duty of non-resistance
must now be emphasized with wearisome reiteration,
if the State was to retain the allegiance, of those
large numbers, who were gazing with longing and
regret at the old order. From the year 1570, of the
Bull of excommunication there is a king ' across the
water' claiming allegiance, threatening and sometimes
organizing descents upon the coast. Every patriotic
Englishman must henceforth affirm, that his own
princess is the lawful recipient of obedience, with
as good or better title than that of the Pope; in a
word that she is Queen by Divine Right. If the
Pope had excommunicated Council or Parliament,
men might have urged the divine authority of the
Sanhedrim or God's favours to the chosen people.
But since it was the Queen who was deposed; the
Queen must be defended, and the rights of the
Crown shewn to exist by a Divine decree.

Effect of the death of Mary Stuart. Lastly, it may be observed that the position of
affairs in respect of the succession had undergone a
change towards the close of the reign. It was no

longer necessary to speak of hereditary right with
bated breath. So long as Mary Stuart lived, to
enforce the claims of strict right might be to
countenance immediate rebellion; certainly it would
pave the way for a Papal reaction that was likely
to prove more lasting than that under Mary Tudor.
But now that the young King of Scotland was
heir according to strict rule, there was nothing to
prevent the national sentiment in favour of legitimism exerting its full force. Besides, it is the *Papalists
now oppose*
Roman writers who now begin to attack the doc- *doctrine of*
trine. Doleman's *Conference about the Next Succession* *hereditary*
succession.
to the Crown of England* (written by the Jesuit 1593.
Parsons) proclaims in strident tones the new alliance
between Papal sovereignty and popular rights. The
author repeatedly declares that " Propinquity of birth
or blood alone, without other circumstances, is not
sufficient to be preferred to a Crown[1] "; that forms
of government are variable and may be established
and changed according to the will of the community[2];
that "the succession to government by nearness of
blood is not by Law of Nature and Divine, but by
human and positive laws only of every particular
government, and consequently may upon just causes
be altered by the same[3]." The basis of the author's

---

[1] *A Conference about the Next Succession*, 1; cf. also 11, "It
[that any prince hath his particular government or interest to
succeed by institution of nature] is ridiculous, for that nature
giveth it not, but the particular constitution of every commonwealth within itself."

[2] *Ibid.* 10. " The Commonwealth hath power to choose their
own fashion of government, as also to change the same upon
reasonable causes." [3] *Ibid.* cap. i. title.

political theory is frankly utilitarian; Doleman asserts that "the Commonwealth hath authority to dispossess them that have been lawfully put in possession, if they fulfil not the Laws and *Conditions* by which, and for which their dignity was given them[1]." He upholds the right of resistance, although, with a shrewd eye to the Papal supremacy, he forbids it to be exercised by "private men," who are inferior to the Prince; whereas the Commonwealth is superior to him[2]. The importance of the Coronation oath as implying the conditions of allegiance is insisted upon.

In this book there is found the complete expression by an Englishman of the doctrines of the right of resistance, of popular sovereignty, and the merely official character of kingship. These are proclaimed purely in the interests of the Papal monarchy, without the smallest enthusiasm for liberty. The book appears to have been widely circulated, as the ability with which it was written deserved. Doleman is the most frequent subject of attack by supporters of James, and his work is evidently regarded as the most salient exposition of the treasonable character of the Papal aims. Speed, in describing the peaceful accession of James, goes out of his way to make a thrust at this treatise in particular. "Let Doleman therefore dote upon his own dreams, and other like traitors fashion their bars upon the People's forge; yet hath *God and his right* set him on the throne of his most lawful inheritance[4]."

By the irony of fate the work was not only

1611.

---

[1] *A Conference*, 26.   [2] *Ibid.* 58.
[3] *Ibid.* Part i. Ch. 5.   [4] Speed's *History*, 911.

hashed up in the interests of the Puritan party in 1647; but had the fortune to be reprinted by the supporters of the Exclusion Bill as the best compendium of arguments against the doctrine of inherent right[1]. It was strange that a work written to exclude a Protestant prince from the throne of England should have exercised its most effectual influence in all but causing the exclusion of a Papist[2].

From this time forth, anti-papal writers will feel bound to attack the notions of popular sovereignty put forward by the great Jesuit controversialists in order to serve the occasion. Doleman, Bellarmine and Suarez are the *bêtes noires* of Anglican divines. Against them as the preachers of resistance and inventors of the theory of original compact the heavy artillery of the royalist pamphleteers is always directed. The attempt of the Jesuits

Use made of the book in later times.

Anti-Roman writers henceforth strong supporters of absolute monarchy.

[1] Halifax charges the author of the *History of the Succession* with plagiarism from Doleman, from whom he asserts all his arguments to have been drawn.

[2] Cardinal Allen's *Defence of the English Catholics* is based upon a similar theory of popular rights to that of Parsons. The purpose of the book, however, is to justify the deposing power, and the succession is not discussed. Yet Allen's insistence on the importance of the coronation ceremony as conferring rights upon the Pope is interesting. Once more it is in the necessities of Papalist controversy that originates the theory that the coronation oath proves the existence of a compact between king and people. "Upon these conditions [the oath to preserve the Catholic faith] therefore, and no other, kings be received of the Bishop that in God's behalf anointeth them; which oath and promise not being observed, they break with God and their people; and their people may, and by order of Christ's supreme minister their chief Pastor in earth, must needs break with them; heresy and infidelity in the Prince tending directly to the perdition of the Commonwealth" (113).

to manufacture anti-monarchical sentiment in the interests of the Papal claims could only have as its main result the effect of causing orthodox English churchmen to attach an increased value to kingship and to emphasize the peculiar importance of hereditary succession.

cir. 1600.   Heywood's *Royal King and Loyal Subject*[1] reaches perhaps the high-water mark of sixteenth century loyalism. The plot and general development of this play have no other object than that of illustrating the virtue of absolute obedience under oppressive and tyrannical treatment. To the King of England is attributed arbitrary and unlimited authority. Loyalty could hardly go further than the unbroken submission of the Earl Marshal, nor could caprice ever make more unreasonable demands, than the King in this play. The author evidently wrote his work with the one aim of inculcating this lesson of royal omnipotence and perfect obedience. Nor is the play evidence of Heywood's sentiments only; its success testifies to those of his audience. Assuredly no other motive but that of loyalty could have led to such a play being 'acted with applause,' as we are told that it was. Despite the recent panegyric on the author by a republican critic[2], it may be questioned whether this production is not too deficient in dramatic power and poetic interest to have afforded pleasure to an audience that

[1] For the probable date of the play see J. Payne Collier in Introduction (p. vi) to the reprint by the Shakespeare Society.

[2] Mr Swinburne in *Nineteenth Century*, Oct. 1895 (400), *The Romantic and Contemporary Plays of Thomas Heywood*. It is fair to say that *The Royal King* is not placed on a level with most of the author's works.

was not steeped in royalist sentiment. Of *The Maid's Tragedy*, which was a little later, the same cannot be said. Yet it also proves how strong was the popular belief in the mystical nature of kingship and in its claims to unquestioning obedience.

Thus, then, it appears that by the close of the sixteenth century events have done much to strengthen the monarchy, and to generate notions of its Divine institution; and that there has been elaborated a theory of the unlimited jurisdiction of the Crown and of non-resistance upon any pretence, which will not be brought to the test of popular criticism until the next century. These notions have all arisen out of the necessities of the struggle with the Papacy, although the Civil Wars of the previous age have doubtless produced by way of reaction a sense of the necessity of securing strong government and universal obedience to the law. English controversialists, in answering the theory of the Papal supremacy, were driven to propound a doctrine of the Divine Right of secular governments, which is in its essential meaning no other than the Imperialist theory of two centuries and a half before. To the Empire ancient and mediæval they go for the historical justification of their position, and for the rest build up their argument with texts and illustrations from Scripture. Theories of inherent rights of birth as governing the succession are latent rather than expressed. But the sentiment in favour of indefeasible hereditary right has been steadily growing, and will appear triumphant, so soon as "England's Empress" shall have left the way free for a successor, reigning by right of birth alone.

CHAPTER VI.

HENRY OF NAVARRE AND THE SALIC LAW.

Similarity of political controversy in England and France.

THE political and religious questions which occupied the minds of Englishmen in the seventeenth century find their counterpart in controversies evoked during the French Wars of Religion[1]. In the theories of Huguenots, Lorrainers and *Politiques* appear most of the ideas, of which we hear so much in England a little later. France indeed was a soil peculiarly suited to the development both of regal and papal theories. From the position of the king, as eldest son of the Church, men might demonstrate his subjection to the Pope. The deposition of Childeric by Pope Zacharias was the earliest exercise of the deposing power, and was alleged by the supporters of the league against both Henry III. and Henry IV. as conclusive proof, that this power had been recognized in the past. In no other country is the connection of politics and theology more intimate and vital. Of pure politics there is even less than there is in England in the next century. Political theory is never developed, save with the object of strengthening some theological position.

The pretensions of the Huguenots to be taking up arms against their prince by the authority of God

752.

[1] On this point and the position of Henry IV. see the remarks in Seeley's *Growth of British Policy*, I. 68.

exemplify the fact, more patent later in Scotland and England, that the Presbyterian and the Papal theories of politics are at bottom identical.   The essence of both is the claim put forward by an ecclesiastical organization to control and direct the action of the State.   Huguenot Preachers and Presbyterian Disciplinarians are like their Papalist enemies in this, that they would place the secular power under the heel of the spiritual, or else would claim the exercise of sovereign rights for a portion of the community. It was as a danger to the State, claiming for themselves an *imperium in imperio*, that the Huguenots as a political power were finally crushed by Richelieu, while religious liberty was preserved to them.

Again, in the position assumed by the League with regard to Henry III., there is much that is parallel to the relation between Charles I. and the Long Parliament.   Henry is lawful king; no one doubts it.   Yet he must be restrained and coerced by force of arms in the interests of the Crown which he wears.   The distinction between the personal and political authority of the Crown first arose, as has been shewn, in England under Edward II., and will reappear during the Great Rebellion.   But the conception of their office entertained by the ultra-royalist rebels of the League is precisely similar. They too claim to be taking up arms against the person of their king in support of his authority.

Lastly, the reign of Henry IV. is the supreme triumph of legitimism, and far outdoes in importance the accession of James I. to the English Crown. James I. had the sentiment of the whole English nation at his back; and the very few disloyal

Catholics are a negligeable quantity compared with the League. Henry of Navarre, with almost everything against him save his right as legitimate heir by the Salic law and the grant of God, yet made good his claim to the Crown. His success finally disposed of any claims of the right of election or of the Papal sanction, and testified to the depth of the sentiment in favour of hereditary succession by rule of law. Yet the issue was in one respect different from any possible question of English politics. The strength of Henry's position was not as that of James I. or Charles II., the indefeasible right of the heir according to the rule of primogenitary succession. It was the Salic Law, as commonly understood, that gave him his claim, and its inviolability is of the essence of all arguments in his support. He was not the heir by primogeniture, and had the Crown descended, as in England, the Duchess of Savoy[1] must have worn it.

Hence there will be an important difference between French and English theories of Kingship. The inviolability of the succession "as by law established" will play a much greater part in French controversy. Supporters of Henry IV. can hardly develop such a theory as that of Filmer, for the Salic law is an artificial institution; and it can scarcely be claimed, that it has the author of Nature on its side. At least, the Divine Right of the law of

---

[1] Catharine, who married Charles Emmanuel the Great, was Philip's elder daughter by Elizabeth of Valois. The claim to the throne of France was however put forward on behalf of Isabella, the second daughter. The reason apparently was that she was as yet unmarried.

succession is less plausible a doctrine in France than
in England. We must expect then to find French
theory more legal than English. The Salic Law
is "the peculiar institution" and especial glory of
France; but universality cannot well be claimed for it.
In Filmer and Leslie we have what purports to be a
universal system of politics. This will not be possible
in France. French theory is in many respects identical with English but in this matter it must differ
from it. French thought will be less theological, less
transcendental, more legal and local than English.

But against the claims of the Pope, Gallican *Position of*
doctrine will be as uncompromising as Anglican. *France in regard to*
Its historical justification is indeed stronger. French *the Pope.*
authors can look back to a long series of triumphs
over Papal aggression, they can point to conflicts
no less acute and more successful than any which
England had witnessed in pre-Reformation days.
The triumph of Philip the Fair over Boniface VIII.
is the most impressive event in the relations between
France and the Papacy; whereas in power to strike
the imagination the submission of John to Innocent
III. far outdoes any of the successful efforts of the
English kings. A Frenchman can detail with pride
the relations of Charles VI. to Benedict XIII., or of
Louis XII. to Julius II.[2], and can even point to the
recent refusal of Henry II. to admit the validity of
the Tridentine decrees[3]. Whereas in England the

---

[1] King James remarks, "Most notable is the example of Philip
the Fair, and hits the bird in the right eye" (*Works*, 412).

[2] See especially Toussaint Berchet, *Pium Consilium super
Papae Monitorialibus*, Pars I.

[3] *Apologia Catholica*, 186, 7. "Interea vero dum legitimum

Popes had constantly protested against all legislation directed against their autocracy, their partial recognition and reluctant endurance of the Gallican liberties[1] may be adduced to prove, that in the case of France all claims to political supremacy have been expressly renounced by the Pope.

Yet there were difficulties in the position of French Catholics to which neither Imperialists nor Anglicans were exposed. For they admitted the

illud concilium expectatur neque Rex Francorum neque supremae ipsius Curiae Concilii illius Tridentini decreta unquam in hoc regno mandari voluerunt, nec nisi ab Ecclesiasticis, qui Pontificiae Monarchiae subsunt, fuerunt recepta. Contra Rex Henricus II. piae memoriae certam legationem misit, qua huic Concilio (prout Concilium esse volunt) obsisteret et renuntiaret se nullo pacto id probaturum esse. Etenim revera illud accipi non potest, quin eadem opera corrumpantur et jura authoritasque Francorum Regis, et vetera decreta in summis Regni Ordinibus constituta pragmaticae sanctionis nomine et sanctissimae libertates Ecclesiae Gallicanae, quibus florentissime hujus regni dignitas conservatur."

[1] On the Pragmatic Sanction, see Creighton, *History of the Papacy*, II. 198, 9 and 423 sqq. "It was a memorial of national opposition to the theory of the Universal Church. It expressed the claim of a temporal ruler to arrange at his pleasure the affairs of the Church within his realms." Louis XI. first abolished the Pragmatic Sanction and afterwards restored its provisions by royal ordinance. "The Pragmatic Sanction rested on the basis of the power of General Councils, of an inherent right of self-government in the Universal Church, which was independent of and superior to the Papal monarchy" (*Ibid.* IV. 231). Although the Pragmatic Sanction was superseded by the Concordat of Francis I. with the Pope, yet the sentiment it enshrined was preserved: the new arrangement gave no further rights to the Pope, but relieved the Crown from the fear of being thwarted by the leaders of the Gallican Church. So to say the Pragmatic Sanction had affirmed the independence of the nation, the Concordat secured the supremacy of the Crown. On this aspect of the Concordat see Kitchin, *History of France*, II. 182, and Armstrong, *French Wars of Religion*, 122.

spiritual claims of the Papacy, and it is far from easy to do this, while denying *in toto* its pretensions to political supremacy. It was impossible for the supporters of the king to take the line of the Imperialists and boldly to claim that the Pope was amenable to the jurisdiction of their master. To admit, as did French Catholics, that the Pope is a sovereign prince, and that he further has spiritual authority over the orthodox in every nation, is to grant him a power of interference, out of which very little ingenuity is required to construct a theory of universal supremacy. Nor on the other hand can the *politiques* boldly cut the knot in the Anglican method, by denying that the Pope is head of the Church. The inconsistency of their position necessarily affected their theory. Since it was hard for French writers to reconcile the liberty claimed for the French king, with the authority allowed to the Pope, they may be expected to be less clear than either Englishmen or Imperialists in their statement of the necessary unity of the sovereign power. Save in the case of writers with a Huguenot bias, this notion is far less prominent in French than in English or mediæval opponents of the Papal claims. A little want of harmony and consistency in this matter was to be expected from the circumstances of the case. With this brief account of the causes, which led to the growth in France of a theory similar in its main scope, though different in certain details from the English doctrine, the study of the chief controversialists may be approached.

In the *Vindiciae contra Tyrannos* and the *Franco-Gallia* are to be found the ideas at the bottom of all theories of popular rights until the *Theories of popular rights.*

eighteenth century. The doctrine of an original compact appears full-blown in the *Vindiciae*, although it is worthy of remark that the compact between King and people is here regarded as not the first but the second contract involved in the institution of civil society. The first compact is that between God on the one hand and King and people on the other as contracting parties; this was discarded by later writers. The second compact is the ordinary contract of government, and is identical with that of Hooker or Locke. From it are drawn the usual proofs that the right of resistance is vested in the people and may be exercised upon a breach of the contract by the sovereign. This compact may be express or tacit, but it is inviolable and unchangeable in its terms; no oath or consent of either party or of both can abrogate it[1]. The basis of the argument throughout the book is the principle of utility[2]. It is contended, just as in the manner of Locke, that the King can have no power over either the life or the property of his subjects, for it is contrary to *the principle of utility* for men to give power over their life or property into the hands of another[3]. For such a purpose men, who are naturally free, would never have set up a King. There are the very same

[1] "Inter regem et populum mutua obligatio est, quae sive Civilis sive Naturalis tantum sit, sive tacita, sive verbis concepta, nullo pacto tolli, nullo jure violari, nullo vi rescindi potest." *Vindiciae contra Tyrannos*, 147.

[2] "Hic considerandum est imprimis certissimum totius huiusce disputationis fundamentum, quo reges utilitatis publicae causa constitutos fuisse statuimus. Eo enim posito tota lis finita est." *Ibid.* 112. The author repeatedly has recourse to the principle of utility as the final proof of his position.

[3] *Ibid.* 112 sqq.

erroneous beliefs in the artificial nature of government, and in the possibility of limiting the 'sovereign,' which Locke was afterwards to render famous.   The author shares with the great Whig philosopher the inability to see that in any developed state there must exist some ultimate supreme authority, to whose action no legal limits can be affixed.   Both Locke and Languet think they can "put a hook into the nose" of the Leviathan[1].   The law is for them endowed with Divine Right, eternal and immutable, the breath of God rather than man, controlling sovereign and subject alike[2].   This of course is to miss the con-

[1] It is hard to overestimate the resemblance between the ideas of Locke and the author of the *Vindiciae*, e.g. "Primum sane palam est, homines *natura liberos*, servitutis impatientes et ad imperandum magis, quam ad parendum natos, non nisi magnae cuiusdam utilitatis caussa imperium alienum ultro elegisse, et suae quasi naturae legi, ut alienam ferrent, renunciasse." *Vindiciae contra Tyrannos*, 98. The question as to whether the *Vindiciae* should be attributed to Languet or Du Plessis Mornay need not be here discussed.

[2] "Rexne, inquam, a lege an Lex a rege pendebit? * * * Itaque est quod reges legi ipsi pareant, eamque tamquam reginam agnoscant. ......Quis vero ambigat, quin legi, quam regi parere, id est, homini utilius et honestius sit? Lex est boni regis anima; per hanc movet sentit vivit Rex Legis organum, et quasi corpus, per quod illa suas vires exerit, sua munera obit, sua sensa eloquitur. Animae vero, quam corpori, parere, justius est. Lex est multorum prudentum in unum collecta ratio et sapientia. Plures autem oculatiores et perspicaciores sunt, quam unus. Tutius itaque est Legem, quam hominem, quantumuis perspicacem, ducem sequi. Lex est ratio sive mens, ab omni perturbatione vacua, non ira, non cupiditate, non odio, non studio mouetur, non precibus, non minis flectitur. Homo contra, quantumuis rationis particeps sit, ira, vindicta, aliove subinde appetitu vincitur rapiturque, et ita variis affectibus perturbatur, ut sui ipse compos non sit: nempe, quia ex appetitu et ratione constat, quin hic interdum vincat, fieri nequit.* * * Deni-

ception of sovereignty, for the argument will apply to any form of government. Locke saw and boldly admitted, that his theory was as fatal to Parliamentary omnipotence, as it was to royal prerogative, but the author of the *Vindiciae* appears to confine his views to kings.

In another respect the author of the *Vindiciae* is as curiously at one with Whig Englishmen of the seventeenth century, as he is at variance with modern feeling. He is emphatic in his rejection of the right of private individuals to resist the prince on any pretence whatsoever[1]. Passive obedience is their duty, prayers and tears their one resource. Only to corporate bodies, integral parts of the kingdom, does the *Vindiciae* grant the right of resistance. To private individuals Christ's patience is held up as an example; and the precedents of tyrannicide in the Old Testament are explained away, as the result of direct Divine inspiration. Anyhow the view is closely parallel to the English

que lex est mens, vel potius mentium congruata multitudo : mens vero diuinae aurae particula, ut qui legi paret, Deo parere, Deumque arbitrum quodammodo facere videatur. Contra vero, quia homo ex mente divina, et anima illa belluina constans, sibi saepe non constat, saepe dementat, et insanit: cum vero ita afficitur non jam homo sed bellua est; qui Regi parere mavult, quam legi, belluae quam Dei imperium malle videatur." *Vindiciae contra Tyrannos*, 108.

[1] *Ibid.* 65 sqq., 178 sqq. No supporter of Passive Obedience could be more emphatic in his denunciation of any general right of insurrection than is this upholder of popular liberty. If the aristocracy lend their support to a tyrant, it is by God's command, and the only lawful weapon is prayer. This notion is of course exactly similar to the royalist contention, that kings are frequently "given in wrath."

doctrine, that resistance is unjustifiable on the part
of private persons, but lawful, when commanded by
the "inferior magistrate." Probably the doctrine
is a relic of feudal theory. Its appearance in
Huguenot theory with its strange exaltation of
municipal and provincial authority, seems to carry
us back to the days of provincial sovereignty and
semi-sovereign *communes.* Certainly under any
form of government great dangers would arise, if the
rights ascribed by 'Brutus' to the municipal organizations were admitted. His theory would reduce
the State to a confederation of semi-independent
bodies. It would be quite in accordance with the
doctrine, if the London County Council were to direct
an insurrection in favour of the principle of better-
ment, or the Leicester Board of Guardians to
organise rebellion against the Vaccination Statutes.

There are some points of similarity to Papal
theory in this book. God is the true king, and
therefore must be supported against the earthly
king, who is merely God's vassal. Just as a single
city of the empire would be within its rights in
supporting a duly elected Emperor against a usurper,
so a city of France may support God against a
king[1]. Moreover, kings hold their dignity by Divine
right, therefore they are amenable to God's authority,
and in support of God's truth they may be resisted[2].
The author argues that if the maxim *nullum tempus
occurrit regi* be true, it is *a fortiori* evident that no
prescription can touch the inalienable sovereignty of

---

[1] *Vindiciae contra Tyrannos*, 57 sqq.   [2] *Ibid.* Qu. 1.

the people[1]. Indeed the notion that sovereignty is inalienable finds expression on all sides, whether the doctrine advocated be the ultimate authority of Pope, of king, or of people. Nor is this surprising. Practical necessity rendered it essential for each side to insist much upon the doctrine. For neither party could shew such an unbroken series of precedents, that they could make their position secure without asserting that while examples might support their own view, precedents against them will avail nothing.

Hotman's Franco-Gallia.

The *Franco-Gallia* of Hotman is a work of a different order. It is a purely historical argument to prove, that the Frankish kingdom was in the earliest stages of its development, a limited mon-

[1] *Vindiciae contra Tyrannos*, 96. The following passage, summing up the whole argument, may be quoted: " In summa, ut hunc tandem tractatum concludamus, principes eliguntur a Deo, constituuntur a populo. Ut singuli principe inferiores sunt : ita universi, et qui universos repraesentant, regni officiarii, principe superiores sunt. In constituendo principe intervenit foedus inter ipsum et populum, tacitum, expressum, naturale, vel etiam civile, ut bene imperanti bene pareatur, ut reipublicae inservienti omnes inserviant...... Huius vero foederis seu pacti regni officiarii vindices et custodes sunt. Qui hoc pactum perfide et pervicaciter violat, is vere exercitio tyrannus est. Itaque regni officiarii ipsum et secundum leges judicare, et renitentem vi coercere, si alias non possunt, ex officio tenentur. Hi duorum generum sunt. Qui regni universi tutelam susceperunt, quales Comes stabuli, Mareschalli, Patricii, Palatini et caeteri singuli per se caeteris conniventibus aut colludentibus, tyrannum coercere debent; qui alicujus partis, regionisve, quales duces, marchiones, comites, consules, maiores tyrannidem tyrannumque ab ea regione urbeve arcere jure suo possunt. Porro singuli sive privati adversus tyrannos exercitio, gladium non stringent; quia non a singulis, sed ab universis constituti sunt " (182, 3).

archy. The inference is that the present power of
the Crown is an usurpation and may justly be
abolished in favour of a return to the old state of
things. The notion that governs the whole course
of the argument, is the same as that held by English
writers of all schools in the next century. Constitutional arrangements, whether they consist in the
sovereign rights of the Crown or in the power of the
people are believed to be unchangeable, a 'fundamental law' which no lapse of time or development of
circumstances can abrogate. Thus the primitive
system of government, whatever it be, is the only
rightful one. Whatever powers originally belonged
to the people, they still possess, however long be
the period since they were recognised as effective.
Whatever rights were vested in the Crown at the
beginning, it still has, and no amount of constitutional development can check them. Hotman's
conclusions are similar to those of the *Vindiciae*
and of Whig writers. To him the king is a mere
official created by the People for their own behoof[1].
Like Locke and Rousseau he will allow omnipotence to no government, and would apparently like
Rousseau regard all forms of constitution as liable to
change at the will of the sovereign people. The
basis of the argument, where it is not historical,
is utilitarian, and Hotman has frequent recourse
to the maxim *Salus populi suprema lex*[2].

[1] "Deinde cum illi populi Regem sibi crearent, (sicuti et jam
prius dictum est et postea dicetur) perabsurdum est existimare
populum a Rege potius, quam Regem a populo denominatum" (58).

[2] It is noticeable that Hotman adduces in proof the limited

*Compari-
son with
English
theories of
resistance.*

Here, then, are the same ideas as were at the bottom of English theories of popular rights in the seventeenth century. Proclaimed first of all by Huguenots, they passed over to the ultramontane supporters of the League, when the death of the Duke of Alençon left Henry of Navarre the heir to the French Crown. Henceforward they become identified with Papal pretensions. The great treatise of Barclay *De Regno* is directed against Buchanan, Brutus, and Boucher, the Scotch, the Huguenot, and the Papalist opponents of the rights of the Crown and of the inviolability of the Salic law[1].

*Theory of
Divine
Right of
Kings.*

It is now, in the later years of Henry III. and the earlier of his successors, that there appears a well-defined theory of the French Monarchy. Against the Papal claims to interfere with the internal politics of France and to alter the succession as by law established, the Divine Right of Kings and the fundamental character of the Salic law are emphatically asserted.

*Similarity
to English
doctrine.*

The main arguments are similar to those employed by English controversialists. Kings are of Divine appointment, all resistance to them is there-

character of the French monarchy, the admitted fact that the Salic law was unalterable, and that the treaty of Troyes was invalid for that reason. It is curious how completely this weak point in their position escaped the notice of most supporters of the Divine Right of Kings. In one and the same breath they assert that the succession is fixed by a fundamental law, and that the king is absolutely sovereign.

[1] For a complete account of Huguenot and League politics see Armstrong, *The Political Theory of the Huguenots (Eng. Hist. Rev.* IV. 13) and *The French Wars of Religion.*

fore sin[1]. The Pope has not and never had authority
to depose princes[2]. Since the king's rights come
directly from God, the Pope can have no power to
take away what he never granted[3]. The deposition
of Childeric was merely the formal ratification of a
change that had long ago taken place and affected
the name, not the reality of kingship. It was
effected with the consent not by the authority of the
Pope. Perhaps the deposition was not quite justifiable and were better forgotten; it was a case of
doing a little wrong, that a great right might result[4].
The instances of royal repudiation of Papal interference are duly recorded; and the usual Scriptural
passages and illustrations are brought into play[5].
The position of the Emperor in regard to the Pope
is affirmed to be one of superiority. This is an
important element in the controversy; for the
Carolingian monarchs are regarded as kings of
France. The translation of the Empire is thus invested with significance, from the French, as from
the Imperialist standpoint, and the treatment of
Julian by his subjects receives, as usual, its meed of
attention[6]. It is not easy to single out any one

[1] Barclay, *De Regno*, 113.
[2] E.g. Toussaint Berchet, *Pium Consilium*, Pars I.
[3] Berchet (Goldast, III. 163).
[4] Masson, *Responsio in Franco-Galliam*, 126.
[5] The following is a specimen of the mode of argument: " Nec
enim solum propter iram id est metu poenae illis [regibus] obedien-
dum est, sed propter conscientiam, quia nimirum omnes scire
oportet, id est divina voluntate et constitutione fieri debet."
Servin (Goldast, III. 200).
[6] Barclay, *De Potestate Papae* (Goldast, III. 635).

name as preeminent, in the case of a doctrine so widespread. Yet the fact that the theory of the Divine Right of Kings was in its origin a weapon of anti-papal controversy, is made plain by the treatise of Berchet in favour of Henry IV. and comes out in the collection of Gallican writings made by Pithon[1].

Points of difference between English and French doctrines.
 Special points, for comparison with English theory, may be indicated. In the first place comes the difficulty (before alluded to) inherent in the circumstances of French Catholic writers. Barclay and others are clearly hampered by the necessity of admitting the spiritual claims of the Pope and his title to the obedience of the clergy. Barclay is unable to take the same line as Imperialist or English writers and to affirm the absolute necessity of unity in the sovereign authority. He is content to admit that the Papal and regal power are equal, and must respect one another[2]. He will, however, allow no exemptions to the clergy from the operation of the ordinary law, and even hints a wish that excommunication should be unaccompanied by civil disabilities[3].

 Other writers, such as Du Moulin[4] and Servin[5] are found arguing like Ockham or Marsiglio, that Christ's kingdom is not of this world, and that the whole doctrine of papal sovereignty is based upon a fallacy. But all alike are clear, that the prince is to be obeyed, although he be excommunicate or a heretic. All affirm that kings are accountable to God alone, and above the restraints of civil law; only

[1] *Les Libertez de l'Eglise Gallicane.*
[2] Barclay, *De Potestate Papae* (Goldast, III. 645).
[3] *Ibid.* c. xxxiv. [4] Goldast, III. 63. [5] *Ibid.* 241.

natural law can lay commands upon a king, says
Servin[1]. All are agreed that subjects must obey
for conscience' sake, and not merely for wrath.
Servin also has a lengthy argument to prove 1592.
that coronation and unction are mere ceremonies
and no essential part of the regality, and that
the coronation oath gives the people no rights
against him. It is a pious custom only; it will not
affect Henry's authority, though the Archbishop of
Rheims refuse to crown him, as a heretic[2].

In regard to the Salic law more than one line is *The Salic*
taken. Du Moulin finds in it evidence of the per- *Law.*
fection of the French monarchy, as founded on the 1561.
model of the Davidic kingdom[3]. Bodin seeks a
philosophical justification for it as the ideal mode of
succession[4]. Most writers content themselves with
the declaration that the custom is a fundamental
law and may not be violated by the king. They do
not, as a rule, lay claim to any special Divine
sanction for it, but declare, that the law of succession
in all kingdoms is of merely human origin; obedience
to the lawful successor is a Divine ordinance[5]. The

---

[1] His argument is strange; the Pope is *solutus legibus*, therefore
a fortiori the king is also. Servin, *Vindiciae* (Goldast, III. 197).

[2] Goldast, III. 209 sqq. Cf. also *Apologia Catholica*, 100 sqq.
Bodin takes a similar view, supporting it by the maxim *The king
never dies.* This aphorism, as a proof of inherent right, is a
favourite argument of French, as of English writers; it is the
most effectual way of disposing of any claims, that kingship is
elective or founded on compact.

[3] Du Moulin, *De Monarchia Francorum* (Goldast, III. 51).

[4] Bodin, *De la Republique*, VI. 5.

[5] "*De jure divino est servare veram fidem et religionem; de jure
autem humano est, quod hunc aut illum habemus regem.*" Barclay

Apologia Catholica is clearest in its exposition of the
point.　There can be little doubt, that the stress
necessarily laid on so plainly artificial a rule as that
of the Salic law, gives to the French theory a far
more legal aspect than had the English.　Past
struggles and present necessities alike rendered
necessary this emphatic assertion of the binding
character of the Salic law.　Not only was it the
ground of Henry's claim, but it was the source of
the independence of the French monarchy.　For
Edward III. was undoubted heir to the French
Crown, had there been no such rule.　Thus the
sentiment in its favour had to strengthen it every
feeling of patriotic pride at the successful issue of
the Hundred Years' War[1].　It is a commonplace
with French writers that the treaty of Troyes was
invalid, for it gave to Henry V. and his heirs the
reversion of the Crown, and a treaty to violate the
Salic law is void[2].　The vividness with which men

quotes these words from Bellarmine, and says that he ought to have
added, "Ubi hunc vel illum regem semel habeamus, de jure divino
est, ut ei in civilibus causis cum omni honore et reverentia pare-
amus."　*De Potestate Papae* (Goldast, III. 659).

[1] Du Moulin thus describes the close of the Hundred Years'
War: "Tandem vero Angli spe sua frustrati, *a lege antiquissima
Salica* dejecti sunt."　Goldast, III. 51.

[2] Servin, whose main source of inspiration is hatred of
Spain, declares that even if the League could make good its point,
there would be no advantage gained by Spain, for England's
claims would have been valid, if the Salic law were not binding.
"Sed ista dicentes non animadverterunt se non tam Hispaniam et
Guisianam causam, quam Anglicam defendere" (Goldast, III. 206).
It was no wonder that the Salic law awakened such passionate
enthusiasm; for if the Hundred Years' War be taken into account,

realised the distinctive character of the rule of succession, as giving to the French monarchy a perfection lacking to other kingdoms, made it the more impossible for them to claim universality for so peculiar a system. There is no such attempt as that made by Filmer, to seek for hereditary monarchy a foundation in the natural constitution of society. It is of Nimrod rather than Adam that we hear as the founder of kingship. Certainly we come across comparisons of a kingdom to a family, and of kings to fathers. But they are never the basis of the theory, as in the *Patriarcha* or *The Rehearsal*. If agnatic kinship had been regarded as primitive or universal, there would have been stronger grounds for a French patriarchal theory of kingship, than there were for the English. But it does not appear that the possibility of such a theory ever suggested itself. Besides, it would not have been easy to derive the doctrine of the French succession from the common rules of inheritance. Henry IV. was not heir of Henry III. at private law; and much pains is taken by the author of the *Apologia Catholica* to demonstrate that, although the Bourbon prince was too distantly connected with the Valois to inherit their private property, he was yet the lawful heir to the throne[1]. The Crown is regarded as

it seems true to say that it was the salvation of France. The claim of Edward III. was far better than that put forward by Philip II. for himself or for his daughter.

[1] *Apologia Catholica*, 20. "Hoc quidem jus regni, inquiunt Doctores nostri, revera non est hereditarium, sed ad familiam pertinet, etiamsi nemo in ea existeret, qui succederet in defuncti bona."

something different in its nature from mere property; and a peculiar custom is needful to regulate the succession to the mystical position of a king. Bodin is at pains to declare that the king succeeds not by right of inheritance or by gift of God, but solely through the rule of law. It is easy to see how different is this view from the English conception of succession, which is always regarded as mysteriously above positive law, founded by God and Nature, and followed in all rightly regulated families.

Bodin, De la République, 1577.

To other French writers Bodin stands in somewhat the same relation, as does Hobbes to the English supporters of Divine Right. Nominally scientific, his treatise has really the same practical aim as those of Servin and Berchet. All his acuteness and philosophical grasp of the nature of government are directed to one end, that of securing the Crown to the next heir, Henry of Navarre. More clearly perhaps than any previous writer French or English does he realise the nature of sovereignty[1]. Of the conception of a "mixed" or limited monarchy he is as contemptuous as Hobbes or Filmer or Austin[2]. Quite in the manner of the last, he describes the notes of sovereignty, and defines law as a command of the sovereign generally binding. Sovereignty he declares to be indivisible and inalienable, and upon the question of customary law

---

[1] *De la Republique,* I. 8, 10.

[2] *Ibid.* II. 1. Speaking on a 'mixed form of government' he says:—" Je respons qu'il ne s'en est jamais trouué, et qu'il ne se peut faire ny mesmes imaginer, attendu que les marques de souuraineté sont indivisibles." p. 268.

comes to conclusions similar to those of Austin[1]. In depth and accuracy of thought his treatise far surpasses *the Leviathan*, and Bodin escapes the pitfall into which Hobbes fell of seeking the origin of sovereignty in a contract. Even a *lex regia* is according to him an impossibility in France, for the people never having possessed sovereign authority cannot have transferred it to the Crown.

The practical part of the treatise is much the same as that of other writers. The authority of the Pope is repudiated, although little is said on the subject[2]. The power of the prince is asserted to come from God, and the usual texts are employed to inculcate the duty of absolute non-resistance[3]. Monarchy is shewn to be the best form of government, in an argument of similar character, to that of Ockham[4]. But Bodin is more emphatic

[1] " La coustume prend sa force peu à peu, et par longues années d'un commun consentement de tous ou de la plus part ; mais la loy sort en un moment et prend sa vigueur de celuy qui a puissance de commander à tous ; la coustume se coule doucement et sans force ; la loy est commandee et publiee par puissance et bien souvent contre le gré des subjects ; et pour cette cause Dion Chrysostome compare la coustume au Roy, et la loy au tyran : *dauantage la loy peut casser les coustumes et la coustume ne peut deroger à la loy* * * * la coustume ne porte loyer ny peine ; la loy emporte tousiours loyer ou peine, si ce n'est une loy permissiue qui leue les defenses d'vne autre loy : et, pour le faire court, *la coustume n'a force que par souffrance, et tant qu'il plaist au Prince souuerain, qui peut faire une loy y adjoustant son homologation. Et par ainsi toute la force des lois civiles et coustumes gist, au pouvoir du Prince Souverain* " (*De la Republique*, 222).

[2] *Ibid.* 190 sqq.

[3] " Qui mesprises son Prince souuerain, il mesprise Dieu duquel il est l'image en terre." *Ibid.* p. 212.

[4] *Ibid.* VI. 4.

in his contention, that since the members of a "sovereign number" may disagree, sovereignty should be vested in a single person[1]. Finally, a philosophical justification is sought for the rule of the French succession, and the Salic law is alleged to be in harmony with the teachings of nature[2].

Summary. Thus it appears that in the writings of French controversialists there is developed a theory, which with slight modifications is identical with the English theory of the Divine Right of Kings. The essential notion is that the king owes his position directly to Divine appointment and is therefore accountable to God alone and not to the Pope. From this naturally arises the sense of the absolute duty of non-resistance upon religious grounds. The king is regarded as above the restraints of positive law, save in the matter of the succession. This, like the English custom of hereditary succession, is regarded as a constitutional or 'fundamental' law, which may not be violated by king or people or both together. In English theory the notion appears,

---

[1] *De la Republique*, p. 968. "Il n'est pas besoin d'insister beaucoup pour monstrer que la monarchie est la plus seure [forme de gouvernement], veu que la famille qui est la vraye image d'vne Republique ne peut avoir qu'vn chef, comme nous avons monstré, et que toutes les loix de Nature nous guident à la monarchie, soit que nous regardons ce petit monde qui n'a qu'un corps, et pour tous les membres un seul chef, duquel depend la volonté, le mouuement, et sentiment, soit que nous prenons ce grand monde qui n'a qu'un Dieu souuerain; soit que nous dressons nos yeux au ciel nous ne verrons qu'un soleil : et jusques aux animaux sociables, nous voyons qu'ils ne peuuent souffrir plusieurs Roys, plusieurs seigneurs, pour bons qu'il soyent."

[2] *Ibid.* vi. 5.

as indefeasible hereditary right, in the French as
the inviolability of the Salic law. The legendary
antiquity of the latter further strengthens the sentiment in its favour, although when Hotman pointed
out the true meaning of the passage supposed to
prescribe the rule, Servin is content to say, that
whatever the origin of the rule it is a custom of long
continuance and may not be broken[1]. Bodin completely developed the theory of sovereignty, but the
position of French writers, as loyal subjects at once
of Pope and king, renders many of their utterances
on this subject less clear than those of Englishmen
far inferior in ability.

How far, then, was English political thought *Influence*
actually influenced by these writings? It is im- *of French*
possible to say. It is however plain that the *upon*
English theory of Divine Right was a plant of *English*
indigenous growth. However much French writers *theory.*
may have done to influence English thought, or to
render general a sentiment in favour of Divine Right,
yet assuredly English theory did not arise out of
French. On the other hand the position of England
as an ally of Henry III. and Henry IV., the unpopu-
larity of the Guises including Mary Stuart, and the
hatred of the Spanish monarchy and of all schemes for
advancing its power would tend in various ways to
attract English sympathy to the side of those who
were defending the French monarchy from Papal
aggression and Spanish intrigue. Further, there is
some evidence of direct influence. The treatise of
Bodin in particular largely formed men's notions of

[1] Goldast, III. 207

government in the next century. It was translated into English and made a text-book at Cambridge. There is no question of the great effect of Bodin's writings upon those of Hobbes and Filmer and Leslie; and he is quoted by various other writers. There can hardly be any doubt, that the comparatively thorough understanding of the doctrine of sovereignty evinced by some of the least able among English writers was due to Bodin rather than to Hobbes, who was hated as an 'atheist' and despised as a believer in the original compact[1].

France and Scotland. A further source of influence is to be found in the relations of France to Scotland. The close connection between the two countries led to the migration to France of some Scotch Catholics, who would look with unfriendly eyes at the attempts of the Presbyterian leaders to dominate the politics of their country, whether by deposing Mary Stuart or menacing her son. The theory of popular government propounded by Buchanan was met by a reply *Apologia pro Regibus.* from Blackwood, a Scotsman settled in France. Buchanan is again one of the chief objects of attack

[1] It is worthy of note that Bodin in more than one place expresses himself in the strongest terms on the subject of the sovereignty being vested in the English king. In the coexistence of the privileges of the English Parliament and of the unlimited authority of the Crown, he finds evidence of his contention, that conciliar assemblies, whatever their power and antiquity, are no legal check upon the 'sovereign.' From Elizabeth's treatment of the House of Commons in respect to the succession he infers that Parliament has no real power to control the action of the Crown. *La Republique,* I. 8, pp. 189 sqq. "La souveraineté appertient pour le tout sans diuision aus Roys d'Angleterre, et les estats n'y ont que voir."

in the *De Regno* of Barclay, another Gallicised Scot. *De Regno.*
That Barclay should have announced upon the title-
page that his book was a reply to a Scotch Presbyterian, a Huguenot, and a French Papalist writer
is evidence of the connection between the political
ideas of France and Scotland. This book was dedi-
cated to Henry IV. But Barclay never forgot that
he was a Scotsman and that James I. needed to be
defended in the exercise of his Divinely granted
authority. Had it not been for the latter making
it a condition that Barclay should renounce Catho-
licism, he would probably have returned to Scotland,
there to find a new field for controversy in the sacred
cause of monarchy[1]. But the influence of both
Barclay and Blackwood upon the mind of James is
unquestionable, and through this channel if no other
they must have influenced English thought. Filmer,
indeed, singles them out along with Heywood as
his chief forerunners, and regards their utterances
as a complete expression of the rights of kings.
Barclay's treatise *De Potestate Papae* was translated
into English in 1611, a proof that his influence was
not confined to France. Thus there is a chain of
connection between the English and French theories
of Divine Right. French theory and practice must
certainly have influenced these Scotch writers. They
could hardly enter into the controversy against
' Brutus' or Boucher, without taking account of
French writings in support of monarchy. Nor could
Scotsmen, living in France, remain unaffected by
what was going on around them and by the circum-

[1] *Dict. of Nat. Biog.*, III. 178.

stances which led to a large body of French Catholics supporting the Divine right of Henry IV. There can be no doubt that the earlier struggles of Huguenots, Leaguers, and *Politiques* all contributed to the development of English political thought in the seventeenth century, whether in the direction of Divine Right or of the original compact.

Black-
wood.
Blackwood's two works, *De Vinculo Religionis et Imperii* and the *Apologia pro Regibus*, are instances of the double aspect of the theory. The former treatise was written in order to emphasize the connection between the true faith and the doctrine of non-resistance. Its first two parts published in 1575 are written to shew that Calvinism involves a theory of resistance and is therefore false. The book is a protest from a strong Roman Catholic against the clericalism of the Presbyterian system. Exactly as Anglican divines affirm the Papal claims to be heretical, because they tend to dissolve the bond between sovereign and subjects, so Blackwood contends that Calvinism is proved to be false by its teaching of resistance[1]. He complains that the new system takes away all freedom from states: whereas true religion is ever the support of government, and forbids resistance even to tyrants[2]. The inference

[1] "Religio quae semper hucusque regnorum conservatrix fuit, nunc temporum in reges armatur. Ex quo apparet *veram non esse religionem*, sed larvatam hypocrisim et perfidiam personâ religionis indutam, eo detestabiliorem, quo meliore se auctore jactitat." (*De Vinculo*, 261.)

[2] "Quae, vestram fidem, conscientiae libertas quae in effraenam progressa licentiam, nihil imperio, nihil reipublicae, nihil mori-

is that religion is the only security of States,—that there will be an end of law and order if false sects are permitted to exist.   It is a sense of the political danger involved in toleration that prompts the author to write.   The aim of most writers is to inculcate the religious duty of obedience, that of Blackwood is to assert the political necessity of persecution.

The third part of the book was not published until after the assassination of Henry IV. and is notable as containing a very strong condemnation of the League.   The author is nearly heartbroken to think that any Catholic should have borrowed the maxims of Protestants.   The interest of this treatise is great, for it affords complete justification for the manner in which Anglican divines identified Papist and Dissenting principles of governments.   Blackwood makes the same identification from the opposite point of view.   His argument is that no true Catholic can approve resistance, therefore all who profess to approve it in defence of the Catholic cause are in reality on the side of the Protestants. The Anglican view is that no true Protestant can approve resistance, and therefore that those Dissenters who allow it in the cause of Protestantism are Papists in disguise.

The *Apologia pro Regibus* is interesting in a different way.   Whether or no it be out of compliment to the reputation of Buchanan, as a classical

bus, nihil legibus liberum reliquit?" (*De Vinculo*, 262.) "Jamne religione perfidiam velabant suam? At religio servat ac tuetur, non labefactat, non evertit imperia." (*Ibid*. 289.)

9—2

scholar, the inspiration of the book is largely classical[1]. Although Scripture is sometimes cited, the bulk of the illustrations and arguments are from classical history or philosophy. Appeals to Roman law are frequent and the secular tone of the whole is remarkable. Perhaps Blackwood thought that his former work said enough upon the religious side. Or it may be, that the cause lay in the position of the writer as a Roman Catholic defending against Presbyterian subjects a king who was known to be a heretic. The book is further interesting for its references to England, which to Blackwood as to Bodin, is a clear instance of undiluted absolutism. Certainly if the derided principle of a mixed monarchy were proved to have no force in England, it would hardly be thought to exist in France or Scotland. Blackwood, who is a strong Anglophobist, declares that neither in England nor certain other

[1] Blackwood's position as at once a strong royalist and a devoted Papalist is remarkable. In the last part of the *De Vinculo* he extols the Pope's power, but avoids all reference to the deposition of Childeric or any disputed case; he is careful to confine himself to the perfectly harmless instances of royal reverence for the person of the holy Father. But in the *Apologia pro Regibus* his views come out more clearly. He cannot understand why Buchanan should object to the Pope doing what he approves in his own ministers. (121). The deposition of Childeric was done not at the bidding but with the consent of the Pope, and therefore implied no popular rights against the prince (p. 197). He ascribes sovereignty to the Pope and declares him to be as far superior to other monarchs as they are to their subjects. Yet he admits an ultimate power in the council to depose for heresy. But since this power is never exercised save in cases of Papal heresy, no inference of popular sovereignty can be drawn from it. The people are no judge of truth (201–4).

countries can the people be admitted to share the
sovereignty, even with the consent of the king[1].
He denies the validity of Henry the Eighth's testamentary devolution of the crown; for the succession
descends by an immutable law to the next of kin,
not as his father's heir, but as the legitimate ruler
of the kingdom[2]. Blackwood's theory of sovereignty
is complete with this exception. Monarchy may not
be divided or shared in any way. Yet he regards
force as the origin of kingship, a view curiously unlike
that of other writers, while Nimrod is of course
the first king[3]. He is so anxious to assert that the
king is above the law, that unlike Justice Berkeley
he denies that he is *lex loquens*. He declares that
all laws only retain their force through the tacit
assent of the sovereign at his accession[4], while in
regard to local laws and customs he approaches the
Austinian maxim, " Whatever the sovereign permits,
he commands[5]."

[1] *Apologia*, 6.

[2] *Ibid.* 78 sqq. "Reges non regum sed regni sunt heredes"
(112).

[3] *Ibid.* ch. vii.   [4] *Ibid.* ch. xi.

[5] "Neque tamen eam vim ac firmitatem habent, ut a principe
mutari non queant, cuius tum in leges, tum in homines potestas
nulla ratione definiri potest " (*Ibid.* 110). Buchanan desired a mixed
form of government, in which the king should have the supreme
executive, the judges interpretative, the people legislative power.
Blackwood ridicules this, and pertinently asks, " Non attendis
legis interpretationem legis vim obtinere?" (ch. xiii.). He shews
that there could be no supreme power in Buchanan's ideal state
with its three ultimate authorities independent of one another.
" Regem populo subesse iubes, quem populo vis inuito legem im-
ponere. Populo summam rerum attribuis, quem reluctantem et
inuitum regis imperio subiicis. Sed qui fieri potest ut idem

Previous enquiry necessary to the understanding of seventeenth century controversy.

This long preliminary investigation has shewn the causes at work in mediæval England, in the conflicts within the Holy Roman Empire, in the French Wars of Religion, and in the circumstances of the English Reformation, which contributed in various ways to the development of a theory of kingship more uncompromising, narrow, and absolutist than had yet been prevalent in England.

It is now possible to approach the political controversies of the seventeenth century, with some prospect of understanding why they took the shape they did. The ideas have arisen of Divine Right, of a 'fundamental law' of succession, of sovereignty, and on the other hand of the original compact, and of the duty of resistance at the bidding of the Church. It remains to view these notions welded into harmonious theories, to trace the process by which they were superseded, and to estimate the practical effect upon later ages of their once having been prevalent.

patiatur et agat? idem dominatur et serviat?" (295) The whole of Chapter xxxiii. is an argument in favour of monarchy as the expression of the principle of unity in all States. It is noteworthy that he regards this as the supreme effort of art, not nature; he apparently regards the family as an artificial organization. He finds it necessary to point out to his opponent that all states contain some supreme authority, that the Roman or Athenian democracy or the Venetian oligarchy ruled with exactly that 'regal,' i.e. sovereign power which Buchanan thinks it possible to eliminate from the commonwealth (193).

CHAPTER VII.

FROM JAMES I. TO THE JACOBITES.

THERE were many reasons why James I. should *James I. and the Theory of Divine Right.* hold the doctrine of the Divine Right of kings in its strictest form. His claim to the throne of England rested upon descent alone; barred by two Acts of Parliament, it could only be successfully maintained by means of the legitimist principle. Further, it was disputed by the Roman controversialists who had not sufficient hope of converting James to make them love his title. Doleman's attack on the hereditary principle is written from the Papalist standpoint. But it was not only from the Roman side that the position of James was threatened. Presbyterianism in Scotland, as expounded by Knox or Buchanan, and inwoven with politics by Murray and Morton, was a system of clericalism as much more irritating and meddlesome, as it was stronger and more popular in its basis than that of the Papal sovereignty. Even had there been no question of the English throne, there was enough

in the position of a king, thwarted and insulted on
all hands by the ministers of an upstart and narrow
communion, to bring him into approval of a theory,
which asserted against Papist and Presbyterian alike
that every soul without benefit of clergy is subject
to the royal authority, for the secular power is ordained by God alone and may not be controlled by
Pope or minister. Nor could the influences at work
also in England and France, which led to the theoretical exaltation of monarchy, have been devoid of
effect upon the mind of James. Thus it is no matter
for surprise, that at a time, when the sons of Zeruiah
were too strong for him, and he felt his authority a
mockery before the insolent representatives of ecclesiastical bigotry, James should promulgate with
logical completeness and grasp with the tenacity of
a narrow but clear-sighted intellect the theory of
the Divine Right of kings. In the *True Law of
Free Monarchies*, which saw the light five years
1598. before the death of Elizabeth, is to be found the
doctrine of Divine Right complete in every detail.
On his accession Parliament passed a statute which
purported not to give James a title, but merely to
declare his inherent right[1]. This would seem evidence that the theory of Divine Right was by this
time generally prevalent. Yet though, as was shewn
above, approaches had been made to it in more ways
than one, it does not appear as yet to have taken

---

[1] 1 Jas. I., c. 1. See Appendix A. Cf. also Coke's *Reports*,
vii. 10 b: "The king holdeth the kingdom of England by birthright inherent, by descent from the blood royal, whereupon
succession doth attend."

much hold of the popular imagination or even to *Incon-*
have been fully grasped by those who professed to *sistency of*
believe it. *popular*
opinion.

Evidence of this is to be found in *Overall's Con-*
vocation Book. This was avowedly intended to be
an authoritative exposition of the doctrine, but it
exhibits a curious inability to understand, what it
actually involved, and is very different from the perfectly harmonious system of the royalists of the
Restoration or of James himself. The Canons are
emphatic on the divine authority of *de facto*
governments[1]. The language of the book on this
point so alarmed the king that he wrote irritably to
Archbishop Abbot, bidding him not to meddle in
matters too high for him[2]. James was perfectly
justified in declaring that, should Philip of Spain
succeed in conquering the country, his right to the
throne would be Divine on the principles of the
Convocation Book, and Englishmen would be pre-
cluded from ousting the usurper in favour of the
lawful king. The compilers were so imbued with
the root idea of the theory of Divine Right, that
secular government is lawful without Papal or
clerical confirmation, that they were unable to
attach due importance to the 'organic details' of the

[1] Canons xxviii—xxxiii.

[2] The letter is printed in the edition of the *Convocation
Book* in the Library of Anglo-Catholic theology. The book was,
on account of this, not published until 1690. There is a strange
inconsistency in the letter of James; for he complains of the
Canons as not affording a justification of England in assisting the
United Provinces.

doctrine, or to distinguish between claims founded on force and the right of conquest.

James on the other hand met with a rebuff, when he attempted to expound his views of the inalienable character of sovereignty. The irritation of Parliament at his assertion, that, since all its privileges were originally granted by the Crown, they were liable to be revoked by the same authority, may be taken as fairly representing the general sentiment at this time. Further, the answer of Coke to the king's request that he might sit as judge in the courts of law, is a precursor of the coming breach between the supporters of the sovereign rights of the Crown and the upholders of the Common Law. However, in Calvin's case the personal character of allegiance was asserted to the full[1], and the decision of Bates's case[2] affirmed the doctrine that no king may materially

---

[1] The unanimous opinion of the judges decided that allegiance is due by the law of nature and God and may not be altered, and is due to the person of the king, not to his politic capacity. It was greatly to exalt the position of the king to declare that the mere fact of his being king of England and Scotland so united the countries that henceforward no one born in one of them was an alien in the other. And the language in which this is declared still further exalts the Crown: "Whatsoever is due by the law or constitution of man may be altered: but natural legiance or obedience of the subject to the sovereign cannot be altered; *ergo* natural legiance or obedience to the sovereign is not due by the law or constitution of man. Again, whatsoever is due by the law of nature, cannot be altered, but legiance and obedience of the subject to the sovereign is due by the law of nature; *ergo* it cannot be altered." Coke's *Reports*, VII. 25 a.

[2] Prothero's *Statutes*, 340–353.

diminish the rights of sovereignty, therefore that the statutes of Edward I. and Edward III. prohibiting unlimited customs did not bind their successors.

Mainwaring's Sermons published in 1628 are evidence at once of the prevalence of the doctrine and of its slow progress. The preacher asserts the Divine basis of royal authority and the right of the king to satisfy his necessities as seems good to him. Laud, however, thought the publication of these sermons inexpedient and endeavoured to prevent it[1]. When the character of Laud's own opinions as to royal authority are taken into account, this fact is significant of the popular attitude on this subject. As yet the country would not swallow the doctrine that was so palatable to it during the latter half of the century. Not that there was much disloyalty. Up to a much later date the nation as a whole was profoundly loyal to the monarchy. But it was not until extreme theories of popular rights aroused the antagonism of the large class who held to the old order, that counter theories of a royal sovereignty uncontrolled by custom became at all widely prevalent.

From the time however that the conflict between *The* king and Parliament entered upon its acute stage *doctrine grows into* there grew up a passionate sentiment of loyalty to *popularity* the Crown, which would be satisfied with nothing less *during the* than the doctrine of Divine Right in its extremest *Civil War.* form. As a popular force in politics the theory

---

[1] See Gardiner, *History of England,* vi. 208, 9.

hardly exerted much influence until the time of the
Long Parliament. Henceforward Divine Right becomes the watchword of all supporters of the rights
of the Crown, at least until the Revolution. The
most servile Parliament of Henry VIII., or that
which recognised with such fulsome redundance the
flawless title of James I., would scarcely have suffered
the employment of such terms, as those which in
1640 gave expression to the sentiment of the great
majority of the clergy :—

"The most high and sacred order of kings is of
Divine Right, being the ordinance of God Himself,
founded in the prime laws of nature, and clearly
established by express texts both of the Old and
New Testaments. A supreme power is given to
this most excellent order by God Himself in the
Scripture, which is, that kings should rule and
command in their several dominions all persons of
what rank or estate soever, whether ecclesiastical or
civil. * * * For any person or persons to set up,
maintain or avow in any their said realms or territories respectively, under any pretence whatsoever,
any independent coactive power, either papal or
popular, (whether directly or indirectly,) is to undermine their great royal office, and cunningly to overthrow that most sacred ordinance which God Himself
hath established ; and so is treasonable against God
as well as against the king. For subjects to bear
arms against their kings, offensive or defensive, upon
any pretence whatsoever, is at least to resist the
powers which are ordained of God ; and though
they do not invade, but only resist, yet S. Paul tells

them plainly they shall receive to themselves damnation[1]."

It will be observed that there is no mention here of indefeasible hereditary right. None was needed. So long as Charles I. was king and his right to reign undisputed, there was no cause to linger over any question of hereditary right. Only, when the notion is expressly rejected by an influential section of the community will it become necessary to reaffirm it. It is a truism that dogma never takes definite shape, save as a result of its denial by some thinker or leader. Thus the enthusiastic attachment to the notion of Passive Obedience was due to the Civil War and to the anarchy and tyranny that followed it.

Before that time men might well have misgivings about the duty in extreme cases. But henceforward all who have suffered through the war will entertain no doubt, but that obedience to the most oppressive of regular authorities will lead to less misery than will resistance. So with hereditary right. It was the execution of Charles and the exclusion of his heir that led men to dwell upon the distinction between a *de facto* and a *de jure* authority. The logical mind of James I. would have found nothing to shock it in royalist pronouncements of this period. The confusion apparent in *Overall's Convocation Book* has now disappeared from the popular mind. No one now, whichever party he favours, but has a clear enough sense that it is possible to assert Divine Right for the lawful heir without predicating it of an usurper.

[1] Cardwell's *Synodalia*, I. 889.

There was now present every condition necessary
for awakening men to the sharp distinctions between
de jure and *de facto* authority and between passive
obedience and active resistance however slight. On
the one hand there were the recollection of the arbitrary rule of Charles I. and the general hatred of the
methods of Strafford and the Star Chamber.   These
would serve to keep men in mind that a lawful
government might be intolerably oppressive, and
that therefore complete or active obedience would
not always be a duty. On the other hand there
was the existence of an upstart military autocracy,
claiming to be the inheritor of the secular traditions
of the English constitution and demanding universal
allegiance as though there were no question about the
legality of its acts.   This would sufficiently ensure
that every royalist and every opponent of Cromwell
and the Major-generals should realise, that an
usurper can have no moral claim to obedience, and
that it may be a sacred duty to restore the dispossessed heir. Passive Obedience and Indefeasible
Hereditary Right were no new conceptions; they
had long been in the air, and the necessity of com-
bating Papal claims had brought about a doctrine of
which they were merely the logical expansion.   But
as a force in English politics they largely owe
their importance to the Civil War and the successful
usurpation of Cromwell. The horror which was
awakened by the execution of Charles, and the
melancholy reverence which *Eikon Basiliké* won for
the Martyr, would tend to deepen in men's minds
their sentiment in favour of royal power, as clothed

with mysterious sanctity, and separated by a gulf from all other forms of government. Thus, while the origin of the theory of the Divine Right of Kings is earlier and due to other causes—for no real additions are made to the doctrine expounded by James,—its widespread prevalence was certainly due rather to the Civil War than to any more remote causes. It is the sentiment that brought back Charles II. to his father's throne, and finds expression in the Act of Uniformity[1].

In the Tudor period the doctrine is seen in the making. It is forged as a weapon in the great conflict with ecclesiastical aggression. The character given to it by that controversy remained ever its most essential quality. But the theory of government was developing at the same time and partly through the same causes. In the seventeenth century the real value of the theory in the development of political thought appears. Retaining still its antipapal character it yet exhibits itself more completely, as the form in which was expressed the discovery of sovereignty. The controversies which rage round the origin of law become now prominent. And the supporters of the doctrine of Divine Right are constantly found fighting for their contention, that law cannot exist independently of some lawgiver, and

Three stages of the doctrine.
1. Religion in sixteenth century.

2. Political in seventeenth century.

---

[1] Declaration to be made by schoolmasters &c.,: "I A.B. do declare that it is not lawful upon any pretence whatsoever to take arms against the king, and that I do abhor that traitorous position of taking arms by his authority against his person or against those that are commissionated by him," 14 Car. II. c. 4. 13 Car. II. c. 1, makes it an offence to declare that either or both Houses of Parliament have any legislative power without the king.

that the ultimate legislative authority in any State is necessarily above all positive law. The value of the theory as a political force is due not to this purely scientific element, but to the testimony it bears to the need of continuity in national life and to the paramount importance to a State of a law-abiding habit. It is easy to deny the doctrine. But those, who do this, should bear in mind that the singularly orderly character of English constitutional development, its freedom from violent changes, would not have been obtained but for the influence of this doctrine.

In contemplating the earlier stages of the Reformation, we are driven to regard with gratitude the men, who alone made possible a justification of the position of independence assumed by the English monarchy against the Pope. But the Divine Right of Kings is more than the effective expression of Gallicanism. It has a purely political side, which comes out most strongly in the middle of the seventeenth century. From the writings of that period we learn how it has stamped upon the English mind the conception of sovereignty, and thereby rendered a service which can hardly be overestimated by all who value clearness of political vision. Further, in contemplating the Restoration and the period of the Exclusion Bill and the Revolution, we are driven to express the debt of modern times to the faith, through which alone men weathered the storm of political change and achieved the ends of freedom and good government with less of bloodshed and anarchy than has been the lot of any other nation. This passionate sense of the need of continuity in national institu-

tions is perhaps the dominant note of the pamphlets
and sermons which poured forth in a deluge, when
men were debating the question of a Popish successor
to Charles II., and weighing in a balance the risks
of persecution and the advantages of an unbroken
succession.

A further impulse to enthusiasm was afforded by *The Exclusion Bill.*
the Exclusion Bill. The controversy, which raged
round that ill-fated measure, was the source on the
one hand of the most emphatic expressions of belief
in indefeasible hereditary right and passive obedience,
and on the other of the clearest exposition of the
theory of popular rights. Doleman's pamphlet was
reprinted. The theory of original compact and of
the purely official character of the kingly dignity
was elaborated. While the discussion on the position
of Julian the Apostate reveals the similarity of the
arguments employed to those of French and Imperialist thinkers, and is evidence, that the popular
party had no fault to find with the dialectic method
of their opponents.

In *Julian the Apostate* Johnson argues that *Johnson and his opponents.*
the inference commonly drawn from the obedience
of the Christians to an unbelieving Emperor is
false, for as a matter of fact they did not recognize
his authority, and S. Gregory Nazianzen had fears
that his father the Bishop would have kicked
the Emperor[1]. To this it is replied in *Constantius
the Apostate*, that the assertions are unfounded
and are a libel upon Christians; further, that if

---

[1] Johnson's *Works*, p. 21.

they were true, it would not affect the argument,
for Christians recognized Constantius and obeyed
him, although he was an Arian. Thus the duty
of obedience to a heretic sovereign is demonstrated.
The acknowledged dangers to be apprehended from
James lead men to emphasize the duty of *passive*
obedience. Tears and prayers are repeatedly declared to be the only lawful weapons against a
tyrant. It was felt that there might ere long be
need of them. The Doctrine of the Cross, as it is
called, is written up with much enthusiasm in a
host of pamphlets and sermons.

1681.
*Filmer's
Patri-
archa.*

It was shortly after this time that Filmer's
Patriarcha was first published. The work won great
and deserved popularity as the ablest justification of
the extreme royalist doctrine. Filmer had the
acuteness to see that of the two modes of argument, that of relying upon a medley of Scripture
texts, forbidding resistance and asserting divine
sanction for kingship, and that of claiming that
monarchy is in accordance with the teachings of
nature, the latter rested upon a far more solid
basis. It is always possible to explain away single
texts of Scripture. Indeed no one nowadays but
knows that, when S. Paul and S. Peter enjoined
obedience to established government as a religious
duty, they were far from considering the question
of men's duty in extreme cases, and had no notion
of discussing the right of insurrection. Whether
or no Filmer was aware of this may be doubted.
Probably he was not, as in another place he
founds an elaborate argument on the thirteenth

of Romans[1]. But he was instinctively conscious
that this was not the best method of establishing his position. In his treatise the textual method
of argument falls quite into the background be-
fore the prominence given to the conception that *Changed mode of argument.*
monarchy is founded in nature. The idea is not
new. It was introduced with more or less of completeness by most of the supporters of Divine Right.
But with them it is rather an illustration or a figure
of rhetoric than the basis of an argument. Filmer
rests his whole system upon it. He attempts to find
the origin of kingship in the natural constitution of
society, and bases it neither on force nor on popular
sanction, but on human nature, as formed by the
Creator. Most writers regard the fact that kingship is founded by Divine ordinance, as proved by
the institution of the kingdom of Israel or by
isolated phrases in Daniel or Proverbs; to this proof
they are content to add that kingship is indeed
natural, as may be seen in a family or the animal kingdom among geese, or sheep. Filmer on the other
hand contends that kingship is natural, and that
therefore it must be ordained by God, the author
of nature. His whole argument depends on the
identification of the kingdom with the family, and
of royal with paternal power. That the king is
the father of his people was a metaphor frequently
employed by writers in favour of monarchy. Filmer
expands the metaphor into an argument, and founds
upon it the only rational system of absolutist
politics. The patriarchal conception of society is far

---

[1] Preface to *Observations on Aristotle*.

Many writers do not make the patriarchal theory the basis of the doctrine. from being of the essence of the theory of the Divine Right of Kings; it is merely the best argument by which it is supported. Some supporters of the theory scarcely refer to the idea, most however do so, but employ it very loosely, and clearly without the notion that it was a far better justification for their opinions, than the. phrase, "By me kings reign, and princes decree judgment." King James uses the analogy avowedly as a metaphor. Sir Dudley Digges declares that the king is "without a metaphor the father of his people," evidence that the comparison is commonly regarded as a mere figure of speech. Like other authors he regards the marriage tie, as equally typical of the bond between king and people, and is ready with the argument against resistance, "What God hath joined, let no man cut asunder." Sanderson, like Bodin, declares that kings have more powers than parents, and that a monarch is "a brother and something more." Mainwaring regards the bond between king and people as fourfold, consisting of the ties that bind (1) The Creator and the Creature, (2) Husband and Wife, (3) Parents and Children, (4) Masters and Servants[1].

These are only a few instances of the general view, which is merely that allegiance is the strongest of all bonds and includes all other human ties. Of any general patriarchal theory of kingship there is little evidence before Filmer[2]. It is his merit to have

[1] *Religion and Allegiance*, 3.

[2] S. Thomas Aquinas, who regards the family as something similar to the kingdom, is the type of most thought. Sanderson says "the master or *paterfamilias* is a *kind* of petty monarch there" (*Judgment in One View*, p. 106), and argues that "what power the

discovered that the common metaphor contained within it the germ of a system far more substantial in its basis than the ordinary hotch-potch of quotations from Scripture.   The popularity of the book is further evidence that the idea came to most men with the force of a discovery.   For its sole contribution to the theory is the careful elaboration of the patriarchal conception of kingship.   If the notion had previously been regarded as a necessary element of the doctrine it would be hard to account for Filmer's reputation.   Men clutched at the chance, given them by the *Patriarcha*, of grappling with their opponents on better terms than were afforded by the weapons with which they were familiar.   At the same time Filmer can hardly be said to have been the discoverer of the conception.   His book was certainly the occasion of its prevalence, but so widespread a metaphor as that of the king being *pater*

master hath over his servants for the ordering of his family no doubt the same at the least, if not much more, hath the supreme magistrate over his subjects for the peace of the Commonwealth, the magistrate being *Pater Patriæ* as the master is *Pater familias*" (p. 108). And again, "A governor is a brother too and something more; and duty is charity too and something more. If then I may not offend my brother, then certainly not my governor" (p. 112). *Vox Populi*, a pamphlet against Spain of 1624, is an instance of the loose way in which the patriarchal power is regarded, even by a writer who seems to approach Filmer. "Amongst all nations the rule of a family or country was *conferred* upon the eldest. Until there were kings they were instead of such, and when there were kings, either they were *chosen out* of these, or these were their substitutes in such families and places where they resided" (7). *The Royal Charter granted unto Kings* regards the Divine origin of kingship as proved by the case of Melchisedec, who was "without father, without mother" (6).

patriae is sure to be pressed to its full extent by some writers. The arguments of Bodin in favour of monarchy and the phrases employed by Williams, Bishop of Ossory, in a little pamphlet *Jura Magistratus* are an indication that men were feeling their way to a system akin to that of Filmer[1].

1644.

The constructive theory of Divine Right.

The importance of Filmer in the history of the doctrine is indeed great. But he deserves to be remembered not so much as the most perfect exponent of the theory as the herald of its decadence. It is an easy transition from the conception of government as directly established by Divine command to the notion that since God is the author of nature, whatever is natural has His sanction. Yet the change is great. For direct Divine Right has been substituted a constructive theory of Divine approval. The theological conception of politics is giving way before what may be termed the naturalistic. In this disguised form the theory of Divine Right, as the only possible justification for any political system, lingers on until with the present century the notion of natural rights has fallen into discredit. In a sense it may be said, that Filmer paved the way not only for Locke, but for Rousseau. It is plain that the theory of natural rights, whether vested in king or people, is the next stage of development to the conception that all political systems must find their sanction in the Bible, as the

Transition to natural rights.

[1] *Jura Magistratus*, 15: " Every master of a family that ruleth his own household is a *petite* king"; and again, "A kingdom is nothing else but a great family where the king hath paternal power," 22.

complete Revelation of the Divine Will.   Whether
the theory be one of Divine Right in the older sense,
or of natural rights as a proof of Divine sanction, the
motives which lead men to adopt it are the same.
It is the desire to find some immutable basis for
politics and to lift them above considerations of mere
expediency, that prompts men to elaborate systems
of Divine or natural rights.   They are haunted
with the hope of finding a universal system, superior
to time and circumstance, untrammelled by considerations of historical development or national
idiosyncrasy.   And to both schools, that of the
believers in Divine right, whether of Pope or
Presbytery or King, and that of the upholders of
natural and inalienable, i.e. Divine rights of nations
or individuals, the same objections apply.   No system
of politics can be immutable.   It is impossible in
framing a doctrine of government to lay down
eternal principles, which may never be transgressed.
A universal theory of the state is a chimæra, for
historical development and national character are the
most important of all considerations in investigating
the laws of political development.   The arguments,
with which Burke annihilated the vain dreams of the
Revolutionary idealists, are equally applicable to the
theories of Bellarmine on behalf of the Pope, or of
James I. or Filmer in favour of monarchy.   The
theory of natural rights is the old theory of Divine
Right disguised.

Yet it was disguised.   There is no denying the
great transformation thought has undergone when
controversialists have abandoned the habit of un-

Motive to believe in a theory of Divine or natural rights.

Fallacies of theories of natural rights.

critically compiling a cento of Scripture phrases for arguments. No longer is the Bible regarded as the sole source of political theory. Instead of this, an attempt, however imperfect, is made to seek in the nature of man and the necessity of human society the changeless principles of civil government and inviolable laws of political duty. Once the project of finding an immutable system of politics be granted as worthy of undertaking, it is certainly more reasonable to seek it in the teachings of nature, than in the doubtful import of a fortuitous concourse of Scripture texts. At least it is one step further towards a utilitarian or a historical system of politics, for nature certainly would seem to approve the principle of utility, and it distinctly indicates the importance of development according to the law of an organism. The first fact, that utility is in accordance with the law of nature, was recognized by Locke and Sidney, while Filmer has certainly more of the historical spirit than any of his opponents, or than some of his predecessors, such as Blackwood. In any case it is the merit of Filmer to have seen, that a natural system of politics was more likely to prove well-founded than a purely theological scheme; or rather to have regarded theology as pointing to nature as the teacher of political philosophy.

Filmer's change of front really gives up the ground. Yet the credit due to him as a political thinker, is not clearly his as a supporter of his own theory. His method paved the way for its overthrow. The older mode of arguing from Scripture texts, as direct Divine injunctions, had this advantage, that it was impregnable to the assaults of criticism, and that neither natural law nor the principle of utility could

avail aught against it. In partially deserting the
old method of argument Filmer has in reality
surrendered the case for Divine Right. In appearance his position is far stronger than that of his
predecessors. The reason of this is that his argument
approaches more closely to those with which we are
familiar. Filmer's theory of Divine Right was
expressed in a syllogism :—

What is natural to man exists by Divine Right.
        Kingship is natural to man.
Therefore Kingship exists by Divine Right.

This is a sounder mode of procedure than that
of collecting a few texts and illustrations from the
Bible and ignoring or emptying of their meaning
any that make for the contrary view. Yet Filmer's
position is far more open to attack than that of the
older controversialists. The verse 'they that resist
shall receive to themselves damnation' is apparently
of unmistakeable import, which can only be evaded
by sophistry. No arguments from expediency, no
fresh reading of history could affect the elaborate
accumulation of texts made by Mainwaring in support
of his doctrine. The only possible way to meet him
was to deny the interpretation or the applicability
of the passages quoted. In fact considerations of
utility or historical circumstances could not affect
the ordinary argument for Divine Right. But
with Filmer's arguments this is not the case. For
the whole question of what constitutes the law of
nature is involved, and it is easy to argue as did
Locke for the principle of utility, the instinct of self-
preservation, as of natural and therefore Divine

origin. Both Locke and Sidney indeed elevate their
own principle of natural rights above any considerations of temporary expediency, and would not allow,
that the legislature in a state is sovereign, even
though it were manifestly expedient that it should
be so. But the principle of utility governs much of
their thought, and they are justified in regarding
its dictates as being every whit as much a law of
nature, as the necessity of obedience to government.
The theory of natural rights and original compact
propounded by the Whig opponents of Filmer is less
well-founded and more artificial than the Divine
Right of Kings. But the speculations of Locke and
Sidney have this of value, that they recognize to some
extent the importance of considerations of utility in
framing a practicable theory of politics. It is the
failure to see this, not the elaboration of an absolutist system, that is the real ground of the
puerilities of the royalist school. But in appealing
to law natural Filmer was paving the way for the
use of this principle of utility to overthrow his
idealist system. With those of the old school it was
useless talking of utility. They regard the Bible as
containing in set terms an emphatic prohibition of
resistance, and they put this in the forefront of
their argument. Against such a contention no
argument from the inexpediency of absolute non-
resistance can have any hope of success. The
arguments drawn from isolated texts seem to modern
readers the most absurd part of the theory of Divine
Right. They are in reality the strength of the
position. If the arguments be absurd, it was not

easy to prove it.   But for Filmer the Bible is no
mere storehouse of texts, though he will be ready so
to employ it on occasion.   It is the one historical
document which gives authentic information as to
the nature of primitive society.   In the early
chapters of Genesis he finds evidence, that society is
as old as humanity, that kingship is an expansion of
family life, and that monarchy is the inalienable
natural power of the father.   The value of the
conception is great; it is far less unhistorical or
artificial than the Whig idea of the state, and
contains by implication the pregnant truth that the
state is an organism not a machine.   Yet the
Divinity claimed for kingship is, as has been pointed
out, purely constructive.   The protection afforded by *Filmer's*
direct Divine injunction is abandoned; the inspira- *position*
tion of the Bible is of service, only so far as was *open to*
needed to authenticate the account of society given *attack.*
in Genesis.   The truth or falsehood of Mr McLen-
nan's theory of primitive society would have been a
vital matter for Filmer.   Had the theory of the
former been accepted, the system of the latter would
have fallen like a house of cards.   But the *mutterrecht*
would have had no bearing on the common arguments.   Nothing was easier than to meet Filmer
on his own ground, and Locke did so.   He asserts
that Filmer has misconceived Genesis, that, as a
fact of history, no such kingly power as was claimed
for him, was ever held by Adam, that, if it had
been, it could have no possible reference to the
power of modern kings.   Locke then interrogates
his own consciousness, as to what are the natural

instincts of men, and infers, on the same ground of
natural law as Filmer, a totally opposed conclusion.
Filmer's political theory is in brief this. Natural
rights are Divine rights. There is one natural right
only, the authority of the father. This is preserved
in the sovereign power in all states. All men are
born slaves. Locke on the other hand asserts, that
all men are born free and equal, with inalienable
rights granted them by God; that states are founded
upon compact from motives of utility, and are not
given unlimited authority, for that would be to
contradict the law of self-preservation. The point
of view of both Locke and Filmer is in reality
identical. Both believe that there existed a state
of nature, and that true principles of politics
may in some way be discovered by investigation into it. Both believe that whatever rights
belong to man living in a state of nature are
inalienable and may not be taken from him by any
form of organized society. Filmer believes that the
one inalienable right is the power of the father.
He saw what Hobbes and Locke and all believers in
the original compact failed to see, that political
society is natural and necessary to men, and is no
artificial creation of their choice. But his method
of proving this is by finding the state of nature in
the patriarchal society described in the Bible. He
indeed believed that there was irrefragable evidence
to prove that his state of nature was a historical
fact. While Locke and Hobbes were content to
urge on à priori grounds that theirs must have
existed, although there was no evidence to shew it.

In both cases there was the same impassable *Gulf*
gulf between the present condition of society and *between*
actual
what was believed to be the primitive state. The *society and*
the state
theory of compact is Locke's method of bridging the *of nature.*
gulf. Filmer in this point is less successful. He
admits that the heir of Adam is not now to be found,
and only escapes the difficulty by means of the
principle that possession gives the best right where
none else is to be found. But, as with Locke the
rights of man in the state of nature still subsist to
be the foundation of political liberty, save in so far
as they have been partially surrendered to the civil
government, so with Filmer the rights of the father
are the foundation of all political society and of the
title of every government to the obedience of its
subjects.

Locke of course had no difficulty in pointing
out, that it is a strange proceeding to argue Divine
appointment for a number of monarchs, who are
admittedly the descendants of usurpers, merely on
the ground that their ancestors were less scrupulous
than those of other men. Locke's destructive
criticism is completely effective, owing to the slender
bond of connection between the primitive family
and modern political society. Thus Filmer's work
forms the transition stage between the older views
and those of Locke in more ways than one. Not
only does it afford the necessary link of development
between theories of Divine and of natural right; but
it approaches the schemes of Locke and Rousseau
in its singular idealism. It is almost grotesque to
treat political theory as though all its problems

could be solved by an appeal to the primitive family.
The attempt to find in patriarchal authority the
sole source of all political rights, and to derive the
modern state directly from the Adamic society gives
to Filmer's work an air of unreality, which is not
shared by that of earlier writers. While Filmer's
method was sounder, his system was more artificial than that of his predecessors. The same
might be said of Locke with reference to Filmer.
His system is as much more unhistorical in its basis,
as it is more reasonable in its conclusions, than
that of Filmer.

Stages in the development of the theory and subsequent ideas.
The change which had thus come over the
royalist method of conducting the controversy is
significant. The theory of the Divine Right of
Kings takes its rise as a doctrine of the right of
secular governments to be free from clerical interference. In its essential idea the doctrine has been
at work in English politics from the days of
Henry VIII. So long as there was much to be
apprehended from the side of those who claimed a
divine right to control the state in the interests of
an ecclesiastical organization, it was necessary to lay
stress on the religious side of the argument for
kingship. But as this danger tends to disappear,
and the doctrine has begun to do its work, secular
politics will be free to develop on their own lines.
Theological systems of politics and purely theological
arguments will be no longer needed to meet the
claims of Pope or Presbytery, and politics will enter
upon the modern stage. The theory of natural
rights is inevitably the next stage of development.

It abandons the attempt to discover in Scripture the sanctions of civil society, and its direct institution by God. Yet it retains the conception of an immutable system of politics, rooted in the nature of man, and not to be changed through motives of mere expediency. Like the theory of Divine Right, the doctrine of natural rights is an attempt to determine à *priori* the nature of government, the limits of obedience, and the principles which should govern state action. Less even than the theory of Divine Right does it take account of circumstances or historical causes. It proclaims a system of politics, clear, universal, and unalterable, based not on the uncritical study of Scripture, but on what are believed to be the teachings of nature and the dictates of pure reason. The supporters of Divine Right confined their view to special states, and peculiar circumstances, whatever their system might claim of abstract truth and universality. The supporters of natural rights paid no regard to racial characteristics or external conditions, but proclaimed a doctrine that should last for all time and be valid for all stages of civilisation. Yet if they erred greatly, in seeking an eternal system of rights and duties to govern the fleeting arrangements of political constitutions, at least their plan of seeking political theory in nature had this merit; that they could not altogether ignore the principle of utility, so plain to natural reason. Thus they are one step nearer to modern political theory.

At this point considerations of utility will begin once more to be of importance. While a further

stage will be the abandonment of the attempt to
find an immutable political theory; and politics will
become, as they are at the present day, purely utilitarian or historical. It was the work of the supporters
of the Divine Right of Kings to make this possible. It
was impossible for the state to develop its principles,
so long as its very existence, as an independent
power, was constantly threatened by clericalism.
To set it free from ecclesiastical control it was
needful to claim Divine institution for its .head.
But when this purpose was realized, and independence attained, the state secure in its new-found
freedom may develop principles of politics without
reference to theology. Before, it would have been
at once dangerous and useless so to do. The main
work of the theory of Divine Right was drawing to
a close, although a little remained to be accomplished. It was natural that its supporters should
alter the basis upon which their theory rested.
Men do not desert a belief, until some time after its
main purpose is fulfilled. As has been seen, there
were still potent causes to attach men to the
doctrine. So long as the recollection was vivid of the
martyrdom of Charles and of the tyranny of Oliver,
men would continue to assert the theory. Besides, all
danger from Rome or Scotland was scarcely over as
yet. But the latter has sufficiently diminished in
magnitude, to admit of the transition from the purely
Scriptural to the sociological argument on behalf of
Divine Right[1].

[1] A proof that this was the case is afforded by the writings of
Bellarmine. The Cardinal repeatedly allows to kingship the con-

The changed method of conducting the con- *Nalson.* troversy appears in a work written later though published earlier than *The Patriarcha*, Nalson's *Common Interest of King and People*. The title of 1678. this book sufficiently indicates the main line of argument employed. The author begins with an elaborate account of the principle of self-preservation and of the desire of happiness, as the ruling motives of human nature. No terms could be stronger than those in which the writer sets forth the universality of this law of nature, and save for the excellence of the style the first few pages might have been written by Bentham. The basis of the theory, unlike that of Filmer, is avowedly utilitarian, although other proofs are not discarded. There is a short exposition of the patriarchal theory, but this is not made the foundation of the system. Monarchy is proved to be the most perfect form of government by reason of its antiquity, its universality, its conformity with human nature, and of the fact that it satisfies the great ends of all action, the instinct of self-preservation and the desire of happiness. So far the tone is strangely modern. Then in a short passage the writer reverts to the older mode of argument, and adduces the fourth of Daniel as clear evidence of the Divinity of Kingship. The book is remarkable for

structively Divine character of being rooted in natural necessity. But he declares that the Pope has an immediate commission from God, which kings have not. Their right is indeed Divine, for it is natural, but it is not, as the Pope's power is, founded on direct Divine injunction. Against Bellarmine the older writers assert that the king does hold his power by a direct Divine grant. But Filmer partially abandons this argument.

its lucidity and grasp of principles. It is further to
be observed, that it contains an elaborate demonstration of the incompatibility, not merely of the
Papal sovereignty, but of the Presbyterian system
with the independence of the secular authority and
with the liberty of the subject. Nalson is convinced
that Presbyterianism, if allowed a free hand, is
destructive of the freedom of Crown, Parliament, and
individual alike. Here again with all his ability,
which invests the work with an interest lacking to
the usual hash of texts in royalist pamphlets and
sermons, the author has yet surrendered his whole
case by his adoption of the utilitarian standpoint.
In a case like that of James II. will it be possible
seriously to maintain that his continued reign would
be agreeable to the principle of utility? Doubtless
it might be the case, for, as Hobbes thought, the evils
attendant on the most peaceful Revolution may out-
weigh every benefit attained thereby. But such a
view could never become popular. Unless the doctrine
of non-resistance has something higher than considerations of utility to recommend it, it cannot hope
to hold its ground. The mass of mankind will never
be convinced, that it is useful to maintain in power
a government, which is oppressive beyond limit.
But they may be persuaded that it is their duty to
do so. If acuter minds have come to the conclusion
that a revolution is always inexpedient, the only
method of making their opinion practically effective
will be by inducing the vulgar to believe that it is
always iniquitous. This was the great source of
strength to the upholders of Passive Obedience, as

the plain teaching of the Gospel. If Christianity be
indeed a doctrine of the Cross in their sense, and
every kind of tyranny is to be endured by true
Christians, there will be no use demonstrating the
inexpediency of non-resistance. The more foolish it is
from a common-sense point of view, the more clearly
is it the duty of those who look beyond this world.
What has convenience to do with God's direct
command? But with Nalson's system these considerations lose their force, and in his book even more
than that of Filmer we see the beginning of the end.
But Filmer's patriarchal theory was the necessary
transition to the next stage of development, that
represented by Locke and Sidney, while Nalson's
thought rather looks forward to a yet further day,
when natural rights themselves shall be scouted as
ridiculous, and political theories shall be constructed
on utilitarian principles alone.

Both Filmer and Nalson were a little in advance *Yet the old*
of most contemporary writers. They do no more than *method*
is still
foreshadow the decadence in store for the old modes *popular.*
of thought and argument. Meanwhile, these remain
with little diminution in popularity for some time to
come. The majority of the supporters of Divine
Right, even after the Revolution, use arguments that
differ but slightly from those of the time of the
Commonwealth. Indeed, one effect of the Revolution
was to turn the eyes of all who did not love it on
the past and to deepen for a time the sentiment in
favour of the purely Biblical method of political *Third*
stage of
theory. The nonjurors had been beaten by accom- *the theory-*
plished facts. Like all supporters of "lost causes *romantic.*

11—2

and forsaken beliefs," they draw their main inspiration from the past. The very fact that men are beginning to discredit their modes of reasoning as obsolete, will cause them to cling to them with greater tenacity, as the loved relics of the order which has passed away. The *raison d'être* of their party is the sentiment of romantic attachment to old modes of thought and feeling, to outworn theories, and to ideals which practical men have forgotten. The Jacobite will be more, not less inclined to lay stress upon the religious duty of Passive Obedience and upon the direct appointment of kings by God, than was the controversialist of the Restoration, who had, as he hoped, not merely to justify the past, but to carve out the future. To the one Divine Right was a force of practical value, and its employment part of the business of life. To the other it was a memory and a vain regret.

Prevalence of the belief even after the Revolution. The Revolution and the Act of Settlement disposed for ever of the doctrine of indefeasible hereditary right, and made it all but impossible to maintain the theory of non-resistance. Yet these results were by no means immediate, so far as the bulk of Englishmen were convinced. The doctrine indeed could not die out all at once. And the existence of a wide-spread feeling in favour of the Stuarts is evidence that it did not do so. The Revolution threw on to the side of the Stuarts the whole latent sentiment in favour of all institutions or beliefs of which the life is decaying. The great practical reason for supporting the theory of Divine Right no longer exists. At last all danger to the

State from clerical interference is at end. It becomes
moreover increasingly clear that the doctrine as a
pillar of government has done its work, and that the
leaders of thought and action, with whom rests the
future, have far other aims in view than the conduct
of politics in accordance with theological theories of
kingship and obedience.   But all this will tend to
beget a sentiment, that shall invest the Stuart line
with a dignity, which it never had when in possession,
and to bestow upon it a charm, to which no reigning
dynasty can lay claim.   From 1688 the Stuart
cause is the expression of the 'passion of the past';
and the theory that supports it suffers a like change.
All men's hatred of what is new because it is new,
their dislike of conquering ideas because they are
winning, their love of the antique for no reason than
that it is not modern, will draw them to the side of
the 'king over the water.' The Divine Right of
Kings has reached its last stage.   At first a method
of meeting in argument a foe, whom it was impossible
to conquer by force, it grew in weight and efficiency
until it became one of the chief means whereby men
justified to themselves the rejection of that Papal
supremacy that threatened to retard the free development of the national states.   The deep sentiment
of anti-clericalism which it enshrined saved men from
the danger of submitting to another and a yet more
blighting tyranny of ecclesiasticism, that threatened
to suck the life out of State and people with a net-
work of inquisitorial jurisdiction and with a narrow
code of life and morality.   In the political conflicts of
the seventeenth century, in which religion played so

large a part, the Divine Right of Kings had been the form in which expression had been found for men's reverence for tradition and for their instinctive sense that progress can never be by trampling on old institutions. Thus the theory was the bulwark of the Restored monarchy, by rallying sentiment round the king as the ancient centre and symbol of national life. It had preserved the continuity of the constitutional system, and was probably a main cause of the tranquillity, which marked the English alone among the Revolutions of history. By a fiction, as expedient as it was transparent, the sentiment in favour of obedience to law was prevented from receiving any shock, and those who smile at the falsity of the assertion that James II. 'abdicated the throne' would do well to bear in mind that it is far easier to shake the law-abiding sentiment by an admitted break with the legal system of the past, than it is to repair it by any improvement in the constitution. But, if with a certain amount of ingenuity the doctrine of non-resistance might still be maintained to be a principle of English constitutional life, it was not so with indefeasible hereditary right, which after suffering a shock at the Revolution received an irretrievable blow in the Act of Settlement. Nor was it possible any longer to contend that the king was absolutely sovereign, and accountable to God alone. Henceforward the Divine Right of Kings is the expression of regretful aspirations, and in no sense of actual fact. From a practical force it has become a romantic sentiment. Pity for the unfortunate and loyalty to a forlorn hope were now the main elements in the faith. Its true cha-

Effect of the theory in maintaining the continuity of the English state.

racter is to be found in that burst of lyrical *The* lament, that echoed with pathetic melancholy of *Jacobite Songs.* tone the longings of men, who were ever "looking backwards." It is in this rather than in sermons or treatises that we must seek the source of such lingering vitality, as still remained to the doctrine. No fresh development in argumentative method was possible, and the writings of Leslie are in many respects little more than an expansion of Filmer. But perhaps in the very brilliancy of the nonjuring controversialist, in his pungent satire and acute criticism we may have an indication, that the defence of the doctrine is becoming rather a *jeu d'esprit* than a serious labour. Once an intellectual weapon against the assaults of Rome, the by no means contemptible expression of a very practical determination to ensure for the State a free hand, the doctrine in losing its value as a force has acquired a certain æsthetic interest. The feeling which keeps alive is partly artistic, partly sentimental, and becomes vivid to us in the song for the blackbird, and the legendary halo surrounding Bonnie Prince Charlie. This phase of the belief is enshrined for ever in the novels of Sir Walter Scott. The use, which more recent writers of romance have made of the Jacobite sentiment, is a further proof that the main interest of the belief after 1688 is æsthetic. This aspect of the doctrine is indeed so familiar to us, that it is hard to realise that it ever possessed any other. We find it easy enough to regard with a certain tolerance a faith, which is to us a mere romantic pose. But it is not so easy to recognise, that this was only the

latest phase in the history of a theory, which had
been a force of great practical importance, the
expression (in obsolete forms) of deep truths of political philosophy and of a necessary stage of political
development. That all this was the case there is
ample evidence to prove. But the practical work of
the doctrine was done before the Revolution, and it
is well to realise that the tendency to hold it after
was the inevitable feeling, that touches all dying
causes with a sunset charm. It is those, who find
artistic gratification in contemplating with half-simu-
lated regret an order which is no more, who will
more and more make up the diminishing band of
Jacobite enthusiasts.

It is worthy of remark that Swift and Bolingbroke, the two most brilliant practical politicians on
the Tory side, have neither of them anything but
contempt for a doctrine which they regard as absurd
and as emptied of all effectual influence. Swift's
pamphlet, *The sentiments of a Church of England
man*, save in the assertion that the supreme legislative power may never be resisted, is utterly unlike the
work of earlier royalist writers. Nor does Bolingbroke like the theory any better. Indeed his criticism
is far more modern in its tone, than that of any
other writer with views resembling his own. His
assertion that "a divine right to govern ill is an
absurdity; to assert it blasphemy[1]" might have
been written a hundred years later, and exhibits the
same sort of ignorance to be deplored in most criti-
cisms of the doctrine. The real point of it is entirely

[1] *The idea of a patriot king.* Bolingbroke, *Works*, II. 879.

missed, and a faith, which had at least in the past exercised great influence, is exhibited as though it had never been more than antiquarian pedantry.

Just in so far as for practical men the theory is ceasing in the reign of Anne to have any interest, it begins to have a value for all who with whatever motive are in love with what is antiquated and is passing into tradition. There is always a sense of attachment to a dispossessed house, and some men still cling to Divine Right as investing with a certain glamour of mystic import the ancient line and its God-given title. The Divine Right of the Stuarts becomes the symbol and the sacrament of the contrast between right and might, between the favour of men and the justice of God, between the romance of the past and the sordid turmoil of the present, between the ideal of a state and the reality of politics. Perhaps it is not too much to say, that the doctrine yet survives as an influence through the peculiar melancholy interest, that is still felt to surround the ill-fated race, whatever be the light in which their rule is regarded.

Yet even as a practical force the doctrine was by no means dead for some time yet. In this connection, the nonjurors may perhaps be disregarded as a small body of idealists. But the insecurity of the new order, the constant intrigues with the court of S. Germains, the perpetual fears of Jacobite risings are a proof that the feeling in favour of the dispossessed dynasty as alone possessing a lawful title has by no means spent its force. The incidents of the Sacheverell case are alone evidence that the

Yet the theory had still some vitality.

nation had not as yet made up its mind on the question. Mr Lecky[1] is of opinion that the Revolution was brought about by a small minority of men far in advance of the general body of their countrymen. Had Bolingbroke been the victim of an idea, and proclaimed the Pretender, as Atterbury wished, there would in all probability have been a peaceful restoration of the Stuarts. On the other hand the failure of the rebellions of 1715 and 1745 shews how little of practical vitality there was about the Jacobite creed. Yet it may well be, that if a great leader had arisen, he might have brought about a successful reaction. Men may follow a statesman in carrying to a successful issue a cause, for which they will not move a finger in doubtful circumstances. Yet it is something that the belief in hereditary right should have been strong enough to cause the only High Church schism in the history of the English Church. At the Sacheverell trial Divine Right is clearly a popular sentiment. Even as late as 1747 a pamphleteer is found lamenting its continued prevalence.

It must not be forgotten, that the English clergy claimed the phraseology of the Bill of Rights in support of their contention that the Revolution did not transgress the principle of non-resistance. The strength of popular belief in the principle is attested by the very insertion of the word "abdicated" in that document. Again, the fiction of the supposititious birth of the Pretender is a proof of the influence the Whigs felt it necessary to counteract.

[1] *History of England*, i. 19.

Further, it was possible by skilful omission for the
clergy to continue to preach the duty of passive
obedience to the established government. Sacheverell is able to allege in his defence that the
Revolution was not a case of resistance[1], and that
those who brought it about have grossly lied, if they
claim that it was. Many, then, even of the loyal
clergy are still found maintaining the doctrine of
non-resistance. Of the nonjuring controversialists
Leslie and Hickes are the most interesting.

Berkeley's *Discourse of Passive Obedience* is *Berkeley,*
worthy of note as a specimen of the later method *1709.*
of argument. Nothing is said therein of hereditary
right, which cannot well be defended by a supporter
of the Act of Settlement. The argument is that
government is natural and necessary to the well-
being of mankind, that obedience is a natural law,
that to natural laws there is never any exception.
If once hard cases be admitted as a ground for
disregarding the rule, it will be as easy to prove the
convenience of murder in certain circumstances, as it
is to justify resistance to a tyrant. The transformation of method, which Filmer was found beginning
and Nalson carrying a little further, is thus completed
by Berkeley[2]. He deliberately drops the old mode of
argument, because, as he plaintively remarks, men

[1] Speech of Dr Sacheverell, 4: "My Lords, the Resistance in
that passage by me condemned is nowhere by me applied to the
Revolution, nor is it applicable to the case of the Revolution, the
Supreme Power not being then resisted": cf. also Leslie, *The Best
Answer* and *The Rehearsal, passim.*

[2] Berkeley's theory applies to the supreme power in all governments.

will no longer suffer it. He hopes, however, to
prove his case by employing the law of nature to
endow with immutable and inviolable authority the
principle of passive obedience.

At the close of this enquiry may be quoted
Bishop Butler[1], whose speculations on government
and subjection shew what was the residuum left by
the Doctrine of Divine Right. Human society and
government are in his view part of the constitution
and course of nature, and therefore divine. Obedience is also a part of the law of nature and has
therefore Divine sanction. He contends that government, as distinct from mere force, necessarily
implies reverence in subjects, and that reverence will
be liable to disappear, if it be not founded on the sentiment that authority is the ordinance of God. The
duty to obey the prince is however on the same
footing as all other general obligations, which are none
of them absolute or without exception. Butler is
clear that the possibility of exceptional cases arising
ought to be as little brought to mind as may be.
Rather there should be inculcated the duty of
Christian subjects to obey not only for wrath but for
conscience' sake. This view, similar to that held by
Hooker[2], is a fair specimen of the point of view of
the eighteenth-century divine. It is evident that
by this time all sense of the original purport of the

---

[1] Butler, *Sermons on Special Occasions*, III. and v.

[2] Hooker, *Supposed fragment of a sermon on civil obedience* and
Ecclesiastical Polity, Book VIII. *passim*, e.g. "God doth ratify the
works of that sovereign authority which kings have received by
men." Ch. II. § 7.

theory has been lost, and, since its work is done and facts render it impossible of support by any loyal subject, its edge has been taken off. Yet, whittled down to a few harmless truisms, it still remains to stimulate the sense that obedience to law has some sanction higher than mere personal convenience.

To sum up: out of the sentiment common to *Summary*. all Christians that subjection to lawful authority is in general a religious duty, since authority is part of the natural and Divine order, the Papacy developed a claim to complete supremacy, as the only Divinely ordained government. This claim was met by a counter-claim to Divine Right on behalf of the Imperial dignity. In the sixteenth century the doctrine is elaborated with greater rigidity,—the principle of absolute non-resistance is seen to be necessary to protect secular government from clerical interference. In combination with other causes, this theory gives birth to a theory of indefeasible hereditary right whose prevalence is largely due to the fact that both Henry IV. of France and James I. of England obtained their thrones by right of birth alone and without Papal sanction. In the seventeenth century the political side of the doctrine came out most strongly, and it is seen to be the form, in which alone could become popular the theory of sovereignty. It further accomplished a work in softening or preventing political changes. Its work done, it begins to become obsolete at the Revolution, and tends to pass into a mere sentiment. Meanwhile the older method of argument by means of a medley of Scripture texts has given place to the

contention that monarchy and obedience are a part
of the natural order and therefore divine. The basis
of the theory is no longer Biblical and theological,
but historical and utilitarian. Yet on this basis the
ground cannot be maintained; and the theory gives
way before the doctrine of natural rights of the people
propounded by Locke, which is only the Divine
Right of Kings in a disguised form. There is however far more weight allowed by Locke than by Filmer
to the principle of utility. This conception may be
expected to overshadow and then to supersede the
artificial fiction of the original compact and the
dream of natural inalienable rights. The doctrine of
Divine Right not only was transformed by imperceptible degrees into the theory of natural rights, but
it left behind it a legacy, in the sense that government in general is divine, because it is natural,
and that obedience to law is a religious duty.

CHAPTER VIII.

PASSIVE OBEDIENCE AND THE CHURCH OF ENGLAND.

THE doctrine of the Divine Right of Kings has now been considered in respect of the process of its development and decay. It remains to regard it *Divine* statically, so to say, to view it in relation to rival *Right to* theories of government. It must be remembered *be con-* first of all that the import of the phrase "Divine *relation to* Right of Kings" is mainly negative. It implies *theories.* that there is no foundation for the pretensions advanced by certain other authorities to supremacy by God's especial grant. The notion of Divine Right is in the air; all theories of government are theories of Divine Right, and most of them admit so much[1]. The Pope claims by Divine Right, so do the Presbyterians. Even the author of the *Vindiciae* contends, that since kings hold their crowns by God's grace, they may be judged by the people, as interpreters of the original Divine compact[2]. Again, the English writers on behalf of resistance most of them assert for law and custom a claim to absolute authority by

---

[1] On this point see Leslie's able paper, *The Rehearsal*, no. 58, *Divine Right in Government acknowledged by all.*

[2] *Vindiciae contra Tyrannos*, Quaestio I. *passim.*

Divine Right. The theory of natural rights is but
the theory of Divine Right under a changed guise,
a fact of which the writings of Rousseau form the
clearest evidence. Algernon Sidney contends that an
unjust law ought not to be obeyed, since it cannot
bind the conscience and lacks Divine authority[1]. This
view is one, which only admits law to be law "simply
and strictly so-called," when it is believed to be in
accordance with the Divine will. Sidney's notion, that
the sovereignty of the people is inalienable, as being a
grant from God, which neither human ordinance nor
the people's own consent may alienate, is every whit
as much a theory of Divine Right as the views of
All theories of seventeenth century are theories of Divine Right.
Mainwaring or Sacheverell. The doctrine under
investigation does not differ from contemporary
theories of politics in alone claiming Divine Right
for the supreme authority, but in claiming that the
king is the supreme authority. All the theories
alike are at variance with modern political philosophy, for they all assert or imply a claim to Divine
Right. In this respect, they differ from the thought
of to-day, but agree among themselves. If the
Divine Right of Kings be, as is so often asserted, the
stupidest of all theories of politics, it cannot be
because it seeks to find a Divine authority for
government. We have no right to condemn it
beyond other theories for a notion, which they all
hold in common. The point to consider is, how far
it was a specially stupid theory of politics, as compared with other views prevalent in the sixteenth
and seventeenth centuries.

[1] *Discourses on Government*, III. § 11.

It will be convenient to examine the theory first *Religious side of the theory will be here discussed.* of all in relation to those doctrines, which most directly controvert it and assert a Divine Right for some ecclesiastical authority. In this chapter the religious aspect of the theory will be the main element considered. Afterwards it will be examined on its political side, and its relations to other views of politics investigated.

From the foregoing investigation it must have *Its anti-papal origin.* appeared sufficiently that the theory arose out of the reaction against the Papal pretensions. It was the need of a controversial method to meet the claims of the spiritual power, which produced the doctrine of the Divine Right of Kings. This has been shewn to be the case in the Empire, in France, and in England. If further evidence be required, it is only necessary to take up at random any tract or pamphlet in behalf of royal rights written during the seventeenth century. In all probability the name of either the Pope or Bellarmine will be prominent on the first page. The royalist authors have the Pope on the brain. Whoever be their immediate antagonist, the Pope is always in the background, and it is against him that the long struggle is waged. Preachers on Jan. 30th assert that the martyrdom of Charles was really the work of the Jesuits, or they open their sermons with an elaborate proof not that resistance is a sin, but that Papal interference is against the laws and liberties of this realm of England[1]. Filmer was perhaps less

[1] In a sermon preached before the King on January 30, 168¾, Dr Turner's first thought is of the Pope and of the advantage to

antipapal in sentiment than most of the supporters
of the theory. Yet his *Patriarcha* opens with an
attack on Bellarmine. Hobbes was the one great
writer of the time, whose thought was not dominated by the notion of Divine Right. Yet Hobbes
devotes a whole book of *The Leviathan* to the
consideration of *The Kingdom of Darkness*, or the
Roman Church. Besides, the commonest term for a
Identifica- Dissenter is Jesuit. This is used with a definite
tion of intention and is not merely vague vituperation. The
Dissenters Jesuits are regarded as *par excellence* the teachers
with of the doctrine of resistance. All the special tenets
Jesuits. of the Society go for nothing beside this one striking
fact, that its members deliberately weaken the bonds
of allegiance and argue that under certain conditions
a nation may resist and even depose its sovereign.
Now the Dissenters teach the same doctrine, and
therefore they may without injustice be dubbed
Jesuits in disguise. It is not possible to read the
numerous pamphlets and sermons, in which this
view is set forth, without seeing that the royalist
writers were sincere and believed themselves to have
made an important discovery, as to the true nature
of Dissent. Rome would for its own ends permit
subjects to resist. Dissenters would for the good of
the Commonwealth permit the same. Therefore
Dissenters are in reality Romanists, and only play at
Protestantism. The dominant feeling is that the
supreme heresy of the Roman Church was the claim
put forth on behalf of the Papacy to a political

Rome of the execution of Charles. "Is the greatest misgovern-
ment sufficient pretence for any Pope or consistory on earth to
depose a Sovereign Power?" (23.)

supremacy over all kings and princes. The sense
of this dwarfs everything else, and all the other defects of the Roman system are viewed as nothing in
comparison with the cardinal iniquity of the Papal
sovereignty. Every sect, which in any way approaches
to the claim of Rome to limit the "true law of free
monarchies," is thus regarded as consciously or unconsciously Roman in its tenets. It is impossible
to deny that intense hatred of the Pope and the
Jesuits, as his chief supporters, was the animating
motive of the upholders of the Divine Right of
Kings. Yet the hatred, be it observed, is rather
political than religious. Comparatively little is said *Jesuits are attacked*
of the erroneous doctrines or corrupt practices of the *on politi-*
Roman communion. Here is not the place for such *cal rather than*
discussion. What is attacked is the Papacy as a *religious*
political authority, claiming universal Empire, and *grounds.*
dissolving the bonds of national allegiance. A burning
and fanatic hatred of the Society of Jesus is another
note of all these writings. Yet here again it is not
as the servants of a system destructive of morality
or inimical to truth, that the Jesuits have won for
themselves their monumental meed of execration.
This is not the ground of their evil name. That
comes of their ardent support of the Papal claims.
It is not as believers in Roman Catholic doctrine[1],
but as Papalists, that they are attacked. The

---

[1] For Bellarmine's theory of the indirect political supremacy
of the Pope see *De Romano Pontifice,* L. v. especially cc. 4, 6;
also his contemptuous brushing aside as irrelevant of Barclay's
refutation of the theory of the canonists in *De Excusatione Bar-
claii,* cc. 1, 2.

Jesuits, above all others, have devoted their energies
to an elaborate defence of the Pope's position.
Whether, as the canonists claim, his political power
be direct, or, as Bellarmine argues, it be merely
indirect, certain it is that far the weightiest arguments in his favour are those of Jesuit writers[1].
Others, who think themselves loyal enough to the
Pope, may reason and refine away his political power,
and argue in favour of the oath of allegiance. But
of all this the Jesuits will have nothing. They
assert on behalf of the Pope pretensions, which would
have shamed neither Boniface VIII. nor John XXII.,
and they met their reward. This is the head and
front of their offending; and it is for this cause
that they have won for themselves a name among
Englishmen, which those who hate them most nowadays would least of all be able to interpret. It may
well be that the shouts of applause, with which a
present day audience at Exeter Hall would greet
an attack on the iniquities of Ignatius Loyola, are a
tribute unconsciously but none the less really paid
to the Divine Right of Kings. And, when the
members of the Protestant Alliance or the Church
Association devote a field-day to the exposition of
the evils and dishonesty of Jesuitry, they are,
though they think it not, uniting with Andrews

---

[1] Besides Bellarmine, there stand out more particularly
Mariana, who approves of tyrannicide in general and of the
murder of Henry III. of France (*Del Rey y de Institution Real*, I.
6) and decides against the power of the prince to legislate in
matters of religion (*Ibid.* 10); and Suarez, *De Legibus*, L. III., *De
Lege Positiva*, cc. 7, 34, and L. IV. *De Lege Canonica*, especially
cc. 9, 19.

and Bramhall, with Taylor and Jackson in repelling an assault which is dangerous to the State rather than to the Church, and are exhibiting a relic of that patriotic indignation, which, in days when the political claims of Rome were real and formidable, had a meaning and a value. Anyhow in the seventeenth century there is little evidence that the Jesuits are attacked, because their system is disliked or their teaching believed to be immoral. The polemic against the conquering Society is not the lofty indignation of a Pascal, denouncing a casuistry which is debasing the moral standard and destroying all principles of right action. The spirit of the English royalists is as far inferior to that which breathes through every page of the *Provinciales*, as is the form in which it is embodied. But if the irony of the believer in Divine Right be lacking in the polish of the "letters," his declamation at least surpasses them in the blind force of passion. The English hatred of the Jesuits is the narrow but fervent enthusiasm of patriots disgusted at claims, which fetter the free action of the nation, and enraged with those, who presume to justify such claims with the pen or to put them into practice with the sword. The Jesuits are villains—that the royalists believe. But the cause is not that they believe or teach false dogmas in theology, not that they are paving the way for moral scepticism, nor that they (in general) urge and permit immoral actions, but merely that they are traitors guilty of high treason against the sovereignty of nations, seeking to wrest the diadem from the imperial crown of England, that they may place it on the brows of a priest : *Le clericalisme c'est l'ennemi* is the governing thought of those who cry for *Jus Divinum* and Non-resistance.

Teaching of resist- ance regarded as main element in Popery and Dissent.

As was said, it is this sense, that the essence of Popery is a claim to political supremacy that is the cause of the numerous accusations for holding Jesuit or Papist views, that are levelled against the Dissenters. Filmer tells us that "the main and indeed the only point of Popery is the alienating and withdrawing of subjects from their obedience to their Prince[1]." It is not, then, surprising that Hickes is of opinion that "Popery having apparently corrupted the Gospel in the doctrines of obedience, and submission, and the divine authority of the supreme power, especially of Kings; they cannot be sound and orthodox Protestants, who hold the very same destructive principles to regal government, by which the Papists have corrupted the Gospel in these points. No they are not sound, and orthodox Protestants, but Protestants popularly affected, Papists under a Protestant dress, wolves in sheeps' clothing, rebellious and Satanical spirits transformed into angels of light[2]." Of this well-known passage quotations similar in spirit might be multiplied a thousand-fold[3]. The

---

[1] Preface to *The Anarchy of a Mixed Monarchy.*

[2] Hickes, *Sermon on Jan.* 30, 168½. Another sermon describes Jesuits as *Rome's Fifth Monarchy Men*; Mr Gardiner's account of the Fifth Monarchy is a proof of the appositeness of this description (*History of the Commonwealth and Protectorate*, I. 32).

[3] We have one pamphlet directed against *The Six Popish Pillars, Anabaptists, Quakers, Presbyterians*, etc. (1690). Jewell writes, "Why hath he [the Pope] and his complices (like Anabaptists and Libertines, to the end they might run on the more licentiously

reiterated charge that Dissenters are all Jesuits at heart is only to be explained upon this view of what was really the mind of the Anglican divines. The term is not employed merely as an opprobrious epithet. It is the expression of a deep sense, that since the real object of Jesuitism is to loose the bonds of civil allegiance, all who hold doctrines of resistance are believers in the only essential and distinctive doctrines of Loyola and Rome[1]. The

and carelessly), shaken off the yokes, and exempted themselves from being under all civil power?" (*Apology*, 75). In *The Apostate Parliament* occurs the query, "Setting aside the Romish faith and the vow of blind obedience, tell me wherein these men differ from the disciples of Ignatius Loyola? Why only these are Popish and they Protestant Jesuits?" See Appendix C.

[1] The taunt levelled at all who taught that resistance was justifiable, that they were at heart Jesuits, has this much of justice in it; that the Jesuits in arguing for the Papal claims had evolved most of the doctrines which were dear to the Whig controversialist. It may be doubted whether Suarez and even Mariana are not even as political thinkers vastly superior in lucidity and grasp to Locke and Sidney. We have a complete description of the state of nature in Mariana, "En un principio los hombres como las fieras andaban errantes por el mundo; ni tenian hogar fijo, ni pensaban mas que en conservar la vida y obedecer al agradable instinto de procrear y de educar la prole. Ni habia leyes que les obligasen ni jeles que les mandasen etc." (*Del Rey*, I. 1). Suarez emphatically asserts that all men are born free and equal (*De Legibus*, III. 1, 2). He anticipates Rousseau in teaching the sovereignty of the people (*Ibid.*), and Mariana is equally of opinion the power of the community is inalienable and superior to the king (*Del Rey*, I. 8). His classing the incapacity of the crown to alter the succession with other limitations on sovereignty is noteworthy; for that it is a limitation is not perceived by the believers in Indefeasible Hereditary Right. "No puede el principe oponerse á la voluntad de la multitud, ni cuando se trata de imponer tributos, ni quando se trata de derogar leyes,

purely theological points on which Dissenters differ
even more widely than Anglicans from the Roman
Church may be ignored as mere details, which do
not concern the main position.

Some
Noncon-
formists
agree with
Rome
only in
allowing
resistance.

But here a distinction must be made. The theory
of most English Nonconformists and of the average
Whig politician, is open to the taunts of the royalist
on the score of its likeness to the Jesuit doctrine
of resistance. If resistance in any form for any cause
be damnable, and if it be Popery to teach it, then
Whigs like Locke and Sidney, and Parliamentarians
like Prynne may be accused of Popery. It is true
that religion is one of the main grounds for resistance in practice, but at least neither Whigs
nor Independents believe that the State is to be
controlled in the interests of a religious body. They
would not fetter its action, as the Papalist would do.

ni mucho menos cuando se trata de alterar la sucesion del reino."
Neither Mariana nor Suarez appears to be so wedded to the notion
of a "mixed monarchy" as Whig theorists; they escape the
fallacies of the Whig theorists by their clear conception, that on
a theory of popular rights the sovereign power must be placed
in the community; the king is obliged by the laws, because they
emanate from the nation rather than himself (*Del Rey*, I. 9).
Even their notion of Papal supremacy does not lead them into
any such absurd attacks on the idea of sovereignty, as those
of Locke and most Whig theorists. Similarly, Bellarmine asserts
the origin of the state in the general will (*De Verbo Dei*, III. 9);
"[Potestas Ecclesiae] non enim est similis civili potestati, quae est
in populo nisi a populo transferatur in principem " (*De Rom. Pont.*
I. 6; cf. also *De Translatione Imperii*, I. 3). He is strongly imbued
with the advantages of 'mixed monarchy ' (*De Rom. Pont.* 3); he
will not allow that unjust laws are laws properly so called (*Ibid.*
IV. 15). Bellarmine is nearer to the common Whig theory, and a
less acute and logical thinker than Suarez or Mariana.

Indeed as the notion of toleration begins to develope, any general theory of clerical supremacy becomes an impossibility. That men view the mere teaching of resistance as evidence of Popery is indicative of a state of feeling, difficult for us to bring into imagination, when non-resistance is regarded as the most essential element of religion.

But in regard to one ecclesiastical system other than the Roman, the taunt of Jesuitism is more truly justified. Presbyterianism, as exhibited in Geneva or Scotland veritably claims, as did the Papacy, to control the State in the interests of an ecclesiastical corporation. The cardinal error of the royalist writers, when viewed from the modern standpoint, is that in formulating the theory of the Divine Right of Kings against that of the Pope, they were driven into the position of supporters of despotism and oppression. However much this is to be condemned, it was probably inevitable. Certainly it may seem to us a strange thing that in defending the secular power against the spiritual, men should ignore or minimise the dangers of the secular power itself becoming a tyranny. But it is not strange, that those who were inspired by a passionate indignation at the preposterous assumptions of the Papacy, should have been no less hostile to the political side of the Presbyterian system. "New presbyter is but old priest writ large" is a maxim of deeper import than is sometimes imagined. It is the felicitous expression of men's sense of the danger still to be apprehended from clericalism. The same mischievous claims to place secular

Presbyterian advances claim similar to those of Rome.

A theory of clericalism in politics.

governments under the heel of an ecclesiastical
organization, as had led to so much conflict in
the Middle Ages and were only finally overthrown
by the Reformation, had reappeared in a yet more
irritating form in the Presbyterian system. The condition of Geneva under Calvin was an object-lesson,
which neither statesmen nor patriotic churchmen
were likely to ignore. Affairs in Scotland would
form a sufficient warning, if any should be tempted
to fall out of the frying-pan into the fire, and after
throwing off one ecclesiastical tyranny to rivet upon
their necks another, which would differ from it
mainly in being narrower, more searching, more
inquisitorial, more ubiquitous, and less careful
of the larger needs and hopes of humanity, less
likely to force upon states and their rulers the sense
that sectional and local interests are not the only
rule of right. The Papacy, whatever might be said
against it, was at least a standing witness to the
need of international morality, and might be supposed to have the advantage of viewing political
problems from a universal standpoint. Despite the
evils and mischief attendant on the political claims
of the Popes, it might be contended with some
plausibility that these claims were the only security the mediæval world possessed for something
like justice and fair-dealing between kings and
princes. The fear of Papal excommunication undoubtedly tended to confine aggression within limits
and to make rulers temper expediency with right
reason. No such defence could be made for the
Presbyterian system. It would have controlled the

action of the State more completely than did the
Papacy, while it would have strengthened instead
of diminishing all the tendencies that made for a
narrow patriotism, and that would lead men to regard
local and provincial feeling as all important. The position of the Papacy could not fail to lift it in a great
degree above the limitations, that must surround
and sometimes fetter the thought and action of the
national statesman. But there was no such cause at
work in the Presbyterian system, and its rulers would
so far as politics were concerned, have exhibited
most of the defects without any of the merits of
clericalism. Unless it be contended, that their
possession of a purer system of theology, would
ensure the wisdom of their political action, it can
hardly be doubted that the Presbyterian system,
if allowed to run its course, would have made
greater havoc of politics, than did the Papacy. It
would have subordinated all state action to considerations at once narrowly local and rigidly ecclesiastical.
Thus it is not surprising that the ablest defenders
of the doctrine of Divine Right are at pains to
shew not merely that the Papal claims would dissolve
the bonds of civil society, but that they go on,
as does Nalson, to prove that the "Presbyterian
Discipline" is equally destructive not merely of
royal power, but of Parliamentary authority and the
liberty of the subject[1]. The two systems of Papal

[1] "There may be many particular interests which may be
disadvantageous to the safety, security and happiness of the
Imperial Crown of this Realm of Great Britain, and its other
dominions, as well as to the liberty and property of the People;
but there are two which are directly and fundamentally opposite
and contrary to them, both in their principles and practices, and

supremacy and Presbyterian "discipline" are both clerical in essence. They both assert a claim by Divine Right for God's minister, whether he be the Pope or the office-bearers in the Presbyterian body; this claim is to be superior to all civil government whatever. Bishop Bramhall's tract *A warning to the Church of England* is an able exposition of this view. In this is shewn the political danger of Presbyterianism, as an ecclesiastical system claiming dominion by Divine Right over the secular power. The latter part of Nalson's *Common Interest of King and People* is a singularly lucid and well-balanced statement of the same position.

Illustra-tions of Presby-terian theory. Cart-wright.

Nor do these writers attribute to the Presbyterians any pretensions which they do not make for themselves. Cartwright's works are almost as full as those of Bellarmine of the claim to control the State in the interests of the Church; in many respects they form an exact parallel to Papalist pretensions. The magistrate is the Lord's officer, and must wield the sword as the Church directs, persecute all "idolatry" at its bidding, and grant no pardon upon the recantation of a heretic. He is to be guided by the example of Constantine the Great, who persecuted in favour of orthodoxy[1]. The

these are the pretensions of a universal supremacy and spirituo-temporal monarchy of the Church of Rome or Papacy on the one hand, and the Democratic Presbyterian on the other. That both these are utterly inconsistent with the safety and very essence of monarchy and particularly with that of these nations, as also with the peace, happiness, liberty and property of the subjects is that which I hope to prove " (Nalson, *The Common Interest of King and People*, 178).

[1] Cartwright, *Second Reply*, cxv. sqq.

'discipline' is universal and immutable[1] and is to be maintained by the magistrate[2]; the civil magistrate is to provide some sharp punishment for all who contemn the censure of the Church[3]. In fact the State is to wield the temporal sword, and the Church to dictate how it shall be wielded. The civil magistrates as they are the nurses, so they are the servants of the Church and must throw down their crowns before it[4]. Since the Church is prior to the State, the constitution of the latter must be fashioned and made suitable unto the Church[5]. Church government is to be the model of the civil State. Cartwright knows that the 'discipline' is regarded in the light of a new popedom and tyranny in the Church; but so to term it is blasphemy[6]. The author's views are as definitely theocratic, as those of the mediæval Papacy. He is not merely using phrases to emphasize the spiritual subjection of the Prince as a layman, to the officers of the Church; but he teaches that the prince is merely the minister and executant of the Church's decrees. Finally, his object being to move the people to obedience, he shews no sort of inclination to popular government or liberty as such. The only liberty he desires is the liberty of the office-bearers of the Church to control the action of the State and to use its forces at their will. The duty of private individuals is merely that of obedience[7].

Still stronger are the views of Christopher Goodman.

[1] *Declaration of Discipline*, 13.   [2] *Ibid.* 187.

[3] *Second Admonition to Parliament*, 49.

[4] *Reply to Whitgift*, 144.   [5] *Ibid.*

[6] *Demonstration of Discipline*, 75.

[7] *Declaration of Discipline*, 185. The passage is quoted below, p. 220.

Goodman. His book *How to obey or disobey* was
written in 1558 against the tyranny of the 'idol-
atress' Mary, and the monstrous regiment of women,
although there is flattery of Elizabeth, "that godly
lady and meek lamb void of all Spanish pride and
stranger blood." Goodman will have nothing of passive obedience[1]; idolatry must be resisted by force[2].
Like the papalists, Goodman conceives of God as
the true recipient of civil obedience, and of all earthly
governments as subordinate to His rule, and liable to
be overturned at any moment if they transgress it[3].
Of the nature of God's ordinances and of the question
as to whether or no they have been transgressed, he
would apparently make the rulers of the Church the
sole and irresponsible arbiters. For princes are not
to suffer their subjects to be ignorant of God's law,
but to enforce theological doctrine universally[4]. On
this condition obedience is to be paid to the magistrate and no tyranny will absolve from the duty[5].
As in the view of Cartwright, or Bellarmine, the
subject's duty is mere obedience, but obedience to
an ecclesiastical corporation; only secondarily and
under qualifications, will obedience to the civil
magistrate become a duty. The State exists solely
on sufferance; and the officers of the Church may
meddle with its policy and upset its organization at
their pleasure. For no heretic is truly a king; not
the clearest legal right, neither election nor succession can give any title to a claimant unless in the
opinion of this self-constituted authority, he 'be a

---

[1] *How to obey*, 30, 64. [2] *Ibid.* 77.
[3] *Ibid.* 44 sqq., 60, 110, 118, 139.
[4] *Ibid.* 105. [5] *Ibid.* 110.

promoter and setter forth of God's glory[1].' The
contention that neither prince nor people are free
but both are subject to God's law might indeed be
used to-day in an innocent sense; but, as in the
case of all teachers of the political supremacy of
ecclesiasticism, in Goodman's mouth the words imply
a claim on the part of an irresponsible person or
body of persons, not experts in politics, to control
the action of the State, in whatever direction they
please. The king is to persecute and the people
to rebel at the bidding of the Kirk[2]. There is no
appeal from their decision as to the character of the
policy that will promote God's glory or will hinder
it. How far these claims would have been carried
if men such as Goodman had been given a free hand
may be gathered from some hints, which he lets
drop. One of the reasons for resisting Mary is her
foreign policy; since it is plainly forbidden them by
God's word to make war in alliance with Spain
against France and 'their own brethren the Scots,'
all Englishmen are bidden to throw off the yoke[3].
Nor does Goodman stop here, but devotes many
pages to a glorification of Sir Thomas Wyatt, and
the praise of his rebellion[4].

Here, then, in the writings of Cartwright and
Goodman we have clear proof that the political

---

[1] *How to obey*, 51, 58. Goodman's contention is that an
idolatrous and persecuting king is to be regarded as a mere private
man, to whom no obedience is due (139). This is on a par with
Bellarmine's view that the Pope does not command subjects to
disobey their sovereigns, for the Papal deposition *ipso facto*
destroys the kingly character.

[2] *Ibid.* Chap. xi.   [3] *Ibid.* 178.   [4] 204 sqq.

claims of Presbyterianism were as oppressive, as tyrannical and as preposterous as those of Rome. The two systems Papal and Presbyterian are alike in that they both regard the State as the mere handmaid of an ecclesiastical corporation, and would, in the last resort, place the supreme direction of politics in the hands of the rulers of the Church. They only differ in the character of the theological systems, in the interests of which the policy of the secular government is to be regulated. The history of Scotland affords further evidence of the claims made and exercised under this system. And those who had most to do with the establishment of the Presbyterian Kirk in Scotland are most emphatic in their announcement of their pretensions to subject *Knox.* the policy of the State to their own caprice. John Knox declares that no idolater (by which is meant a person whose theological views differ from his own) ought to be promoted to any public office; that no oath can bind men to obey such an one; and that any prince, who after appointment, becomes an idolater may be justly opposed[1]. In the First Book *First Book* of Discipline it is declared that rulers and ruled must *of Dis-* all alike be subject to discipline[2], and that idolatry *cipline.* and all monuments thereof must be suppressed[3]; that punishment (death for choice) should be appointed for all such as disobeyed the superintendents, and for profaners of the Sacraments[4]. Now when these are

---

[1] *Summary of the proposed Second Blast of the Trumpet. Works,* iv. 539.

[2] vii. 3.   The First Book of Discipline is to be found in the *Works of John Knox,* ii. 183 sqq.

[3] *Ibid.* iii.   [4] *Ibid.* p. 253.

regarded as directions from the Kirk to the State in order to guide its legislation, it will readily be seen how great is the power claimed. In subjecting all rulers to ' discipline,' a civil supremacy is in reality claimed for the Kirk; for excommunication carried with it civil disabilities; it was immediately followed by " letters of horning."

The Second Book of Discipline claims for the *Second* spiritual power an indirect temporal supremacy, *Book of Discipline,* very similar to that claimed by Bellarmine for the 1581. Pope. The method of argument is not very different in the two cases. The magistrate commands external things for external peace and quietness among his subjects ; the minister handles external things only for conscience' sake[1]. The magistrate is to command the minister to observe the rule commanded in the world, and *to punish the transgressors by civil means.* The ministers exercise not the civil jurisdiction, but teach the magistrate how it should be exercised according to the word[2]. Ecclesiastical power is distinguished from civil by the fact that it flows immediately from God[3].

All this may seem little more than a declaration of the freedom of the Kirk, and of the divergent spheres of Church and State. It might be so in an age when all religious opinions are tolerated. But at a time when persecution was recognised as a duty, it amounts to a claim on behalf of the Kirk for complete supremacy. The civil magistrate is bound to suppress all teaching not recognised by the Kirk,

---

[1] *Second Book of Discipline,* x. 11. Calderwood (III. 529 sqq.).
[2] *Ibid.* 14.   [3] *Ibid.* 5.

to enforce its commands, to see to the execution of its views as to the administration of God's Word and Sacraments—all this, according to the theory of Knox and his successors, on pain of deposition. The Kirk is to be the nation in its spiritual capacity, yet over this vast body the State is to have no authority, but is merely in the position of an executive appointed to execute the will of the office-bearers. If the Prince will not obey the officers of the Kirk, and employ all the machinery of government to execute their decrees, he is to be deposed.

We are told that the magistrate is to assist and maintain and justify the jurisdiction of the Kirk. There is no qualification. The ministers, on the other hand, are to assist the Prince in all things agreeable to God's word[1]. Thus to the ministers is left the final interpretation of the limits of obedience, and the magistrate becomes the mere tenant-at-will of the Kirk.

Further, in the Second Book of Discipline the magistrate is bidden to fortify the godly proceedings of the Kirk; to see that its public estate and ministers be maintained[2], and so to secure the Church against false teachers and hirelings, dumb dogs and idle bellies[3]; to punish civilly those that will not obey the censure of the Kirk, " without confounding always the one jurisdiction with the other[4]," i.e. maintaining his allotted position of subserviency. He is to make laws *for the advancement of the Kirk* without usurping anything that pertains not to the civil sword[5].

These constitutions in fact invest the Kirk with

[1] *Second Book of Discipline,* I. 15.   [2] *Ibid.* x. 2.
[3] *Ibid.* 3.   [4] *Ibid.* 4.   [5] *Ibid.* 7.

the absolute freedom and right of establishing its constitution and discipline in matters small and great and then of employing the secular arm to enforce them on a reluctant nation. For where the ministry of the Kirk is once lawfully constituted, all godly princes ought to obey the voice and reverence the majesty of the Son of God[1]. The Book proceeds to quote from the statute declaring that no other ecclesiastical jurisdiction should be acknowledged, but that which is and shall be in the Reformed Kirk and flowing therefrom[2].

It is this that constitutes the real objection from the statesman's point of view to the Presbyterian system, and the justification of the theory of the Divine Right of Kings and of much that seems arbitrary in the treatment of religious bodies by the State. The acts of Henry VIII. and Elizabeth may appear harsh, and the *submissio cleri* may be regarded as depriving the Church of its due rights. Yet no less could have been claimed at the time by any self-respecting monarch. For at that time toleration was not recognised as a principle, and it was a maxim that the nation in its spiritual capacity forms one corporation, subject to one ecclesiastical jurisdiction and one

The belief in persecution is the real cause of the conflict between Church and State.

[1] A power in the Prince of reforming the Church when corrupted is indeed admitted (*Ibid.* 7), but this is merely a saving clause by which a Revolution in favour of Presbyterianism may be admitted. Knox in attacking the Roman Church where established asserts emphatically the claims of the civil magistrate (*Letter to the Queen Regent, Works,* IV. 443). Like the Pope, he will admit the power of the civil magistrate, on condition of its being exercised in subserviency to himself.

[2] *Second Book of Discipline,* XI. 16.

system of discipline. Under such conditions it can
never be other than dangerous for the State to give
the spiritual power a free hand. For it will fetter
the action of the State in a thousand ways and will
be repeatedly claiming to "handle external things
for conscience' sake." It may, as in Scotland, set
up an inquisitorial jurisdiction in every village, and
demand the assistance of the State in punishing
any and every breach of what it regards as the
moral law, from adultery to Sabbath-breaking. It
may claim, as in Scotland, that the royal pardon
shall never issue for capital crimes; it may demand,
as in 1582, that no alliances shall be made with
Roman Catholic powers[1]. The Papacy in the middle
ages claimed to regulate international differences,
and was constantly encroaching upon the sphere of
the State. But hardly at the period of its proudest
exaltation did it claim to make the civil power so
completely its slave or to interfere so minutely with
the private life of individuals, as did the maintainers
of "the discipline." However, opinions may differ
as to which of the two systems was the more
meddlesome and irritating tyranny. But there can
be no doubt that, with whatever differences in
degree, both are alike in kind. Each puts forward
a claim by Divine Right to subject the secular
power to the spiritual, to make the clergy the
ultimate arbiters of political action.

[1] Calderwood, III. 685. The General Assembly demanded that
"no society, league or friendship be made with Papists in France,
Italy, Spain, or other countries, by common or particular outset."
The whole tenor of the articles presented at this time to the King is
expressive of the determination of the Kirk to unfettered supremacy.

And the claim cannot be admitted. The English *The claim*
nation had ever been jealous of clericalism. It had *of clerica-*
lism inad-
refused to surrender the right and liberty of the *missible.*
English crown to the Popes, and had upheld its
independence in matters of politics, unawed by the
majestic traditions and splendid imperiousness of
the mediæval Papacy—this at a time, when the
spiritual authority of the Pope was unquestioned.
England had in the past no quarrel with the
religious pretensions of the Papacy; but she was no
more inclined, than the French King or the Emperor,
to admit its political claims. It was not likely that
she would allow a similar claim, presented in the
unlovely form of the Presbyterian discipline.

Against either claim the same controversial *The state*
can only
method was necessary. It was needful to claim on *meet its*
behalf of the secular power complete supremacy and *opponents*
by claim-
the institution of God. Not until the danger was *ing entire*
passed of a relapse into Popery or Presbyterianism, *supre-*
macy.
can the notion of Divine Right be said to have
accomplished its work. The case of France is
precisely similar. On the one hand the Papacy
claimed to excommunicate and depose the King,
and to keep the rightful heir out of his inheritance.
On the other hand the Huguenots made themselves
the mouthpiece of a recrudescent feudalism, and
strove for an *imperium in imperio* with quasi-
sovereign rights in their strong places. In the
result both in France and England, the central
power succeeded in establishing its supremacy, even
to the point of persecuting the teachers of all
doctrines which it regarded as harmful.

The spiritual power never has the material sword at its disposal.

The passages cited as evidence of the Presbyterian theory may seem patient of a different interpretation. They may be defended as mere humble advice to the State from persons acting with purely spiritual weapons and claiming no coercive authority. John Knox himself could not wield the sword, but was only able to advise subjects in certain circumstances to depose their prince. The Kirk neither possesses nor claims the use of the material sword. It merely demands that it shall be used in its interests. Precisely. Yet the position of the Papacy in regard to European nations was at no time different. Save in the Papal states, the Pope had no direct material power. The army under the immediate command of the Pope or his delegates would scarcely have been sufficient to crush the smallest of recalcitrant sects, and could have made no head against a hostile nation. When the mediæval Papacy is called a tyranny, it is too often forgotten that however mischievous its effects on political action, it was emphatically an instance of government by consent. Whether or no the Popes from Gregory VII. to Boniface VIII. wielded an authority that was both despotic in its nature and oppressive in its incidence, it is certain that their despotism did not rest upon physical force, but upon purely spiritual or moral sanctions. The Papacy never as a matter of practice wielded or claimed to wield the material sword. It merely demanded that physical force should never be employed, save with its approval. Presbyterianism made precisely the same demand. All that the Pope can do by a Bull of Excommunication is to declare, as God's vicar, that men *The spiritual power* are no longer bound in theory and for conscience' sake to obey their sovereign. They may not im- *can only grant or withhold* probably be bound to obey him in practice and by the strength of the material sword. The English *the moral sanctions* Catholics, or those of them who favoured the *of government.* deposing power, were so bound; they were "subject for wrath." But, admitting the Pope's claims, no one will be bound for conscience' sake, so soon as he has launched a bull of excommunication. The *And so with* object, therefore, of the opponents of either system *Presbyterianism.* must be to assert, that, despite the Papal or Presbyterian attempt to exercise the deposing power, *Hence supporters* the sanctions of conscience still remain, and that *of the State must* the moral claim of the State to the allegiance of its *claim that* subjects may not be impaired by ecclesiastical *the moral sanction* censure. Throughout the Middle Ages, in the Wars *is on their side.* of the League, in the plots against Elizabeth, it has been repeatedly proved that the character of men's civil obedience will be affected by other motives than the material sword or the legal sanction of government, "wrath." The success, however partial, of the Popes or of the Presbyterian leaders has proved that the moral sanction, conscience, is a real power in strengthening or loosening the bonds of allegiance. This sanction the supporters of clericalism claim to manipulate at their pleasure. The defenders of the freedom of the State are therefore perpetually driven to assert, that it is not lost or gained according to the theological opinions of the ruler, that the State has a Divine Right to exist despite the disapproval of the Church, that obedience

to the secular power is due not merely for "wrath
but for conscience' sake." Obedience not merely for
wrath but for conscience' sake has been asserted to be
the right of the Church alone. The moral claim
to obedience, as distinct from the physical power of
enforcing it, does not in itself belong to the State,
say the supporters of clericalism, save in so far as
the State is the necessary instrument of the Church.
The theory of the Divine Right of Kings is the
contradiction of this; it asserts that the State has a
claim to obedience on moral and religious grounds,
that it has a right to exist as in accordance with
human nature and God's will, and is based on something better than the right of the stronger. Clericalism makes capital out of its position as the guide
of men's consciences and would subject states and
politics to a meddlesome control. Hence, if political
security is to be obtained, conscience must be asserted to be on the side of civil obedience, and
universal supremacy by God's grant asserted for the
State. Otherwise ecclesiastics will at once step in
and claim to decide the cases in which resistance
may be lawful.

*The State
asserts its
authority
in matters
of reli-
gion.*
Yet in doing this the State makes large claims.
It first asserts its absolute competence to prescribe
forms of religious belief or at least of practice, and
to set up or abolish forms of ecclesiastical organization. It is only when the State consents to be
guided in this matter by experts, i.e. the Church,
that any religious body will allow such a claim in its
fulness. Yet the omni-competence of the State must
be asserted, and asserted as of Divine Right. It

will doubtless be supported in the main only by those who feel morally convinced that the State will not as a matter of fact prohibit their own religious belief.

This is the explanation of the language, that at *Erastian language of certain supporters of Divine Right.* times may seem unduly Erastian, of certain Caroline divines. They exalt the supremacy of the Crown; they declare its competence to prescribe forms of faith; and claim Divine Right for these powers. By this is merely meant a claim of the secular power to be free in theory; there is not intended or implied any claim that the State in practice shall decide religious matters arbitrarily or without consulting the heads of the Church. Doubtless much of Barrow's *Treatise of the Pope's Supremacy* or Jackson's *Treatise of Christian Obedience* will appear Erastian to a modern English Churchman. Yet in reality nothing more is being claimed than the legal omnipotence of the sovereign power. An exponent of the same truth at the present day might well take as an illustration of the theoretical powers of Parliament the undoubted fact that at any moment it might legally abolish the Christian religion and introduce Mohammedanism under the sanction of torture. Yet such a writer would not be held to mean that Parliament could effect this change, or that it would dream of attempting it. Such an act would overpass what have been called the external and the internal limits of sovereignty[1]. Similarly in the seventeenth century, against the clericalism of Rome or of Geneva the omni-competence of the State was asserted. Against the claim of Pope or Presbyter

[1] Dicey, *Law of the Constitution*, 72—78.

to obedience by Divine Right the Divine Right of
Kings must be elaborated. Against the claims to
dissolve the bonds of sentiment or conscience between governors and governed, conscience must be
claimed for the secular government by the theory
of non-resistance, and difficult cases solved by the
doctrine of Passive Obedience.

It may seem strange that men such as Laud,
with high views of the position of the Church and
the power of the priesthood, should have asserted
so strongly a theory, which, as frequently expounded,
involves the assertion of the authority of the Crown
over the forms of Church government and doctrine.
But it must be borne in mind that Laud, like Parker
and Whitgift, was well aware that the political supremacy of the State over the Church was too well-
established a principle to disappear. It could only
change hands. He knew that if this supremacy were
not retained by Charles it would pass over to the Parliament and would be wrested into the protection and
establishment of Puritanism. Laud was not ignorant
that the Church of England "as by law established"
had its strongest supporter in Charles. Although the
Roman controversy was not over he must have felt
that the danger to England from that side was daily
diminishing. The supremacy of the Crown might be
extolled to any extent by a Caroline divine. For it
was known that, as a matter of fact, so long as it
remained in the hands of the King, it would be
used to promote the welfare of the Church. It was
not needful to demand passionately that the King
should maintain the true religion and prohibit false

teaching. Nor was it necessary to fetter the royal
prerogative in order that the Church might be free.
Knox was compelled to both these courses. But in
England the King might be trusted to maintain the
status quo and to guard against the aggressions of
Puritanism. In England the royal authority was
favourable, in Scotland it was hostile to the dominant
religious system. If James VI. ever felt free to
throw off the yoke of the Kirk there can be little
doubt that he would do so; indeed he made various
attempts to strengthen his authority over it[1]. A
shrewd suspicion of this disposition must tend to
drive the leaders of Presbyterianism into hostility to
any doctrine of the nature of the royal supremacy,
even irrespective of their previous theory. James
would be dangerous to the Kirk. His freedom to
touch it must therefore be denied. On the other
hand the greater the freedom of Charles I. the
better would it be for the Church of England, or at
least for the particular view of its character and
ritual taken by Laud. From the time of the
Elizabethan settlement onward the royal supremacy
was the bulwark of the Church of England against
Puritan innovations.

Thus the taunt is not justified, that the theory *Unprin-*
of the Divine Right of Kings was merely the fiction *cipled*
servility
of a time-serving hierarchy, intent upon gaining *cannot*
fairly be
court favour, whatever might happen to the Church. *attributed*
For the belief in this theory was the most trust- *to the*
Anglican
worthy security for the permanence and stability of *clergy.*
that order of things which the clergy had learnt to

[1] Gardiner's *History of England, passim.*

love. They were not serving their King instead of their God; the best defence of the Church was the support of the Crown. Nor is it a cause for blame to the clergy that the theory of Divine Right found in them its strongest and most numerous body of supporters. The theory is, as has been shewn, essentially anti-clerical. Yet for this reason it was necessary, if it were to be effective, that the doctrine should be in the main formulated by a body of clergy. The claims of a system of clericalism, such as the Papal or Presbyterian, might indeed be denied by laymen; but they could not be effectively refuted save by clergy. The element of truth in the Papal claim made it essential that it should be met by clergy rather than laymen. For Bellarmine and Knox were right in asserting that only the spiritual power can give the authoritative decision as to whether men were bound in conscience to obey their rulers. The question as one of conscience must be decided by the spiritual authority. It was not in claiming for a religious body the decision of the moral and religious question, whether or no obedience is due to the State on religious and moral grounds, that the Jesuits erred. Where they were mistaken was in asserting that the secular power as such had no moral claim to obedience apart from the theological accuracy of the opinions which it enforced. The assertion that obedience is a religious duty in all states, irrespective of the opinions of the ruler, was not merely the sole method of rendering politics free from ecclesiasticism; it could only be made effectively by a body of men representing the

spiritual authority. None but the clergy could
meet the Pope on his own ground. It was vain to
denounce ecclesiasticism in politics unless the leaders
of some religious body asserted that the possession
of religious truth was not the one road to political
wisdom, and that a national Church might be truly
of God's appointment without making the civil
magistrate its vassal. That the doctrine in this
country was in an especial degree the product of the
Church of England and her divines is undoubted.
Yet it was equally the product of the Gallican
Church. Indeed the Gallican liberties are one of
the chief sources whence the doctrine could be
drawn[1]. For the ideal of the Divine Right of Kings
in matters of theology is an assertion within limits
of the rights of a national Church. The Pope had
claimed a superiority which rendered nugatory the
name of national Church.

. The Presbyterian system, while asserting national
independence of Papal sovereignty, would have yet
set up within the nation an organization which
would have dwarfed the State and hindered the
growth of the nation's life. A Geneva on a great
scale would not have been a national Church.
Before the Church should have established its
position, the nation would have disappeared. Even
Independency, which seems to leave the whole
matter free, implies a denial of the right of the

[1] See *supra* chap. vi. The connection between the conceptions
of Divine Right and a national Church appears strongly in
the collection of treatises made by Pithou, *Les Libertes de l'Église
Gallicane.*

nation as a whole to an ecclesiastical organization. Had it ever become universal there could not have been a single religious communion claiming to represent the nation on its spiritual side.

The theory belongs to a national Church. If by a national Church be meant a religious body which, representing the whole nation yet leaves its political life free to develop, unaffected by the upas-tree of clericalism, there can be no doubt that the theory of Divine Right was inseparably connected with the ideal of a national Church in the seventeenth century, and that it was necessary to secure its realization in the face of Papal or Presbyterian or Separatist pretensions.

Significance of Passive Obedience. For the theory of Divine Right is a religious as well as a political dogma. The stress laid upon the duty of Passive Obedience is a proof of this. Non-resistance, as an element in a utilitarian system of politics, would probably be taught without qualification. Little would be said of Passive Obedience, even though it should not be forbidden. This is actually the case with the *Leviathan.* But, where absolutist theory is essentially religious, it is inevitable that men should consider the cases where disobedience to law is a religious duty. For, when civil obedience is inculcated as a part of God's Law, the case cannot be ignored of the government's endeavouring to persecute the true religion. Under certain conditions martyrdom is a recognised duty, and this implies the duty of disobedience to the commands of the Sovereign. Unless the qualification be taken into account, no Christian could proclaim the doctrine of

indefeasible hereditary right. Men did not desire
the exclusion of James because they expected that
he would be a tyrant, but because they knew that
he was a Papist. Those who opposed his exclusion
were forced to lay stress upon the duty of Anglicans
in the possible case of his persecuting their religion.

The doctrine of Passive Obedience hampered, in
more ways than one[1], the supporters of the Divine
Right of Kings. They were taunted with shewing
their want of faith in their sovereign, since they
were ever considering the chance of his being a
heretic and a persecutor. It was declared that no
wise upholder of the doctrine of resistance would
dream of inculcating the duty of disobedience as
a general rule, whereas to judge by their language
the supporters of Divine Right regarded the case
for passive obedience as one of constant recurrence.
Besides passive obedience was little better than
active resistance[2]; and its supporters might be

[1] Sanderson, one of the acutest minds who wrote on behalf of
Divine Right, is fully aware of the danger, and endeavours to
minimise to the utmost the duty of Passive Obedience. In all
doubtful cases he declares the responsibility to rest with the
magistrate, and active obedience to be due. He allows that, when
the conscience is clear as to the iniquity of the magistrate's
command, obedience must be withheld, but even here disobedience
is sin; and the case is one of the choice between two evils. " In
such a case certainly he may not obey the magistrate; yet let him
know thus much withal, that he sinneth too in disobeying the magistrate; from which sin the following of the judgment of his own
conscience cannot acquit him. And this is that fearful perplexity,
whereof I spake, wherein many a man casteth himself by his own
error and obstinacy, that he can neither go with his conscience
nor against it, but he shall sin " (*Judgment in One View*, 156).

[2] Hobbes' *Answer to Bramhall*, 127. "Passive Obedience signifies

branded as advocates of rebellion. Hobbes wrote
that, since the Incarnation is the central doctrine
of the Christian faith, the prohibition of that belief
and that alone can justify men in refusing to obey
the laws[1]. No case of the persecution of one
Christian body by another can exempt men from
the normal duty of active obedience. Further,
it might be said, that even in the last resort the
case was not clear, for the Apostles, who declared
that God must be obeyed rather than man, were
eye-witnesses of the Resurrection; their case was
therefore peculiar[2]. Moreover, Elisha had bidden
Naaman go in peace, when he talked of bowing
himself in the House of Rimmon. Taunts of this
sort could easily be levelled at the believers in
Passive Obedience. That there was indeed some
justification for these taunts, is shewn by the sophistical quibble with which the doctrine is wrested to
cover the case of the Revolution and of the acqui-
escence of the clergy in William's reign. The
doctrine of passive obedience could not have loomed
so large save to men for whom politics was a branch
of theology. The cause of its playing so great a
part in the doctrine of Divine Right is that the
latter is bound up with the defence of the Church

nothing except it may be called passive obedience, when a man
refraineth himself from doing what the law hath forbidden. For
in his lordship's sense the thief that is hanged for stealing hath
fulfilled the law, which, I think, is absurd." See also *De Corpore
Politico*, chap. VI.

[1] *Leviathan*, II. 43; the passage is quoted in Appendix C.
[2] *Behemoth*, 86.

of England against its foes. At this time indeed all
theories of politics either have a religious basis or
are framed with the practical object of defending
the true faith. Politics and theology are as yet
intimately connected. And, though in the writings of Locke and Sidney we see politics seeking
to free themselves from their theological vesture, it
is not yet cast away. When the theory of Divine
Right is thus seen to be connected with the existence
of the Church of England and with its position as a
Church at once anti-papal and anti-presbyterian we
shall surely see some justification of the action of
the clergy in 1688. The theory of the Divine Right *James II.*
of Kings is framed for the defence of the nation *tried to*
use the
against Roman claims. It is a weapon forged *theory to*
thwart the
against the Papacy, although it may be used for *purpose*
other purposes. James saw that the weapon was *for which*
it existed.
two-edged, and attempted to use it against the *His*
Church, in whose defence it was formed, and in *failure*
was
favour of the very power it was fashioned to attack. *natural.*
What wonder that the sword broke in his hands!
Whether or no the interpretation of the theory
set upon it by James was logically justified, it ran
directly counter to the intention of all who had
taken part in the making of it. The Anglican clergy
were moved in their action by the clear conviction
that no one could have intended that the great anti-
papal weapon should be used in favour of the Pope.
They must have felt that James was following in
the footsteps of Queen Mary, and was attempting to
use the royal supremacy in order to render it a
nullity for evermore. They refused him their

assistance in this attempt. Who can blame them ?
In neither politics nor theology are men of any age
aware of the whole extent of the ground, which
their theories may logically be held to cover.   Nor
will they ever hesitate about refusing them to carry
a belief to its theoretical conclusion, when the conclusion conflicts with the purpose, for which the doctrine
was first framed.   There are many nowadays who
profess the doctrine *vox populi vox dei.* But it
can hardly be maintained, that they are prompt to
acknowledge an unfavourable verdict of the con-
stituencies as of divine prompting.   If the worship-
pers of democracy are at times betrayed into reading
diaboli for *dei,* or into employing anti-democratic
institutions in order to maintain their position, are
we to find great fault with the supporters of non-
resistance in the seventeenth century, who found
that for once they had been mistaken, and that
on occasion it might be well to exhibit the virtue of
non-resistance, not to a Romanising king, but to
a Protestant invader ?   The theory of Divine Right
had a great work to do in assisting Englishmen to free
themselves from the Papal yoke.   The proof that the
work was done was not reached until in their fear of
Rome, men were ready to cast aside the very weapon
which had hitherto aided them in the struggle.

*Work
of the
doctrine.*   So far remark has been made of the service
performed by the theory of Divine Right, in asserting the profound truth that political institutions
per se are not displeasing to God as the author of
nature; that they ought to be something more
than the instruments of ecclesiastical authority;

that the statesman is not bound to take his policy
from the priest; that the State as such is an
organism with a life of its own, and is subject to
laws of developement distinct from those of the
Church; that the rulers of the Church will not
necessarily be possessed of political wisdom above
the common, and may not without danger be
trusted with the tremendous power of deciding on
questions of national policy with reference to the
aggrandizement of that organization (which itself
has an earthly side), to whose service they are
devoted; or in modern phrase that the "clergy
should not meddle with politics." It is thus clear,
that to the derided Anglican clergy of the seventeenth century are due many of the most cherished
principles of modern life. They may not justly
be charged with pursuing a time-serving and servile
policy. Their aims were not dictated by the interests of a class or section, but were patriotic and
preeminently characteristic of the defenders of a
national Church. They cannot truly be charged
with deserting their principles the moment that
they became inconvenient, for their conduct at the
time of the Revolution, if inconsistent with the
letter of their doctrine, only proves, how deeply
imbued they were with its spirit, and exhibits their
thorough loyalty to the essential principle, which
their theory was framed to express. All this is true,
and has been too often left out of account in the abuse
that has been levelled at the believers in Divine Right.

Yet it must not be forgotten that much was due *The*
to that very ecclesiastical theory of politics against *clerical*

14—2

theory had a value. which men strove in the seventeenth century. That doctrine also had a practical work to perform ; despite much in it that was false and exaggerated and seems to modern notions preposterous beyond measure, it has brought about the recognition of one of the most important principles that can guide the statesman. For the claims of Pope or Presbyter to control the secular power in the interests of the spiritual enshrined in the only form possible to those times the principle of the *rights of conscience.* In ages when the enforcement of conformity by the strong hand is a recognised principle, when all nations profess the same form of religious belief, or when the maxim *cujus regio ejus religio* has become accepted, the only possible method of asserting the rights of conscience and the claims of truth is for the Church to claim superiority over the State. It is inevitable at such times that the perennial problem of Church and State shall take the form of a struggle for supremacy ; for neither can admit the entire authority of the other without the gravest danger on the one hand to truth, on the other to the free developement of national life. If the State be admitted to be omni-competent, while the persecution of error is preached as a duty, an Emperor or King with a theological turn of mind may commit the Church to a heresy and endanger God's truth for all time[1]. For *ex hypothesi* it is recognised that the State is supreme in all

It is an early form of asserting the rights of conscience.

---

[1] On the element of justice in the claims o. the Church see the remarks of Dean Church in the letter to Cardinal (then Archdeacon) Manning of July 1844 (Purcell, *Life of Cardinal Manning,* i. 696).

departments of life; that it is the duty of the State to enforce conformity; and that resistance is unjustifiable. The State may therefore compel the propagation of heresy, and stamp out completely the true faith, for the notion is unfounded, that persecution always fails[1]. If the rights of conscience and the claims of truth are to be respected at all, the Church must make herself the guardian of them and claim supremacy over the State. So long of course as persecution is a recognised principle, truth cannot be secure. But it is at least a step in the right direction that the power which has physical force on its side, shall submit to take its views of truth and error from the power whose force is moral and spiritual only. It is better that the Church should direct the State, as to what forms of faith to enforce or to persecute, than that the State should prescribe religion *proprio motu*. Even this imperfect condition of things is a tribute to the rights of conscience, to the claims of truth, and to the existence of human interests other than those which are merely material and earthly. Toleration involves the principle, that religion is a department of life which the State has no moral right to control, that opinion may not be coerced. Persecution by the State at the bidding of the Church contains the germ of this principle; for it arises from the notion that the State as such cannot meddle with opinion, but must take its views from those who know. It forms the necessary transition between the State-religion of the Roman Empire and the modern ideal of freedom of opinion. In the first stage, the State prescribes

[1] Mill, *On Liberty*, 16.

a religion of its own and compels all men to worship the Emperor. In the second, the State recognizes that it is incompetent to decide upon questions of religious belief, and must go to the spiritual authority to find truth; but it still regards the enforcement of truth as a duty, and persecution as its proper function. The third stage is that of complete toleration of all forms of belief, when the State has given up its claim to meddle with opinion, and regards religious questions as beyond its competence. Now the third stage was not reached at the period which is here being discussed. It will therefore be readily seen that in order to secure the principle which is characteristic of the second stage, and to prevent a relapse into the first, the Church must ever be proclaiming its supremacy in matters of faith and denying the right of the State to meddle therein save at its bidding. This must inevitably lead to some such claim of political authority as was put forward under the Papal or Presbyterian system. If the State admits the right of the Church to dictate to it the true faith to be enforced and to prescribe forms of ecclesiastical organization and discipline, the Church will be found continually encroaching upon the State; many matters, which are of civil import, will be treated as constructively ecclesiastical; and, in the last resort, all freedom will be denied to the State, whose unspiritual character will be made the basis of a claim for its enslavement. The State must then assert its independence; and the form of the assertion is the subject of this essay.

The conflict in- Nor is there any means, whereby the conflict can be brought to a close, until the principle of

toleration be generally accepted. Only when the *evitably lasts, until toleration becomes a recognized principle.*
State has resigned the claim to make religion
coextensive with its authority, can the Church with
safety withdraw from its pretensions to make politics
subservient to ecclesiasticism. When that be the
case, the State by giving up the claim to enforce
truth at the point of the bayonet will have freed
the Church from the risk of destruction. The
claims of the State to omnipotence may henceforward be admitted. The Church will no longer be
in danger with every chance current of thought, that
may sway the sovereign one or number. There is no
longer any need for the Church to proclaim its supremacy over the State, for its activity is recognised as
free from State interference. The State is sovereign.
It may legally do what it pleases. No co-equal
jurisdiction exists. No clerical organization may
dictate to it. That is the principle underlying the
sophistical reasoning and obsolete philosophy of the
supporters of the Divine Right of Kings. Conscience must be respected. Beliefs are free. Men's
forms of ecclesiastical organization must be of their
own choosing. The State must not force their faith
or practice. Religious toleration is to be a practical
limit upon the exercise of the sovereign power.
This is the principle, which out of numberless
impossible claims and anarchical opinions has been
won for modern citizens by those who assert the
Divine Right of Pope or Presbyter. Neither side
saw clearly or completely what was the essence of
its claim. Neither side realized that toleration
alone could set the conflicting claims at rest, and

permit of both Church and State developing without
injuring one another. Both sides argue with passion,
with sophistry, with an uncritical assumption of
God's being on their side, which must seem to us
Pharisaical. Yet each side was right in its main
contention. The State has a right to exist apart
from the favour of the clergy; and politics should
not be governed by ecclesiastical considerations.
On the other hand there are departments of thought
and action with which the State may not interfere
without the gravest injury to the highest interests
of humanity. Both sides were fighting for principles
which have long been admitted to be rooted in right
reason and utility. To throw ridicule upon the
antiquated forms in which these principles found
expression and did their work, to blame the royalist
for servility or the Papalist for bigotry is to blame
men for defending a just cause with the only
weapons that were available. That there was too
much of passion and prejudice on either side may
be admitted. Even modern controversies are
not quite without them. But they are frequently
wanting in those solid results, which give such
cause for gratitude to the controversialists of the
middle ages and the Reformation. The more closely
the subject is studied the greater will be the debt of
gratitude acknowledged to those who by supporting
the Divine Right of Kings have ministered to the
stability and independence of the English State, and
to their opponents to whose labours we owe it that
liberty of thought has become a recognized principle
of modern life.

CHAPTER IX.

NON-RESISTANCE AND THE THEORY OF SOVEREIGNTY.

IT is as a phase in the conflict of Church and *Political* State that the theory of the Divine Right of Kings *aspect of the theory.* possessed its greatest significance and produced its most memorable results. Yet it has a place also in the history of the developement of the theory of government, and must be considered in relation to those political problems which occupied men's minds in the seventeenth century. It is true, that with the possible exception of Hobbes, all the political theorists up to the end of the seventeenth century either have religion for the basis of their system, or regard the defence or supremacy of some one form of faith as their main object. Hardly any political idea of the time but had its origin in theological controversy. To Roman writers in the main are due the theories of the State of nature, and of the original compact[1]. Popular rights and ecclesiastical supremacy are bound up with one another. Yet since all these theological controversies have a political aspect, it is possible to isolate this aspect

---

[1] See especially Suarez, *De Legibus*, III. 4; Mariana, *Del Rey*, I. 1, 2, 8. In the last-mentioned chapter the question discussed is '¿Es mayor el poder del rey, ó el de la republica?' The course of the

for the purposes of inquiry and to investigate the purely political side of the theory of Divine right. There will be the less danger in this course, since the markedly theological character of all seventeenth century politics has already been sufficiently dwelt upon. Further, in the deluge of political literature that poured forth in the seventeenth century, it can hardly be but that views of every sort shall be found here and there in reluctant combination. An attempt to disentangle the main threads of controversy can lay no claim to comprehensive accuracy. Lines of thought apparently inconsistent will at times be united through individual idiosyncrasy. Methods of argument will change sides. Sentiments and opinions will be subject to kaleidoscopic permutations. A sketch like the present can do no more than describe general tendencies of difference or resemblance between opposing schools. It may give a rough estimate of what was the characteristic drift of thought on either side. But it cannot lay claim to finality. Nor must it be forgotten that individual writers may well be found

This chapter can only describe general tendencies.

argument is singularly instructive, and much of it might have been written by Locke. It is notable that, although deciding in Chapter II. that monarchy is the best form of government, Mariana would yet surround his king with all sorts of limitations, so that he really leaves the sovereignty with the people, and thus falls into the error of supporting a "mixed monarchy." "Creo que ha de residir constantemente en la república la facultad de reprimir los vicios de los reyes y destronarlos." (I quote from the Spanish translation of the *De Rege* published in the *Biblioteca de Authores Españoles.*) It is needless to say that, in Mariana's view, one of the main limits on royal authority is set by the freedom of the Church.

whose personal equation obscures the main lines
of controversy, and causes them to overleap the
barriers of thought which separate opposing parties.
Still there are certain well-marked differences in
conception and standpoint between the combatants
on either side; each party appears to represent
certain distinctive tendencies. It seems reasonable
to attempt the exposition of these characteristics,
after thus premising that isolated cases may be
found in which they are not exhibited. It will then
be necessary to consider, whether or no the theory of
the Divine Right of Kings was something more
than the expression of an absurdly romantic sentiment of loyalty; how much it has in common with
other political theories of the time; whether, when
it differs from them, it differs from them for the
worse; and whether it contained within it notions
of the State, its powers and functions, which modern
thought has not discarded.

I.

There is no more universal characteristic of the *Universa-*
political thought of the seventeenth century than *lity of*
notion of
the notion of non-resistance to authority. "To *non-re-*
bring the people to obedience" is the object of *sistance.*
writers of all schools. When resistance is preached,
it is resistance to some authority regarded as
subordinate. Nor is the resistance permitted at
the pleasure or judgment of private individuals.
It is allowed only as a form of obedience, as executing the commands of some superior and ultimate
authority, God, or the Pope and the Law. It has

been shewn already that the Papal theory is in truth a doctrine of obedience to a monarch. Great indeed was the indignation evoked by the airy manner in which Bellarmine or Mariana disposed of the claims to obedience of the secular prince, and fostered principles of popular sovereignty. Yet at least some Anglican writers were capable of seeing that all these notions are developed as part of a theory of obedience and not of liberty, and that the text, "They that resist shall receive to themselves damnation" so far from being discarded or explained away is interpreted as proving the political supremacy of the Pope. As Bishop Jackson puts it, "The principle wherein the Romish Church, the Jesuits, and we agree is this; that none may resist the higher powers; that obedience, at least passive or submissive from the outward man of our bodies, lives, and estates is due to the higher powers; the question is...which be the highest powers on earth."

So with the Presbyterian view. The main object of the discipline is obedience, in Cartwright's view[2]. The strong expressions about duty to the civil magistrates which seem inconsistent when read by the side of claims to depose them are explained by the view, held in common with Papalists and Wycliffe, that resistance for mere oppression's sake is not justifiable, and that no private person may

[1] Jackson, *Treatise of Christian Obedience*, Works, III. 971.

[2] Cf. the following, "Under the name of the Saints are contained all the rest of the Church, which do not exercise any public office or function therein, whose duty as in all others sometimes is only this, to suffer themselves to be ruled and governed by those whom God hath set over them." *Declaration of Discipline*, 185.

resist the sovereign. Only the Kirk, as inspired by God, may direct the removal of an "idolater" in order to secure "freedom" *i.e.* supremacy for itself. Neither Papalist nor Presbyterian contemplates the resistance of individuals[1]; nor does either make any approach to the modern notion, that obedience may be settled by utilitarian considerations.

Even with those who go further than this and look at politics from a more purely secular standpoint, God's cause is almost invariably the sole occasion of lawful resistance. Clearly, the notion of the divine right of insurrection was not one, for which any considerable number of persons were contending in the seventeenth century. Remark has been made of the emphasis laid in the *Vindiciae contra Tyrannos* on the duty of passive obedience incumbent upon private individuals[2]. So long as a tyrant, however oppressive in his acts, is supported by the constituted authorities and estates of the realm, obedience to him is a duty. Nor was the notion confined to France. In England it found expression in the theory that resistance to the Crown is lawful only if it be enjoined by the inferior magistrate. It was pretended that the Parliament took up arms against the person only of the king but in support of his authority. This shews how loth men were to believe that what was legally wrong will ever be morally right. At this time some shadowy legality is always pretended for acts essentially

Modern utilitarian theory of obedience not held in seventeenth century.

---

[1] Mariana is apparently an exception with his theory of the duty of tyrannicide. *Del Rey*, I, 7, 8.

[2] *Supra* 114.

revolutionary. Prynne's elaborate treatise is written with the object of proving that Parliament at the beginning of the Civil War had the law upon its side. The author has no notion that tyranny can justify the abrogation for the nonce of law[1]. The same notion appears more strongly in 1688, in the fiction that James having abdicated the throne the English legal and constitutional system is being developed with no breach of continuity. There is evidence yet more conclusive. Johnson, writing on behalf of the Exclusion Bill, declares deliberately that Christians are bound to submit to persecution in the case where the laws permit it. "When the laws of God and our own country interfere and it is made death by the law of the land to be a good Christian then we are to lay down our lives for Christ's sake. This is the only case ,where the Gospel requires passive obedience, namely, when the laws are against a man[2]." So widespread was this notion that one writer at the time of the Revolution subjects the Whig theory to the following *reductio ad absurdum.* According to the Whig view, if the king persecutes the true faith, he may be resisted. Now on this view if the law took a similar course it might be resisted. But no Whig will admit that this latter case would make resistance justifiable. Therefore it is absurd to claim the right in the former case where the king is persecutor against the law[3]. Nor, again, is the main force of

---

[1] *The Sovereign Power of Parliament and Kingdoms.*
[2] *Julian the Apostate* (Johnson's Works, 33).
[3] *Christianity a Doctrine of the Cross,* 75.

the royalist attack directed against the contention, that resistance to the law may in certain circumstances be justified. Royalists are not concerned to prove that the law may not be resisted on any pretence without grievous sin. Nobody doubts this. Their main position is quite different. They set themselves to prove, that laws derive their binding authority from the king alone, and therefore that he may not be resisted when he breaks them; for he as the source of legislation is himself above positive law, and resistance to the "sovereign" is always sinful[1]. The real controversy between royalists and Whigs is as to the existence of a sovereign one or number not subject to law[2]. The vexed question of Julian the Apostate was a case in point. The Whig argument is that the submission of the early Christians to persecution was owing to the fact that it was legal,

---

[1] See especially the above-mentioned pamphlet, and compare the following passage: "The plea is the same on either side; the Pope says as long as the Prince governs according to the Laws of God and the Church (of which He is the interpreter) so long the censures of the Church do not reach Him; and say the People, as long as the Prince governs according to the Laws of the Land (and of the meaning of those laws themselves are the interpreters) so long are they bound to be obedient: but as soon as the King doth anything that may contradict the Pope, then he is (deservedly say the Romanists) excommunicate, deposed and murdered, and when he usurps upon the People's liberties, then he ought to be deposed by the people; the arguments on either side are the same and for the most part the authorities." *History of Passive Obedience* (1681), 84.

[2] "There is no authority upon earth above the law, much less against it." (Johnson, 30) expresses the whole contention of the Whigs which is opposed to the theory of sovereignty as well as to Divine Right.

while their (alleged) resistance to Julian was due to
the illegality of his oppression[1]. Even Locke evades
the difficulty by denying the omnipotence of "the
legislative" in all States. He will not declare, that
resistance to law is ever justifiable. He merely
denies, that laws which transgress certain fundamental principles, are laws "properly so called[2]."
So with Algernon Sidney. He declares that an
unjust law is not law[3] at all, and gives as instances the persecuting statutes of the Lancastrian
period[4]. No other view was possible to him; for
elsewhere he is content to bow before the majesty
of law. In one eloquent passage Sidney declares that
this [Law] is he to whom we all owe a simple uncon-
ditional obedience[5]." Milton in his *Tenure of Kings
and Magistrates* perhaps comes nearer than most of
his contemporaries to modern utilitarian views. Yet
he places the sovereignty in the people by a fundamental and unalterable law[6]; and thus by a confusion
between natural and positive law, similar to that
made by Locke and Sidney, he thinks to escape the
danger of asserting a doctrine which then seemed so

---

[1] Johnson, *Julian the Apostate*, "The first Christians suffered
according to the laws of their country, whereas these under Julian
were persecuted contrary to law," 28, *Answer to Jovian, Answer to
Constantius the Apostate.*

[2] *Second Treatise of Civil Government*, Chaps. 11, 18.

[3] *Discourses Concerning Government*, III. § 11.

[4] *Ibid.* § 25.   [5] *Ibid.* § 42.

[6] *Tenure of Kings and Magistrates*, Prose Works, II. 11. "The
power of kings and magistrates is nothing else but what is only
derivative, transferred and committed them in trust from the people
* * * in whom the power yet remains fundamentally, and cannot
be taken from them without a violation of their natural birthright."

preposterous as that resistance to law may ever
be morally justifiable.

The law to which obedience is due may be
Canon Law, 'Discipline,' Positive Law, Custom.
But obedience to what is conceived as law of some
sort, truly and not metaphorically speaking, is the
universal maxim.   Nearly all teach the duty of
obedience to positive law, for the law of the Church
will be positive law if its claims be admitted.   That
some of these writers are feeling their way towards
the purely utilitarian theory of obedience held in
modern times is undoubtedly the case.   But they
had none of them reached it.   One and all would
have scouted the bald proposition, fundamental in
utilitarian politics, that a law having all the notes
of law " simply and strictly so called " may yet be
disobeyed, if it be oppressive beyond measure.   The
practical teaching might not greatly differ from that
of a modern utilitarian, for on most of these theories
there would be ample grounds for pronouncing any
law, to which grave objection is taken, as lacking in
some essential property of law rightly so-called.
Yet the theories of the seventeenth and nineteenth
centuries are as wide apart as the poles.   With
very few exceptions, all political thinkers in the
seventeenth century regard as absolute the claims
of law, as they define it, to unquestioning, unvarying
obedience; they teach that to the ultimate authority
in the state, whatever it be, non-resistance is the last
word of duty.

II.

*Causes
of this
general
belief in
the duty of
unvarying
obedience
to law.* Nor is the explanation far to seek. The history
of the Middle Ages is filled with the struggle
between government and anarchy. According to
the Papal theory, secular governments are the anarchical powers, which would teach men to disobey
their true lord in obedience to an inferior authority.
From the point of view of national statesmen it is
on the one hand the Pope claiming the deposing
power, the clergy demanding immunities, on the
other hand the feudal lordships, private jurisdictions,
livery and maintenance, that prevent or check the
unquestioned supremacy of one all-embracing system
of law. In the Wars of the Roses the evils of this
latter tendency exhibit themselves for the last time.
They produce the reaction in favour of despotism
and peace at any price. For a long time after this,
men will have ceased to regard liberty or constitutional rights as of any importance compared with
strong government and the suppression of private
war. Obedience is in the eyes of all men the
supreme duty of the patriotic citizen; and law the
one element essential to the welfare of the state.

*The
Common
Law con-
ceived as
sovereign.* Nor is it of statute law that men are thinking;
but of the Common Law, which, though containing
much that may have originally been directly enacted,
yet possesses that mysterious sanctity of prescription,
which no legislator can bestow. The Common Law
is pictured invested with a halo of dignity, peculiar
to the embodiment of the deepest principles and to
the highest expression of human reason and of the

law of nature implanted by God in the heart of man. As yet men are not clear that an Act of Parliament can do more than declare the Common Law[1]. It is the Common Law, which men set up as the object of worship. They regard it as the symbol of ordered life and disciplined activities, which are to replace the licence and violence of the evil times now passed away. Instead of local custom or special privilege one system shall be common to all. Instead of the caprice of the moment, or the changing principles of competing dynastic policies, or the pleasure of some great noble, or the cunning of a usurper, there shall rule in England a system, older than Kings and Parliaments, of immemorial majesty and almost Divine authority. "Law is the breath of God; her voice the harmony of the world." And the Common Law is the perfect ideal of law; for it is natural reason developed and expounded by the collective wisdom of many generations. By it kings reign and princes decree judgment. By it are fixed the relations of the estates of the realm, and the fundamental laws of the

[1] [Judicial Records and Acts of Parliament] "are but declarations of the Common Law and Custom of the Realm touching Royal Government," *Jenkins Redivivus,* 1; the repeated attempts beginning with 42 Ed. III. c. 1, to declare certain Acts of Parliament unrepealable are another proof of this. Cf. also Bonham's case (Reports 118a). "When an Act of Parliament is against common right and reason or repugnant or impossible to be performed, *the Common Law will control it and adjudge such Act to be void.*" *Majestas Intemerata* contains a long legal argument directed against the omnipotence of Parliament, and contending that "the statute is but declarative" (8). "An Act against payment of tithes is regarded as void" (16).

15—2

constitution. Based on long usage and almost supernatural wisdom its authority is above rather than below that of Acts of Parliament or Royal ordinances, which owe their fleeting existence to the caprice of the King or to the pleasure of councillors, which have a merely material sanction and may be repealed at any moment. It is not wonderful that men should have thought of the Common Law as sovereign by Divine Right; or that they should have deemed that it owed its authority to something higher than the will of the sovereign. In the days when English Law first took shape, men had spoken of it as superior to King and Parliament alike and had dreamed of no sovereign's sanction as needful to make it binding. And so we find many in the seventeenth century who retain the notion, and think, that the word "Law, Law[1]" is enough. For them law is the true sovereign, and they are not under the necessity of considering whether King or Lords or Commons or all three together are the ultimate authority in the State.

III.

With the Reforma-tion a true theory of sove-reignty becomes possible in England. But this was no longer true to the facts. Legislative activity had much increased of late. In Tudor times it effected the most far-reaching series of changes known in English history. The central power had asserted its supremacy over aristocratic privilege and made good its independence against the Papacy.

---

[1] "Truly for these many years last past have the lawyers enslaved both the king and the people by the charm of 'Law, law'." *The Church's Eleventh Persecution*, 7.

At last there is room in English politics for a complete theory of sovereignty. The vast increase of the powers and activity of the legislator could not fail to drive men to seek for the sanction of the law in his will. They were forced to consider the question, whether Kings are anterior to law, or law to governments. Here there is a distinction capable of splitting into two parties the believers in the Divine Right of the law of the land. On the one hand those who believe that custom is the main element in law, and law therefore the king-maker, will naturally claim to make the judges, as interpreters of the law, the supreme power in the state; while, like Bracton, they will themselves fail to see the necessity of a sovereign one or number and will honestly believe that no power in the state is exempt from legal limitation. On the other hand, those who have grasped the truth, now first made apparent by facts, that there must be a sovereign in the state, who may give to laws their efficacy, will claim that he is *ipso facto* above the laws, and cannot be subject to their co-active power. The quarrel between the Crown and the Judges was not only the forerunner of the greater quarrel between King and Parliament; it was inevitable in the nature of things. The Judges, as professors of the Common Law, claimed for it supreme authority, and had their claim been admitted would have made themselves the ultimate authority in the State. For no one denied their right to interpret the law. The King, realising vividly that there must be a sovereign, claimed naturally enough the position asserted for

Inevitable contro- versy between supporters of the Crown and the Common Law.

the Judges. What the Judges really asserted was that all constitutional questions could be settled by a reference to custom, and that they alone were competent to declare it. This, as Mr Gardiner points out, would have given into their hands the decision of the great struggle of the seventeenth century[1]. Coke, like most of the opponents of the King, had not really grasped the conception of sovereignty; he maintained a position, reasonable enough in the Middle Ages, but impossible in a developed state. For his claim and that of all the Common Lawyers was to personify the Common Law as sovereign, and to deny that character to any person or body in the State. Had his ideal been reached, and questions of interpretation (which made the judges sovereign) settled once for all, England would have been in the condition of the Punjaub under Runjeet Singh, as described by Sir Henry Maine, where the person "habitually obeyed" never made a true law and was deemed incapable of making one[2]. The fact, lamented by Clarendon, that the "professors of that great and admirable mystery, the Law" were on the Puritan side, was inevitable[3]. For their view was towards a state of things that had ceased to exist, and they sought to explain the constitution of England as Bracton might have done. But the King had perceived that with the growth of legislative activity and

---

[1] For accounts of Coke's views and the various controversies which culminated in his suspension, see Gardiner, *History of England*, II. 35—43, 242, 279, III. 1—25.

[2] *Early History of Institutions*, 379 sqq.

[3] *History of the Rebellion*, IV. 38—41.

the victory of the central power over its enemies, sovereignty had become a fact, and past history justified him in laying claim to all that was involved in the new state of things. It is the King and his supporters, be it observed, who first saw the change. Parliament, unwilling at first to claim the sovereignty, denies that it exists. On the other hand, if the King had been permitted to retain all his traditional prerogatives, the general recognition of the idea of sovereignty would have made the government a tyranny; as has been said, it was only the lack of this recognition that saved England from falling into despotism in the Middle Ages. Now that the truth was soon to be recognized by the nation at large, Parliament is forced to make new claims and by degrees to grasp at supremacy, lest it should lose old rights or even forfeit equality. With many modifications, the controversies between Whigs and Royalists right up to the Revolution hinge on this question of sovereignty. One side has ever before it the vision of law conceived as a system existing by Divine Right, its origin lost in the past, independent of circumstances and men's caprice, superior to Kings, and controlling Parliament. The other side lays stress on the conception of a sovereign raised above all laws with power to abrogate them, who alone can give binding force to enactments and invest custom with legal sanctions. The supporters of the Crown are repeatedly found arguing that the King must be before and above the law, or how can it be binding? They are enraged at the stupidity of their opponents,

who cannot admit so obvious a fact. The novelty of
the notion of sovereignty is the explanation of the
otherwise unaccountable views entertained by those
judges who favoured the Crown's claims as to the
king's extraordinary power[1]. They saw that law
can never bind the "sovereign" in any state, and
they were therefore driven to enlarge the meaning
of prerogative to an alarming extent. The very
fact that the idea of sovereignty had only then
disengaged itself from a belief in the supremacy of
custom, would compel all those who were imbued
with the idea to treat of the king's prerogative, as the
basis and essence of the whole system of law, rather
than as an aggregate of exceptional powers and discre-
tionary authority allowed to him by well established
custom. Sovereignty presented itself to these men
with all the force of a discovery, and in their
enthusiasm for the abstract conception, they used
language which justified their opponents in declaring
that they were interpreting the law, so as to give
the king a truly arbitrary, i.e. capricious authority.

This question forms the main ground of contro- versy up to the Re- volution. The doctrine of sovereignty was perhaps misconceived in some of its details, or not grasped with
absolute precision. Yet certainly, from the point of
view of political theory, the controversy between
Royalists and Parliamentarians differs merely in its
practical object, from the questions, which every
student of Austin is driven to ask himself, "At what
point does custom become law? And how is it made

[1] See especially the judgment of Chief Baron Fleming in
Bates' case printed in Prothero's *Documents*, 340, and of Berkeley
in Hampden's case in Gardiner's *Documents*, 46.

such?" The point has been much debated of late
years; yet it may be doubted whether there is any
substantial agreement among writers on jurisprudence. If thinkers, whose only object is scientific
investigation, are not yet agreed as to what is the
true answer to these questions, there is no great
cause to blame the disputants on either side in the
seventeenth century. The problem as to the precise
value of the maxim, "Whatever the sovereign permits, he commands" will not improbably continue
to perplex us till the end of time. But this much
is certain. The facts of English history had for the
first time rendered complete sovereignty a necessity
in English national life. The question, in whom
the sovereignty should ultimately be vested, could
only be decided by a century of struggle. The sovereignty of whatever person or body was the highest
authority in the English State became a practical
fact at the Reformation. Only those who were the
least hampered by tradition would be gifted with
the clearness of insight necessary to perceive this.
All whose imaginations were dominated by the past
would fail for a time to observe the change. The
true leaders of progress in this matter were the
believers in Divine Right.

The omnipotence of Parliament is doubtless realised sufficiently at the present day by many persons
who would be at a loss to understand some of the
details of the theory of sovereignty. It is not surprising that the first perception of the notion takes
at first a practical rather than a scientific form.
For most men the idea will be suggested by the

observed fact of the existence of a sovereign.
They will not frame the theory, and afterwards
observe the facts. Now it is unlikely that those,
whose gaze was turned to the England of the sixteenth century, could suppose that sovereignty was
invested in any other person than the King. Here
and there, a man like Prynne or Sir Thomas Smith
may be found arguing that not the King but
Parliament is truly sovereign[1]. Yet most men will
arrive at the idea of sovereignty because they will
seem to see it encircling the diadem of Henry VIII.
or Elizabeth. As has been shewn above, the course
of circumstances would lead men to suppose that
the sovereignty was vested in the Crown and not in
Parliament. The perception of this fact inevitably
leads to the exaltation of the position of the King,

---

[1] The very fact that Prynne knows that his treatise will seem
a dangerous paradox is proof that his views were not generally
accepted (*Sovereign Power of Parliaments*, To the Reader). Bishop
Sanderson again considers the mere words of the oath of supremacy as quite sufficient proof that the sovereignty is vested in the
King and not the Parliament (Preface to Ussher's *Power of the
Prince*). The personal character of allegiance as defined by all the
Judges in Calvin's case was another bar to men's dreaming of
Parliament as the actual depositary of sovereign authority. The
views quoted above as to the possibility of avoiding Acts of Parliament would similarly hinder the growth of a belief in Parliamentary
sovereignty. Nor is there as yet one imperial Parliament; it is
to the King not the Parliament that inhabitants of England,
Scotland and Ireland are united in allegiance. If the three are
to make one realm, it can only be because the King is sovereign.
The United Parliament of Cromwell made Parliamentary sovereignty a possibility. It is noteworthy that theories of popular
sovereignty in the seventeenth century are not in general theories
of technical sovereignty vested in Parliament, but doctrines of the
rights of the people in the last resort.

and to a depreciation of the rights of Parliament and the rules of Law. Only as this took place, would those, who were determined to stand by the rights of Parliament and by the ancient conventions of the constitution, gradually rise to the conception of Parliamentary sovereignty, and find in the privilege of Parliament a treasury of omnipotence not inferior in elasticity and controversial convenience to the undefined possibilities of royal prerogative[1].

IV.

The Divine Right of Kings on its political side *The Divine Right of Kings is the form taken in the seventeenth century by the theory of sovereignty.* was little more than the popular form of expression for the theory of sovereignty. As an abstract theory the idea is never likely to be widely prevalent. But sovereignty seen, as a fact, vested in a person or body of persons may lead men to frame a theory far more generally intelligible and practically effective than the academic analysis of the notion in Austin or even in Hobbes and Bodin can ever become. This is the case with the Divine Right of Kings. Evidence of the fact may be found in plenty. Many of the most strenuous supporters of the Divine Right of Kings declare that similar rights belong to all established governments, and that non-resistance to this authority is equally a duty. On the other hand, the opponents of the theory are frequently found attacking not so much royal authority as the idea of sovereignty. Moreover Hobbes, who has the reputa-

[1] Clarendon traces the process by which the privilege of Parliament was extended by imperceptible degrees to cover an assumption of complete sovereignty. *History of the Rebellion, passim.*

tion of being the first Englishman in the seventeenth century to formulate the complete theory of sovereignty, did not analyse it as a purely scientific notion, but had with his contemporaries the object of proclaiming the duty of invariable obedience and non-resistance to the sovereign in all states. The analysis of sovereignty is only incidental to the practical object of inculating non-resistance. So with supporters of Divine Right.

Divine Right of Kings confused with non-resistance to all established governments.

Bishop Overall's *Convocation Book* was avowedly compiled in the support of monarchy. The object of the book is to assert the Divine Right of Kings, and the duty of non-resistance. Yet it is of all established governments that this Divine authority is really asserted. Arguments in favour of the superiority of monarchy are indeed drawn from the patriarchal theory; yet the statement is made that after rebels have organized a government, its authority is from God. This statement is flatly subversive of the indefeasible hereditary right, and as such was highly distasteful to James I.[1]. It is evident that there was confusion in the minds of the compilers, and that the element in their doctrine which was grasped with lucidity was the idea that some sovereign power existed in all states, that this sovereign power owed its authority to Divine ordinance, and that resistance to it is a sin.

Hickes, who became a non-juror, wrote his *Jovian* in the midst of the Exclusion Bill controversy. Yet he distinctly asserts that all established governments

[1] Overall's *Convocation Book*, Canon xxviii. James' Letter is printed in the preface.

are from God, and that the Biblical prohibitions of resistance are fully as applicable to the subjects of a republic as to those of a monarchy.

The work of Dudley Diggs, *The Unlawfulness of Subjects taking arms against the Sovereign*, is still stronger evidence that the most important elements in the theory of Divine Right are the conception of sovereignty and of non-resistance to the sovereign whether King or Parliament. Save for the addition of the religious sanction to obedience, and for the use of scriptural illustrations, we might be reading a popular abridgment of the *Leviathan*. The theory of the origin of the state held by Hobbes is definitely adopted. The author does not assert that kingship as such is viewed with any special favour by God. Arguments based on the Old Testament and patriarchal society are dismissed as irrelevant[1]. All that is claimed is that England is, as a matter of fact, a monarchy, and that resistance to all established governments is a sin. Ussher, again, argues that sovereignty is a necessary natural fact[2]. Even Laud declares that he has no will to except against any form of government assumed by any State[3]. Although Filmer's sense of the need of unity in the state leads him to regard monarchy as the only true form of government[4], he yet in another

[1] *The Unlawfulness of Subjects taking up Arms*, 16.

[2] "True it is that in several states there are admitted several forms of government." " If this be so, and that nature seeketh always to preserve itself, we may justly conclude that Magistracy is rooted in the Law of Nature and so in the Author of Nature, that is God himself." (*Power of the Prince*, 12, 18.)

[3] *Sermons*, III. (*Works* I. 85).

[4] *Observations on Aristotle*.

place speaks of the supreme power in any state, monarchy or republic, as nothing but the original power of the father[1].

Doubtless such works as the *Convocation Book* and *Jovian* exhibit less grasp of what is really involved in the theory of Divine Right than is the case with the *True Law of Free Monarchies* or the *Patriarcha*. There is confusion in the minds of the writers, yet they believe themselves, and have always been commonly regarded as, supporters of Divine Right. The essence of the theory must therefore lie in those doctrines upon which they lay stress in common with the more accurate expounders of the notion. Those points which are obscured or ignored by so strong a non-juror as Hickes can at most be regarded as "organic details" of the .theory rather than as its main and vital principles[2].

The conception not grasped by the opposite party.

Still more clearly is it evident that the real question in dispute is the fact of sovereignty, and the origin of legal authority, if attention be paid to the repeated attempts made to convince Whig theorists, that no state can be without an ultimate authority, which, because it is sovereign, must be technically arbitrary. "The name of tyranny signi-

[1] *Patriarcha*, 28.

[2] The writings of the non-juror Leslie are the most vivid expression of royalist theory after the Revolution. It is plain that he is moved by no hatred of republicanism, but merely by the dread of anarchy. "There is no medium possible betwixt non-resistance upon any pretence whatsoever and a full licence to resist upon every pretence whatsoever. Because every man is left to judge of the pretence. So that *the whole dispute is Whether government or anarchy?*" (*The Best Answer.*) "For the word King, I mean no more than the supreme authority." (*Best of all.*) See Appendix.

fieth nothing more nor less than the name of
sovereignty," says Hobbes[1]. "There is a necessity
that somebody must be trusted, if you will not
trust one, you must trust more" declares Digges[2].
"There is no such thing as a free state in the
world[3]" is the thesis of another. Laud writes,
"Turn the knot which way you will, all binding to
obedience will be grievous to some[4]." Another asks,
"What State can these rebels have that may not
degenerate into a tyranny[5]?" Indeed during the
troubles of the Commonwealth the notion might easily
be generated that tyranny is no less possible under a
Parliament than under a King. It is a pertinent
question, "The will of one man is contrary to freedom, and why not the will of five hundred[6]?"
Royalists writing on this matter habitually speak
with the half-amazed irritation of a teacher trying
in vain to get wilfully stupid pupils to realise how
chimerical is the dream of a perfect state with no
power in it exempt from legal limitation.

[1] *Leviathan*, 892. Hobbes characteristically adds "saving that
they that use the former word are understood to be angry with
them they call tyrants." In *Behemoth*, 112, Hobbes shews that
all governments are really arbitrary: and goes on, "The true meaning of Parliament was that not the King but they themselves should
have the arbitrary power not only of England, but of Ireland and
(as it appeared by the event) of Scotland also."

[2] *The Unlawfulness of Subjects taking up Arms* (79); cf. also
p. 43, "A necessity to grant impunity to some in all governments."

[3] *Royal Charter granted unto Kings* (Chap. xiv.).

[4] *Sermons*, vi. *Works*, i. 180: cf. with this Mr Sidgwick's
Remarks on the "coercion of well-intentioned adults," *Elements
of Politics*, 623.

[5] ΕΙΚΩΝ ΑΚΛΑΣΤΟΣ, a reply to Milton's *Iconoclastes*.

[6] *Ibid.* There is much more in the same strain.

Locke's Treatise an attack on the idea of sovereignty.

Yet more is this apparent in the most striking exposition of the opposite theory. Locke's treatise is expressly directed against the notion that there is any sovereign power in the state. He realises that the legislative is supreme, yet he sets himself the impossible task of fencing it about with limitations of many kinds, such as the duty of respecting liberty and property, etc.[1]. Locke does not say that the transgressing of these limits is invariably inexpedient or even universally iniquitous. This may be true; certainly it is tenable. But he tries to prove that such action would be illegal. If the 'Legislative' oversteps the bounds which Locke has laid down for it, its authority is at an end, and the state is dissolved. Perhaps it would be hard to mention a single Parliament since the Reform Act which has not overstepped the limits of its competence according to Locke, and by so doing dissolved the State, and broken the continuity of our institutions and the whole system of law and government. The more closely Locke's treatise is studied, the more clearly will it be seen that it is an attack directed far more against the idea of sovereignty than against the claims of monarchy. The notion of legal omnipotence is abhorrent to him; and he is guilty of a confusion between law natural and law positive, from which the extremest and most reactionary royalist would have been free.

Sidney and Milton.

Algernon Sidney's *Discourses concerning Government*, and even Milton's *Tenure of Kings and*

[1] *Second Treatise*, c. 11. Johnson's writings are dominated by a disbelief in the theory of sovereignty.

Magistrates exhibit an almost equal want of insight. The definite ground assumed is that of Rousseau that the people is sovereign, that this sovereignty comes from God and is inalienable. All governments are in their view merely officials carrying out the will of the sovereign people and they may therefore be removed at any time[1]. This view is apparently also that of Mariana and Suarez and is far more consistent and logically defensible than the common Whig theory.

Yet this view is also untenable, for in no state at that time or now can the legal sovereignty be said to be vested in the people. It may be true that it ought to be so vested; but it certainly is not the case in any modern state. The sense in which Milton and Sidney spoke of sovereignty being vested in the people is one which proves them incapable of realising the notion of sovereignty with accuracy. It is with them little more than the expression of the belief in a general right of insurrection against intolerable oppression. To such a belief there would be no objection, if they did not use their loose interpretation of the term sovereignty, as a ground for denying the existence of the thing. They deny the fact of sovereignty save in a perfect democracy. This may be an ideal, but it is not the expression of existing conditions. That the people ought to be sovereign is a tenable view. But to assert that they are so as a matter of fact, and that any state in which they are not so regarded, is not truly a state, is to be guilty of a gross confusion of ideas. Milton's view that " to say the king is accountable to none but God is

---

[1] *Discourses Concerning Government*, Chap. III. *Tenure of Kings and Magistrates*, 14.

the overturning of all law and all government[1]" would
logically lead to the denial of law and government
in the Roman Empire or the French kingdom. The
confusion of Sidney's thought is yet more startling.
After propounding the theory of popular sovereignty
he goes on to assert, quite in the Austinian manner,
that the power of the lawgiver is arbitrary. He
then proceeds to argue that this power is in England
vested in the Parliament[2]. The inconsistency is
glaring. The people is sovereign; yet a small
number of them assembled in Parliament have the
'arbitrary,' i.e. sovereign power of making laws.
Even, if Parliament be held, which it cannot be save
in a loose sense, to govern in the name of the
electors, and if sovereignty be ascribed to them, yet
the electorate was very far from being identical with
the people when Sidney wrote. A still greater inconsistency is to be found in the *Discourses Concerning
Government*. Although admitting the power of the
lawgiver to be arbitrary, Sidney is yet bold enough
to declare that unjust laws are not laws at all[3].

*Theory of
compact.*

Even the theory of the original compact affords
evidence that the popular party had not clearly
grasped the notion of law and sovereignty. Austin
shews how untenable is the notion, that a compact

---

[1] *Tenure of Kings and Magistrates*, 12.

[2] *Discourses Concerning Government*, III. §§ 21, 45, 46. Sidney
regards Filmer's exposition of sovereignty as proving nothing but
"the incurable perverseness of his judgment, the nature of his heart
and the malignity of his fate always to oppose reason and truth."

[3] *Ibid*, 11. Harrington shews similar confusion on the subject
of law and sovereignty (*Oceana*, Preliminaries, Part I.). He approves of a "mixed monarchy," denies that there can be pure aristocracy or pure democracy, and yet would apparently make the people
sovereign, and regards the theories of *the Leviathan* as ridiculous.

can be binding with no sovereign to enforce it. The
widespread prevalence of the theory may therefore
be taken as evidence, that the men who held it
believed in law as resting mainly on moral sanctions,
as independent of physical force and possessed of
Divine authority. The theory that government and
obedience result from a binding compact could only
be credited by men, who instinctively regarded law
as anterior to the State.

V.

From all this it appears that all parties in the *All parties*
seventeenth century are at bottom united in their *unite to*
respect
respect for law and in anxiety to defend government; *law, but*
differ as
although they differ as to the nature of both. Law *to nature*
must be supreme, anarchy at all costs must be pre- *of law*
and sover-
vented. This is the dominant thought of influential *eignty.*
writers on all sides. Yet one party in their reverence
for law would seek to invest it with a quasi-
sovereign authority, and would deny to present and
future generations the power of substantially changing
it. For it is law, as a product of custom and ancient
statutes hardly distinguished from custom, that is
reverenced by the Whigs. The other party had
deeper insight. They saw that in no civilised state
can law exist without a lawgiver, and they deduced
the necessity of a true sovereign. Both sides agree
in inculcating non-resistance to the power which is
regarded as the ultimate authority, whether law or
law-giver. Doubtless the supporters of the monarchy
made mistakes. They pushed to extremes their doctrine of the theoretical omnipotence of the sovereign

power, and seem at times indisposed to recognise the importance of practical limitations on the exercise of sovereignty. Of what have been called "internal limits" on the sovereign power, restrictions imposed by temperament and environment, they admit the wisdom. But their theory of non-resistance forbids them to allow of any external limits. Yet it remains true that the royalist party had in general far clearer notions on law and government in a modern state, than had their opponents, who are often incapable of distinguishing between natural and positive law and are ever haunted by the vain illusion of placing legal limits on the sovereign power.

Funda-
mental
Law.

Once the fact is grasped that the Divine Right of Kings in its philosophical aspect is merely the form given by circumstances to a doctrine of sovereignty, many of its most characteristic notions will present themselves in a fresh light. The phrase "fundamental law" of which so much is heard, signifies what a modern philosopher has classed among "the fundamental conceptions of politics[1]," and indicates merely belief that, if the State be truly such, there must be a sovereign and subjects. Hickes' division of laws into laws positive and laws imperial is another way of expressing the same notion; laws imperial merely mean those facts which are inherent in the nature of the State, and which must exist before laws properly so called arise.

[1] Sidgwick, *Elements of Politics*, Chap. II. It need hardly be said that in the view of all orthodox supporters of Divine Right, the statutes of the Tudor period altering the succession are one and all *ultra vires* and void.

The view that hereditary right is indefeasible *Indefeasi-* is another element in this conception. Or rather it *ble here-* is the form given to that notion of the inalienable *ditary* character of sovereignty, which (however insignificant *right.* practically) is yet sure to arise with the conception of sovereignty. It is doubtless a limitation on the sovereignty to deny the power of the sovereign to alter the form of government. Yet it would be hard to find a better sanction for many branches of so-called constitutional law at the present day, than that the courts will enforce them. So with indefeasible hereditary right; so long as the view could be maintained that the courts would enforce the doctrine, it was not unnaturally regarded as a part of constitutional law.

The doctrine that the rights of Parliament are *Power of* derived from the Crown only as matters of grace *Parlia-* and favour, was characteristic of the mind of *to royal* King James, and became the ground of controversy *grant* both in his own case and that of Dr Cowell. It *recalled.* afterwards became the accepted principle with the royalist writers. The doctrine is really an expression of the sense that sovereignty is indivisible as well as inalienable. So it is used by Bodin[1], who has an elaborate proof that the so-called power of the estates of the realm being merely grants from the sovereign does not imply any diminution or division of his power. He seeks to shew that in the case of England the assent of Parliament to new laws is not really indispensable. It is a maxim, that the donor of a right or privilege may reclaim it at any moment, because sovereignty being indivisible and

[1] *De La République,* 189.

inalienable no sovereign right can be irrevocably resigned. Thus it seemed natural to assert, that because King John granted Magna Charta, all the powers resigned by him still inhere in the King and may be recalled. The repeated historical proof that the Crown was at one time seised of such and such rights and that it still possesses them in theory is evidence of the hold upon men's minds of the notions of the indivisible and inalienable character of sovereignty. They cannot conceive that the King can really have lost any prerogative which can be clearly shewn to have once belonged to him[1].

In the theory of the divine authority of government all sides are agreed. In some form most men hold that non-resistance is a religious duty. It is the theory of sovereignty which differentiates the royalist writers from the popular side and unites them with Hobbes. For the *Leviathan* contains not only a theory of sovereignty, but also a demonstration that monarchy is the best form of government, that the English state is in fact a monarchy, and that resistance to the sovereign is never justifiable. Thus then the affinity between the theories of Divine Right and that of Hobbes' was far closer than is often supposed.

VI.

Hobbes and the clergy.

But how are we to explain the intense abhorrence with which Hobbes was regarded by the believers in Divine Right? Many causes of this dislike may be found. His philosophy, his

[1] *Majestas Intemerata* is a striking instance of this feeling. The author cannot conceive that the King has lost any rights which ever belonged to him.

alleged heterodoxy, his hatred of the Universities, his contempt for Aristotle (of whom Filmer has so great an admiration), his unrelieved Erastianism, his scorn of merely passive obedience, would all tend to deepen the dislike. But the head and front of his offending is different.

In the first place his system of politics is purely utilitarian. It contains far less of the religious sanction, which men of that day demanded for all governments, than do the writings of the opponents of non-resistance. His point of view is eminently modern; and his thought therefore for that very reason tends to be out of relation to that of the time in which he lived. It has been shewn above that in many ways his connection with his contemporary theories of politics is far closer, than was once thought. Yet at bottom his system is divided from all others of his time by a far deeper gulf than that by which they were separated from one another. Alone among the men of his time Hobbes realised, that politics are not and cannot be a branch of theology. The fact that he passed to the other extreme, and committed the error of treating theology, as though it were a branch of politics was unlikely to render him a more acceptable figure[1]

[1] To Hobbes religion was nothing but a "law of the kingdom" enforced for the sake not of truth but of peace, about which there must be no controversy. The duty of the clergy is solely to preach obedience. The Anglican divines could not be expected to view with favour a man who wrote in this style. "We may justly pronounce for the authors therefore of all this spiritual darkness in religion the Pope and Roman clergy, and all those besides who endeavour to settle in the minds of men *this erroneous doctrine,*

in the eyes of those who sought their theory of obedience in S. Paul and found the justification of monarchy in the vision of Nebuchadnezzar.

Theory of original compact denies, believers in Divine Right assert, the organic character of the state.

Yet there is a still greater cause of divergence between Hobbes and the other royalist writers. His theory of government was based upon the original compact. This notion was, however ridiculous, the one clear conception of the opponents of Divine Right and lay at the root of such consistency of theory as they possessed. There is indeed on the Whig side some more or less hesitating recognition of the principle of utility, notably in the case of

---

that the Church now on earth is that kingdom of God mentioned in the Old and New Testament" (*Leviathan*, 383). Now the belief of all contemporary theorists of whatever party was the exact converse of this; they looked to Scripture for a complete theory of politics. The dominant thought of Bellarmine and Suares is that Christ must have appointed for the Christian Church the most perfect form of government; and that political theory may safely be founded thereon. The very first paragraph of the *De Romano Pontifice* is to this effect; Suarez takes the same ground as a proof of the excellence of monarchy, (*De Legibus*, III. 4). Mariana is willing to use the tenable opinion of the council being superior to the Pope in order to prove the subjection of the King to the community; although he guards himself against the retort from the opposite and more common view of Papal autocracy by asserting that the Pope's power comes direct from God while that of the King comes from the people (*Del Rey*, I. 8). Similarly it has been shewn that for most Anglican divines politics are founded upon theology; e.g. Sacheverell's sermons, especially "The Political Union," which is far abler than the better known production, are a striking instance of the belief. "It is impossible for it [government] to subsist upon any other bottom than that of religion." Hobbes would have transposed religion and government; that he arrived at the same conclusion as other royalists is as nothing to the fundamental difference of principle.

Locke, and this connects them with the thought of the future and with the speculations of Bentham and Mill. Yet the basis on which rest all the theories of popular rights in the seventeenth century is not utility but the original compact. It is against the original compact that the supporters of Divine Right inveigh most strongly. For it is the expression of a diametrically opposite standpoint to that of the royalists. Amidst whatever mass of sophistry and error, the conception of the organic character of the State dominated the believers in Divine Right. The theory of compact, whether held by Whigs or Hobbists, is the denial of this. To them the state is an artificial creation. To Filmer or Hickes or Leslie it is a natural growth. In Locke or Sidney or Milton the original compact limits all forms of governments and reduces the state to a mechanical instrument that may with ease be destroyed and manufactured afresh. In the view of Hobbes the machine of state, when created, is indeed to last for all time, but it has no quality of life, no principle of internal development. According to the Whig view the sovereign people may repeatedly upset the constitution of the state, and might, if they were better men, do without one at all. The state in fact is a necessary evil. The popular theories of the seventeenth century are a survival of the notion proclaimed in its nakedness by Hildebrand, but hinted at by Aquinas, and more or less dominant in all the Papalist writers, that the state is a consequence of the fall existing for the hardness of men's hearts. Far different from this is the con-

ception of the supporters of Divine Right. Political
society is natural to man; government and therefore
obedience are necessities of human nature. The
uncritical appeals to the Scripture, to the patriarchal
theory, to past history are all governed by this one
luminous thought, that the state is no mere artificial
manufacture, but a natural organism, and that a
wise handling of its problems can arise only from
the recognition that it has distinct laws of development, which may not be transgressed by tinkering
it, as a machine. The logical issue of the popular
theory is to treat the state as a lifeless creation of
the popular will with no power of development and
with no source of strength in sentiment or tradition.
No theory of government was ever more untrue to
the facts of life than is that of Locke, and the
difference between him and Filmer in this respect
is all in favour of the latter. In Filmer's theory
there is indeed a touch of unreality which is not found
in many of the less famous supporters of Divine
Right. But there can be no doubt that the method
of believers in Divine Right was far less unhistorical
than that of their opponents. The contrast is expounded with striking force of satire and reasoning
in the numerous writings of Leslie. Even Filmer's
theory is based upon the notion that what has
always existed must be natural to man and of
Divine authority and is therefore immutable.

Further, it is worthy of remark, that the supporters of Divine Right differed from their opponents
in being the nearer to the truth. For both sides
agreed in teaching invariable non-resistance to the

ultimate authority and are therefore in error according to the modern views. Neither side admitted the Divine Right of insurrection, as it is very generally held now. Both sides used uncritical methods and misinterpreted Scripture or evaded its meaning. Nor did the supporters of the Divine Right, or at least the majority of them, contend that monarchy is the only lawful form of government and that all republican states ought to set about changing their constitution. Neither side possessed a utilitarian theory of politics. It is possible that on the popular side an individual here and there might be found who taught a theory of utilitarian obedience; while on the side of the King some men might be found who denied God's protection to any government save a monarchy. But in the main this was not the case. Against those who fail to perceive the true nature of law and sovereignty the royalist writers point out with truth the necessity in every state for some supreme authority above the laws. Against those who assert that the state is the artificial creation of an impossible contract they proclaim the profound truth that government is natural and necessary to mankind. The Divine Right of Kings is the expression of the supreme truth of political thought, Φύσει ἄνθρωπος ζῷον πολιτικόν. We pride ourselves on at last realising the truth that the state is organic, or hail with enthusiasm the attempt of Austin and other modern writers on jurisprudence to clear our notions of law and government. We have then little right to charge with triviality those who announced the

same truths in opposition to theories of law that
had ceased to represent facts and to a system of
politics only less unreal and absurd than that of
Rousseau. It is true these notions found forms of
expression that had relation to an order of things
Burke.   that has long since passed away. But if as against
Rousseau prating of the rights of man, of natural
equality, of popular sovereignty, we still pay reverent
gratitude for the polemic in which Burke proclaimed
the historical character of constitutional life, the
organic growth of the state and the value of sentiment and "prejudice," what right have we to blame
Filmer or Leslie, who insist against Locke with equal
truth that all men, so far from being born free and
equal, are born slaves, that government has its roots
deep in the past and that the state has a life which
may not lightly be touched ?

Divine   Lastly, the theory of the Divine Right of Kings
Right
shews a   was the form in which was expressed the sense
belief in   of the need of some bond of moral sentiment and
the moral
basis of   conscience other than the belief in its utility to
the state.   attach men to any government. Burke felt the
same need and expressed it in tones which yet ring
in men's ears. He knew that the influences of
sentiment and tradition are stronger than the cal-
culations of interest to bind a people's allegiance to
its government, and that no constitution can be
stable which makes a merely utilitarian appeal on
men's assistance. He was not ashamed to say that
the dead weight of custom, "prejudice," was the
weapon which all states should have in their hand.
For he felt that an emotional tie must add strength

to the civic reason in order to make it an enduring
support. Now the theory of Divine Right was the
expression of the same truth in forms suited to the
seventeenth century. It may be that our debt of
gratitude to the men of that age is no less great
than that which all are willing to acknowledge to
the great thinker of the last century. Nor should
we be chary of giving their due to the protagonists
in a struggle of which we are enjoying the fruits
merely because their fundamental principles won
ultimate triumph only through the defeat of the practical maxims deduced from them, or because their
methods of argument lack the persuasive charm and
their style is without the majestic flow which have
given to Edmund Burke his unfading laurels.

"It is most true that all available authority is
Mystic in its conditions" says Carlyle[1]. Into the
true nature of the bonds, which unite men in government and subjection Filmer and Leslie and Sacheverell perhaps had a deeper insight than the modern
journalist or member of Parliament. In some form
or other "loyalty to persons springs immortal in the
human breast[2]," and must always survive as the basis
of society, and obedience for conscience sake remain
the chief support of government[3]. The Divine Right
of Kings is but the expression of truths concerning
society and the state of deeper and more universal significance than the trivial banalities of modern politics.

[1] *French Revolution*, II. 2.

[2] Cardinal Newman, *Letter to the Duke of Norfolk* (80).

[3] "There can be no firmness without law; and no laws can be
binding if there be no conscience to obey them; penalty alone could,
can never, do it." Laud, *Sermon* IV. (*Works*, I. 112).

CHAPTER X.

CONCLUSION.

True meaning of Divine Right. IT will have appeared from the foregoing investigation that the theory of the Divine Right of Kings was something different in import and value from the collection of purely ridiculous propositions perversely preached by a servile church, which some have elected to represent it. It was able to gain currency by appealing to some of the deepest instincts of human nature. It gathered up into itself notions of the sanctity of the medicine man, of the priestly character of primitive royalty[1], of the divinity of the Roman Emperors and perhaps of the sacredness of the tribunician power. Yet the doctrine of Divine Right owes much to the common sentiment of Christians as to obedience; and it

---

[1] That this feeling had not died out in the seventeenth century is proved by the following words put into the mouth of Charles; *On their denying his majesty his chaplains:* "It may be, I am esteemed by my deniers sufficient of myself to discharge my duty to God as a priest; though not to men as a prince. Indeed I think both offices, regal and sacerdotal, might well become the same person, as anciently they were under one name, and the united rights of primogeniture." *Eikon Basilike.* This feeling is quite common at the time.

found its most effective material in the practice and teaching of the Christian Church in early ages. The sentiment of obedience to government, as of divine authority, subsisted as a vague notion until the attempt of the Papacy to make use of the notion in its own interests, led men to examine the value of current maxims on the subject and to assert the independent authority of secular governments, in a theory which is in its essential meaning a doctrine of liberty—the freedom of political societies from subjection to an ecclesiastical organization.

It is as an anti-clerical weapon of independence *An anti-clerical theory.* that the theory had its greatest value and fulfilled its most noteworthy function. In opposition to the claims of the Pope to sovereignty by Divine Right, men must formulate the claims of the King to sovereignty by a right that is not inferior. Thus the doctrine is anti-clerical. Yet since it was directed against a theory of clericalism, it was inevitably formed or supported in the main by divines. And the form of the theory was necessary to its success. It would have failed in its object, had it attempted to give to Parliament rather than to the King the sovereignty which it denied to the Pope. Against the traditional splendours of the tiara it would have been vain to set up any lower dignity than the Crown. Indeed no such aim could have been conceived in imagination. It would have been an anachronism. The one country, in which the resistance to the Papal yoke was of purely popular origin, threw off allegiance to the Papacy only to fall under the dominion of a power equally ecclesiastical in its aims and more galling in its incidence. In the sixteenth century it was well if a King had the strength to cast off the Papal yoke, without rivetting another clerical authority on the state. Certainly none but a King had the power.

The theory forms the necessary transition between mediaeval and modern politics.

Again, we see that the theory was necessary as a transition stage between mediaeval and modern politics. It is a far cry from the conception expressed in the Holy Roman Empire, that theology is the source of political theory, and that the State is an aspect of the Kingdom of Christ, to the modern view that politics and theology have little or no relation to one another. Politics are frankly secular nowadays. Even where religion is invoked as a sentiment, theology is not expected to solve the problems of statesmanship. Political theory has ceased to be anything but utilitarian, although it may be a question how far this change is an improvement and whether it is likely to be lasting. At any rate in some form or other utilitarianism governs political thought at the present day. But for this to be the case, a long course of development and conflict has been needful. Before political life can free itself from what may be called the theocratic stage, it must assert for itself a coequal right to exist with theology. It must claim that politics have a proper and necessary function to perform in the development of the human race, and that therefore their independent existence must be as much a part of the Divine plan for mankind, as is the science of theology or the organization of the Church. That the State is the realization of a true idea, and has a necessary place in the world, is the claim, which was explicitly or implicitly denied by the Papalist, and only made good through the theory of Divine Right. For it is only when the claim is put forward by Divine Right, that it can have any practical efficacy against a sovereign claiming as God's vicegerent the overlordship of all kings and princes. That secular politics are as truly God's ordinance and that political organizations have as much claim to exist with His approval as the controversies of Churchmen and the rules of the Canon Law, is the least that can be demanded by all supporters of Divine Right.

In the middle ages all departments of thought *The theory* were conceived as subordinate to theology in such a *an element* way that the methods of theology fettered and *in the Re-* strangled free development in science or art or *formation.* literature. The Reformation is the assertion of the claims of the human spirit to carry on independent work in all branches of inquiry and activity, under the consciousness that truth cannot contradict itself and that the results of every sort of labour carried on with appropriate means and for worthy objects will tend to unity at the last.

Now in politics the rise and prevalence of the theory of the Divine Right is merely the same phenomenon. Theology had attempted unreasonably to dominate politics, and had committed men to an unphilosophical basis and an uncritical method.

The only way to escape from the fetters imposed *Its form* by traditional methods, was to assert from the old *necessary.* standpoint of a Scriptural basis and to argue by the accustomed fashion of Biblical quotations, that politics must be freed from theology and that the Church must give up all attempts to control the State. The work of the Reformation was to set men free in all departments of thought and inquiry from subjection to a single method and a single subject. In the case of politics the achievement of this result was only possible through claiming at first theological sanction for the non-theological view of politics. Only when the result is achieved will politics be free to develope theories which shall be purely philosophical or historical. Not till then will it cease to be needful to find Scriptural authority for political theory, or Biblical counterparts to the ideals of government. Politics were only able to enter upon their modern stage, because the theory of Divine Right having done its work had emancipated them from mediæval fetters and had in so doing become obsolete itself.

Political value of the theory.

Obedience to law.

Again, it has appeared that the anarchy of the middle ages developed in men's minds a sense of the need of law and of the duty of obedience. Further, the Reformation and other causes have contributed to develope so highly the legislative activity of the State, and the checks imposed upon its action by custom or the Pope or feudalism have been so generally removed, that a theory of sovereignty has become the natural expression of facts, and the sense will arise, that law has its authority as being a command of the sovereign. The perception or the denial of these facts has been shewn to be the main point of political controversy between the believers in royal and in popular rights.

The other chief source of difference is that be- *The state an organism.* tween an artificial and a historical conception of the State. The believers in Divine Right teach that the State is a living organism and has a characteristic habit of growth, which must be investigated and observed. Their opponents believe the State to be a mechanical contrivance, which may be taken to pieces and manufactured afresh by every Abbé Siéyès who arises.

Moreover, it has appeared that the doctrine of *The theory fulfilled its object.* Divine Right effected its object. •The political claims of the Papacy have disappeared. Whether or no Rome has technically receded from her pretensions, the temporal supremacy is not now an object for which the most ultramontane Romanist will contend. The claims still put forward by the Vatican to the temporal power in no way involve a claim to political supremacy over all princes. The doctrines of the deposing power and the *plenitudo potestatis* have vanished rather than been disproved. It would not be within the dreams of a modern Papalist to assert them, nor would there be the smallest likelihood of any Roman Catholic nation admitting them, if they were asserted. • The claim to infallibility has been long since explained as in no way involving a weakening of civil allegiance[1].

---

[1] See Cardinal Newman's *Letter to the Duke of Norfolk*; also *Life of Cardinal Manning*, I. 399.

Perhaps the Pope's complaint, that Brandenburg was erected into a kingdom without his consent is the last instance of any attempt to assert the temporal supremacy, unless the coronation of Napoleon be regarded in that light. (Lamberty, *Mémoires*, I. 383).

Further, practical influences, among which the Union with Scotland is probably not the least important, have contributed to reduce to a minimum the claims of the other ecclesiastical body, which disputed with the Roman Church for the palm of imposing upon the State the more stifling touch. The omnipotence of civil governments all the world over is a fact no longer disputed—with one limitation. From the claim by Divine Right put forward by the Church to a freedom which meant supremacy, has grown the doctrine of toleration, by which alone, as a practical limit upon state action, religious freedom can be secured without clerical supremacy.

The theory necessary to the Reformation. That the Divine Right of Kings was not merely useful but necessary to the political side of the Reformation appears to be clearly proved by the evidence. Confirmation of this is afforded by the fact that the theoretical presentment of antagonism to the Papal claims had taken in earlier ages a form which differed but little from the theories of the sixteenth and seventeenth centuries. With the Restoration the last chance of Presbyterianism becoming dominant in England disappeared. The Revolution finally removed all danger from the side of Rome. Only then did the theory of the Divine Right of Kings cease to be useful. As a matter of fact, from a doctrine with a practical aim it begins at this time to pass into a romantic belief enshrining a sentimental regret for the past, and has perhaps a value in literature which it has lost in theology and politics. Perhaps we may see in Burke the survival in substance and transformation

in form of the fundamental principle which gave to
the theory of Divine Right its political value. The
raison d'être for the rival theories was removed by
the statutes of Toleration and Catholic Relief.
On the other hand as soon as the notion of the
original compact has done its work in England
by giving men what they regard as an intellectual
justification for the Revolution, it too begins to
disappear and to give place to the purely utilitarian
theory of politics, which became dominant through
the influence of Bentham.

The theory of Divine Right did not lose its *The belief*
popularity because it was absurd, but because its *died, when*
work was done. There were just as good reasons for *longer*
disbelieving in its validity in 1598 or 1660 as there *useful.*
were at the Revolution. Certainly some writers were
well acquainted with them even at the earlier date,
as is proved by such a treatise as that of Parsons.
The Divine Right of Kings ceased to have practical
importance, not because its doctrines were untrue, *Causality*
but because its teaching had become unnecessary.
The transition stage had passed. The independence
of the State had been attained. Politics having
made good their claim to be a part of the natural
order had no longer need of a theological justification.

Again, if the theory be regarded on its purely *Doctrine*
political side, the conceptions which it enshrined *has*
are become part of our common heritage. To the *moulded*
sense of the organic character of the State and of the *English*
duty of obedience are due the existence of "law- *sentiment.*
abiding citizens" to-day and that dislike of all violent

breaks with the past, which has ever been the peculiar glory of England,

> "Where freedom slowly broadens down
> From precedent to precedent."

It was due to this doctrine that the English Revolution was the most peaceful in history and that English institutions have been developed with scarcely a breach in continuity. To modern ears the "abdication" of James II. must ever seem a fiction only the more dishonest that it was transparent. Yet the phrase was a pledge, that the old laws and customs of the realm should remain, and that no cataclysms should disturb the orderly development of the national life. The phrase was false, but the sentiment it expressed was profoundly true.

Its effect on politics beneficial. Nor again has the doctrine of non-resistance been anything but salutary in its results. It has indeed been superseded by a theory of utilitarian obedience, which, although it may be true, is likely to be fraught with greater dangers than could have attended the firmest faith in passive obedience. It is easy for modern politicians to regard the inculcation of invariable non-resistance as mere nonsense. Yet most sober thinkers would admit that only in the extremest cases can resistance be justified. It may be that obedience is owed to the law on account of its utility, but no one will make every disutility in the law a ground for disobedience. It is not doubtful that a sense of the duty of obedience must be widespread if stability is to be secured for the State. We are willing enough to admit that "force is no remedy," and that in general a certain senti-

ment of loyalty is needful to the well-being and
security of all governments. On what grounds then
can we blame those who found expression for identi-
cally the same views in the maxim that men must
obey not only for wrath, but for conscience' sake ? A
modern thinker has declared that laws and governments need some other sanction than that of military
force. Those who endorse the aphorism "You can
do anything with bayonets except sit on them" can
have little reason for blaming Laud when he declares
"There can be no firmness without law; and no laws
can be binding if there be no conscience to obey
them; penalty alone could never, can never do it[1]."
That government can worthily perform its function
only when obedience is enshrined in the hearts of the
governed, that laws are vain without loyalty, was the
truth for which the men of the seventeenth century
were contending, when they asserted that all resistance was damnable. That government of any kind
was better than anarchy, they were well assured.
Tyranny was in their eyes a more supportable condition than disorder. Despite modern sentiment-
alism to the contrary, this doctrine has never been
disproved. But whether or no it can be maintained
that no caprices of autocracy and no oppression of
democracy can make resistance to a King a right or
defiance of Parliament (or the County Council) a
duty, all will agree that the widespread prevalence
of a law-abiding sentiment is essential to the stability
of the State. It is well that most men should re-

---

[1] Laud, *Sermons* (*Works*, I. 112).

gard resistance to laws, however unjust, as practically prohibited by the moral law. If there be "cases of resistance," they are best ignored.

Dangers of utilitarian theory. Now it is hard to imagine a more effectual method of propagating this view than is the theory of Divine Right. Nor is it at all clear that the widespread popular acceptance of a purely utilitarian basis for obedience may not lead to great dangers in the future. Englishmen have cause for gratulation, that, in a time when the tendency is to loosen the bonds of allegiance and to proclaim (generally out of season) the morality of insurrection, there should still exist in the minds of the great majority of their countrymen a deep sense of the majesty of law and of the duty of obedience. This sense is the priceless legacy bequeathed to our own day by the believers in the Divine Right of Kings.

Errors of believers in Divine Right. It is not contended here that grave errors were not made by these men, that the doctrine of indefeasible hereditary right was ever rational, or that it is now useful. Doubtless extravagant estimates were made of royal prerogative and Parliamentary impotence. Only it is claimed that the main tendency of the doctrine was beneficial and that it was effective. The fault of the royalist writers arose from the attempt to render absolute and universal a theory which was merely relative to particular conditions. They were blind to the fact that kingship, although it had as good a claim to Divine institution as any other form of government, could not without absurdity be made universal. Many of them were unable to perceive that monarchy is only a form of government. Impelled by the need of refuting a theory, which claimed to be founded upon eternal principles, they too strove to find fixed and immutable principles of politics, which circumstances might not affect, nor should they be touched by the hand of time.

Their opponents committed the very same error. Dropping the name of Divine Right, they yet preserved in the theory of natural rights the same pretensions to have found a fixed and eternal principle of politics—inalienable freedom and God-given equality. From Locke the notion passed to Rousseau, and is still wide-spread. Yet surely the main practical lesson of the history of this doctrine is that of the relativity of all political dogma. Theories of politics *Abstract* are the product of historical causes and national idio- *politics are im-* syncrasies. They change with changing conditions. *possible.* If pushed to extremes and treated as truths for all time, they will not therefore be permanent, but will give place when their usefulness is gone to fresh doctrines suited to new conditions. The fact that in the past universal validity has been claimed for theories since discarded is the cause for their former services to mankind to be forgotten; for only their transparent absurdity wins for them a lingering memory. Men tried and failed to transform a temporary instrument in a particular struggle into an eternal truth. Nowadays those who see that neither abstract truth nor enduring potency can rightly be claimed for the theory of the Divine Right of Kings, have forgotten that the doctrine was once a force, and treat a faith which has ceased to be credible as though it were never creditable. Politics are relative, and when men formulate ideal systems based upon eternal principles and laying claim to universal authority, they are apt to come to grief. At least we can learn this much from the theory of the Divine Right of Kings.

Error of seeking theories of the State in the Bible. One other practical conclusion may be drawn. The thinkers of the seventeenth century sought to base their politics upon theology, and to use the Bible as though it were a treatise on law and government. There was much to be said in excuse; and their error was probably inevitable. But they were in error, and their attempt was a failure, which has been the pretext for pouring on them obloquy and ridicule far beyond their deserts. Is there any ground for auguring better success for the attempt only now being made to seek the true system of social organization in the New Testament and to base upon the Sermon on the Mount a new order of things, in which the capitalist will for ever have given place to the Trades' Union?

APPENDIX A.

EXTRACTS FROM STATUTES RELATING TO THE
SUCCESSION.

THE progress of the idea of inherent right and the
complete decay of the doctrine of election may be
illustrated from the statutes passed between 1483 and
1603, which attempt to settle or declare the succession.

(1) In the *titulus regius*, which gave the Crown
to Richard III., we see the two notions of elective
kingship and title by inheritance blended together. It
is noteworthy that the statute seems to regard Parliament in the light of a supreme court competent to
declare the law without appeal, rather than as a
legislative body creating new law. Parliament claims
no right to alter the succession, but merely to declare it,
so as to remove perplexity.

"We consider that ye be the undoubted son and
heir of Richard, late Duke of York, very inheritor of
the said crown and dignity royal, and as in right King
of England by way of inheritance;...and by this our
writing choose you High and Mighty Prince, our King
and Sovereign Lord. *To whom we know it appertain-
eth of inheritance so to be chosen.......* We pray and
require your most noble grace that according to this

election of us the three estates of this land ; as by your
true inheritance you will accept and take upon you the
said Crown and royal dignity with all things thereunto
annexed and appertaining as to you of right belonging as well by inheritance, as by lawful election.......
Albeit that the right title and estate which our
Sovereign Lord the King Richard the Third hath to
and in the Crown...of England...been just and lawful
as grounded upon the laws of God and of nature ; and
also upon the ancient laws and customs of this said
realm and so taken and reputed by all such persons as
been learned in the above said laws and customs ; yet
nevertheless for as much as it is considered, that the
most part of the people is not sufficiently learned in the
above said laws and customs, whereby the truth and
right in this behalf, of likelihood may be hid and not
clearly known to all the people, and thereupon put in
doubt and question.   And over this, how that the court
of Parliament is of such authority and the people of
this land of such a nature and disposition, as experience
teacheth, that manifestation and declaration of any truth
or right made by the three estates of the realm assembled
in Parliament, and by the authority of the same maketh
before all other things most faith and certain, and
quieting of men's minds removeth the occasion of all
doubts and seditious language, therefore &c."—(Speed's
History, 724.)

(2).   The statute granting the Crown to Henry VII.
is far different in its businesslike brevity of tone.   In
this the authority of Parliament to do what it wills
with the succession is unmistakeably implied.

"Be it ordained established and enacted by authority
of this present Parliament that the inheritance of the
Crowns of the Realms of England and France with

all the preeminence and dignity royal to the same
appertaining...be, rest, remain, and abide in the most
royal person of our now Sovereign Lord, King Henry
the Seventh and the heirs of his body...and in none
other."—(*Statutes of the Realm*, II. 499).

(3). The statute declaring Elizabeth queen, although
it admits her title by descent, and is fulsome in tone,
yet has no scruple about regarding an Act of Parliament
as the true title to the Crown.   The second clause
ratifies Henry's testamentary disposition and thus
traverses the doctrine of hereditary succession.

"Your highness is rightly, lineally and lawfully
descended and come out of the blood royal of this
Realm of England in and to......whose princely person
......the imperial and royal estate, place, crown, and
dignity are and shall be most fully...invested and incor-
porated,......as the same were since the Act of Parliament
made in the thirty-fifth year of King Henry the Eighth.
......For which causes......we beseech that it may be
enacted that.   As well this our declaration...as also the
limitation and declaration of the succession contained
in the said Act (35 Hen. VIII. c. 1) shall stand the
law of this realm for ever."—(*Statutes of the Realm*,
IV. 358; Prothero's *Statutes*, 21.)

(4). Lastly, the statute recognising the title of
James I. is saturated with the notion of inherent
birthright, and knows of no other title.   The act
carefully guards against granting the succession, but
claims merely to declare it.

"A most joyful and just recognition of the immediate,
lawful, and undoubted succession of Descent and Right
of the Crown.

"We (being bounden thereunto both by the laws of
God and man) do recognize and acknowledge (and

thereby express our unspeakable joys), that immediately
upon the dissolution and decease of Elizabeth...the
imperial crown of the realm of England...did, by
inherent birthright and lawful and undoubted succession descend and come to your most excellent majesty,
as being lineally, justly, and lawfully next and sole
heir of the blood royal of this realm as is aforesaid."—
(*Statutes of the Realm*, IV. 107; Prothero's *Statutes*, 251.)

APPENDIX B.

THE foregoing essay deals merely incidentally with
theories of popular rights. Yet it is interesting to
trace the germs of the theory in the conciliar movement
of the fifteenth century. It is plain, that the position
of those who were contending for the supremacy of the
councils and asserting their right to judge and, if need
be, to depose the Pope, was closely analogous to that of
all who argued for some authority in the community
at large which could restrain and depose the King.
Williams, Bishop of Ossory, declares in his treatise *Jura
Magistratus* (118) that the doctrine of the sovereignty
of the people came originally from the Sorbonnists,
"who to subject the Pope to the community of the
faithful say that the chief spiritual power was first
committed by Christ unto them, and they to preserve
the unity of the Church remitted the same communi-
catively to the Pope, but suppletively (not privatively or
habitually divesting themselves thereof) retaining the
same still in themselves if the Pope failed in the faith of
the Church, and therefore he was not only censurable but
also deposable by the Council......and to make this more
plausible and probable they alleged how Kings were
thus eligible and likewise deposable by the community

of the people." Evidence of this is found scattered
through Gerson's writings. He argues in the *De
Potestate Ecclesiastica* that the maxim *quod principi
placuit legis habet vigorem* does not apply to the Pope,
who is the head of the best form of government, the
mixed. *Maneat Ecclesiastica politia optimo regimine;
quale fuit sub Moyse gubernata quoniam mixta fuit
ex triplici politia; regali in Moyse: aristocratica in
72 senioribus; et in timocratica, dum e populo et singulis
tribubus sub Moyse rectores sumebantur* (Goldast, II.
1392). So early do the supporters of popular rights
find it necessary to veil the doctrine of the sovereignty
of the people under the illusory ideal of a mixed form
of government. His argument in favour of the latter
is strange. *Omnis idcirco politia ecclesiastica, sive
dominetur unus, sive pauci sive plures boni, dicitur
proprie divina; quia secundum leges supernaturales
debet quilibet regulationem accipere. Et ita perspicuum
est quod tres istae politiae uniuntur in ecclesia aliter
quam in civili politia, propter divinae legis unitatem*
(*Ibid.* 1403). In these last phrases comes out the sense
of the later supporters of the Papacy against the Divine
Right of Kings. The Papalist was ever arguing that
there was a supernatural character in the constitution
of the Church, which raised it above that of secular
States, and enabled it to control them. Here the argument is connected with the claim to make the Church
anti-monarchical. But the idea is the same: royalists
claim that the rights and prerogatives of the King are
as well founded at least as those of the Pope, and
therefore that the Pope has no jurisdiction over him.
Papalists of whatever shade contend that the distinctive
character of the Church raises its ruler above temporal
princes and constitutions. Here the same is claimed

from a different standpoint. The Church is of course
the most perfect form of government in Gerson's view,
for it unites all the three. *Papalis imitatur regalem.
Collegialis Dominorum Cardinalium imitatur aristo-
craticam. Synodalis generalis imitatur politiam seu
timocratiam. Vel potius est perfecta politia quae re-
sultat ex omnibus* (*Ibid.* 1404). Further we find
utilitarianism in the writer's theory of obedience; he
not only declares *Finis autem Papatus est utilitas
ecclesiae* (*De Statibus Ecclesiasticis*, Goldast, II. 1432),
but also (*De Auferibilitate Papae*, c. XIV) he declares
that obedience may cease as soon as it becomes inconvenient. Unlike the supporters of popular rights,
Gerson seems to allow private acts of violence against
the Pope, although he is the Lord's anointed (*Ibid.*
c. X). He describes civil government as a consequence
of the fall, and argues thence the possibility of changing
it. The constitution of the Church is of course unalterable. *Civile dominium seu politicum est dominium
peccati occasione introductum, non competens pluribus
ex aequo retinibile aut abdicabile, servata vel non servata
charitate, fundatum in legibus civilibus et politica; secundum quas potest abdicari vendendo, donando, negli-
gendo, permutando* (*De Pot. Eccles.* Goldast, II. 1403).

Here, then, is a political theory, the acceptance of
which if the Popes can secure, their supremacy in
the Church may readily be made a weapon against
secular monarchs. For it (1) places civil government
on a purely human, utilitarian and changeable foundation, (2) advocates a mixed form of government
as the most perfect, (3) asserts that resistance is
sometimes justifiable, and that the head of the State
may be deposed. It is not surprising that Barclay
should have met the argument which Boucher culled

from Gerson with the retort that Gerson held *Et concilium supra Papam esse, eumque judicare ac deponere posse, quod itidem falsum esse saniore Catholicorum Doctorum judicio convincitur. Ut mirum non sit eumdem Gersonem pari opinionis errore, Principem populo subjicere voluisse, quo Papam concilio (De Regno,* 512). It is the irony of fate that the conciliar movement, which failed in its object of putting limits on the Papal sovereignty, should have assisted to familiarise men's minds with those notions of popular sovereignty and mixed government, which were to be not the least effective of Papal weapons against the recalcitrant Kings. Not only did the conciliar movement fail, but it nearly resulted in adding to the spiritual supremacy of the Pope a universal political sovereignty.

APPENDIX C.

1. *Popery, as involving a belief in the deposing power, a disloyal doctrine.*

"I will not say (though it has been said) the Romanists' faith is faction and their religion rebellion; but this I must say, that they teach and broach such doctrines as are very scandalous to Christian religion, and very dangerous and destructive to Kingdoms and States; as having a direct and natural tendency to sedition, rebellion, and treason."—Duport, *Sermon on the Fifth of November*, 64.

"I do not, I will not, say All our Romanists are enclined to rebellion; I doubt not but there are many faithful and loyal subjects among 'em; but this I must say, As long as they own a foreign jurisdiction, either spiritual or temporal, which they must do if they are thorough-paced; and as long as the Pope usurps the power to depose and dispose, to depose Kings, and dispose of their Kingdoms, and to absolve subjects from their oaths of supremacy and allegiance; so long the Romish religion must needs have a natural tendency to disloyalty; and therefore, if Papists be good subjects,

18—2

no thanks to their Popery; and I fear, 'twill be hard for 'em to be good Catholics at Rome, and good subjects at home; for if they be so, it must be only *durante bene placito*, as long as the Pope is well-pleas'd, but if once he be angry with Kings and call 'em heretics, then have at 'em fowlers, let 'em look to themselves."—*Ibid.* 68.

"The Reformation of our Church was laid upon the subversion of one of the most fatal and pernicious principles to government, that any religion can maintain, namely the precarious conditions of allegiance to the true and lawful sovereign, upon the falsehood and ruin whereof our constitution both civil and ecclesiastical was founded and established."—Sacheverell, *The Political Union*, 54.

The following passage shews how the whole controversy between the temporal and spiritual authority must be viewed from the standpoint of an age, when the enforcement of uniformity in religious practice was regarded by all parties as the duty of the State.

"No king or prince by their [the Romanists'] doctrine can truly be accounted a freeman or denizen in the State wherein he lives, seeing no king can have so much as a voice or suffrage in making those ecclesiastical canons, unto which he, his people, all his laws temporal and spiritual are subordinate and subject. For no man could think him to be a freeman in any corporation, that has no voice in making the temporal laws by which he is to be governed or at least in choosing such of them as have interest in the making of Public Laws."— Jackson, *Treatise of Christian Obedience* (*Works*, III. 909).

"The Jesuits the principal authors of resistance to all higher powers."—*Ibid.* 971.

"The deposing doctrine and placing the power in the people is but the spittle of the Jesuits which our

Whigs and Dissenters have picked up."—Leslie, *The Wolf stripped of his Shepherd's Clothing*, 4.

"Your mobs are all papists, they are for the deposing power, which is perfect popery."—Leslie, *A Battle Royal*, 174.

Papal supremacy divests the prince of his absolute sovereignty, of his legislative power and renders monarchy insecure of possession or succession, by bereaving it of the guard of the laws, of the strength of alliances, of the fidelity of their people. Papal supremacy destructive of the people's liberty and property.—The Common Interest of King and People, Chap. VII.

"These men cry out against Popery, and yet profess, what all good Protestants esteem the most malignant part of Jesuitism."—Dudley Diggs, *The Unlawfulness of Subjects Taking up Arms*, 64.

2. *Identification of Papists and Dissenters.*

"It is most manifest, that all our late horrid civil wars, rapines, bloodshed and the execrable and solemn murder of His Late Majesty, and the banishment of our present sovereign were effected according to the fore-contrivance of the Papists, by the assistance which the Dissenters gave them and the opportunities they had to preach them into rebellion under the pretence of a thorough Reformation, that all late commotions and rebellions in Scotland sprung from the same counsel and conduct."—*Foxes and Firebrands*, 32.

"Let us now come to take a view of the younger antagonists of monarchy, the popular supremacy of Presbytery, that Lerna Malorum, that revived hydra of the Lake of Geneva, with its many-headed progeny, Anabaptists, Quakers, Levellers &c., all which unnatural offspring are as kind to their dam as vipers, and as inconsistent with monarchy, as they pretend to be with the Papacy (with which Presbytery jostles for universal supremacy) or any of them with Loyalty, Royalty or true religion."—Nalson, *Common Interest of King and People*, 201.

"The Puritans were mere tools to the Jesuits (as they are to this day), from them they learned the deposing doctrine, and to set up the private spirit against the Holy Scriptures, and all the authority of the Church."—Leslie, *The Rehearsal*, No. 84.

"Sure the hand of Joab, the Jesuit with his King-killing doctrine, was in all this, and every one of the regicides had a Pope in his belly, to give him a dispensation, and absolve him from his oath of allegiance."—Duport, *Sermon on Thirtieth of January*, 11.

"Those *fratres in malo*, those red-hot fiery zealots o' both sides; your furious hair-brained fanatic, and your perfidious disloyal Loiolite: I join 'em together, *Bithus cum Bachio*, for I know not which is the worse o' the two; and I think they plough with one another's heifer." *Ibid.* 22.

"Do you think our Roman Catholics, at least the Jesuits, were idle spectators all the while and had not a hand in the 30th of January, as well as in the fifth of November? Is it not well known that the train to entangle us in that horrible snare, and intrigue of the late confusions, was laid by a great Cardinal minister of State, and perhaps the whole conclave?......Is it not yet apparent, that the Popish emissaries and incendiaries were sent hither on purpose under the name of Anabaptists, Seekers, and Quakers, and I know not what to blow the coals and foment the flames of our late dissensions?"—Duport, *Sermon on Fifth of November*, 72.

"Our factious, fanatic, turbulent, and schismatical spirits are but the Jesuits' journeymen."—*Ibid.* 76.

3. *Clericalism of the Presbyterian System.*

"Their [the Presbyterians'] Church government is pernicious to Civil Power, grievous to such as must live under it, and apt to distort the Common Peace." —Leslie, *The Trojan Horse of the Presbyterian Government Unbowelled*, 3.

"They claim power to abrogate the laws of the land touching ecclesiastical matters, if they judge them hurtful or unprofitable.......They require the civil magistrate to be subject to their power."—*Ibid.* 5.

"It may be that the general disaffection to regal power, in these distractions, may render some men less apprehensive of the dangerous consequences of this doctrine, and the former claims; as supposing them to have no other drift than to clip the wings of royal prerogative. But this is a gross and dangerous mistake and whosoever shall be invested with that Civil Power, which shall be taken from the King, be it the Parliament or whosoever else, must look to succeed him in the heavy enmity which this Presbyterian power will exercise against the Civil Power (when it doth not comply with them), in what hands soever it be placed. For these encroachments of theirs are not upon the King as distinguished from other magistrates, but upon the civil magistrate in common whosoever he be."—*Ibid.* 8.

"The King and Parliament must be subject not only to their general assembly, but (in subordination to that) to the dictates of every petty parochial session, where their personal residence and abode shall be. Lastly if the King and Parliament will govern contrary to their will and pleasure, their principles will allow them to incite the people to resist them."—*Ibid.* 8.

"They determine that the temporal magistrate is bound to punish adultery with death by God's own law.......They hold it unlawful for the civil magistrate to pardon capital offenders."—*Ibid.* 9.

" By their platform they may deal with all civil causes for a spiritual end, which the Pope usually expresses with this clause *In ordine ad bonum Spirituale*, and these men by the same effect *in ordine ad bonum ecclesiae.* But both he and they do by this distinction usurp upon the Civil magistrate."—*Ibid.* 10.

"This discipline which they do so much adore is the very quintessence of refined Popery, or a greater Tyranny than ever Rome brought forth, inconsistent with all forms of civil government, destructive to all sorts of policy, a rack to the conscience, the heaviest pressure that can fall upon a people, and so much more dangerous because by the specious pretence of Divine institution, it takes away the right, but not the burden of slavery."—Bramhall, *A Warning to the Church of England,* 2.

That it [*the Discipline*] *exempts the ministers from due punishment.*—*Ibid.* Chap. IV.

The Disciplinarians cheat the magistrate of his civil power, in order to religion.—*Ibid.* Chap. VII.

"They ascribe unto their ministers a liberty and power to direct the magistrate even in the managery of civil affairs."—*Ibid.* 25.

"They assume a power in worldly affairs indirectly and in order to the advancement of the Kingdom of Christ."—*Ibid.* 26.

"The Parliament will restore to the King his negative voice; a mere civil thing. The commissioners of the Church oppose it, because of the great dangers that may thereby come to religion. The Parliament name officers and commanders for the army; a mere civil thing. The Church will not allow them because they want such qualifications, as God's word requires, that is to say in plain terms because they were not their confidents. Was there ever Church challenged such an omnipotence as this? Nothing in this world is so civil or political, wherein they do not interest themselves in order to the advancement of the Kingdom of Christ."— *Ibid.* 27.

"This is the Presbyterian want, to subject all causes and persons to their consistories, to ratify and abolish civil laws, to confirm and pull down Parliaments, to levy forces, to invade other Kingdoms, to do anything respectively to the advancement of the good cause and in order to religion."—*Ibid.* 31.

Chapter VIII.   *That the Disciplinarians challenge this exorbitant power by Divine Right.*

Chapter IX.   *That this discipline makes a monster of the Commonwealth.*

"We have seen how pernicious this discipline (as it is maintained in Scotland and endeavoured to be introduced into England by the Covenant) is to the Supreme Magistrate, how it robs him of his supremacy in ecclesiastical affairs, and of the last appeals of his own subjects, that it exempts the presbyters from the power of the magistrate, and subjects the magistrate to the presbyters, that it restrains his dispensative power of pardoning, deprives him of the dependence of his subjects, that it doth challenge and usurp a power paramount both of the word and of the sword, both of peace and war, over all courts and estates, over all laws civil and ecclesiastical, in order to the advancement of the Kingdom of Christ, whereof the Presbyters alone are constituted rulers by God, and all this by a pretended Divine Right, which takes away all hope of remedy, until it be hissed out of the world; in a word that is the top-branch of Popery, a greater tyranny, than ever Rome was guilty of. It remains to shew how disadvantageous it is also to the subject.

" First, to the Commonwealth in general which it makes a monster, like an amphiscian or a serpent with two heads, one at either end. It makes a coordination of sovereignty in the same society, two supremes in the same Kingdom or State, the one civil, the other ecclesiastical, than which nothing can be more pernicious either to the consciences, or the estates of subjects, when it falls out (as it often doth) that from these two heads issue contrary commands."—*Ibid.* 35.

The striking similarity of this passage to the argument of Ockham against the Papacy is plain.

Chapter X. *That this discipline is most prejudicial to the Parliament.*

Chapter XI. *That this discipline is oppressive to particular persons.*

Nalson, *Common Interest of King and People*, Chap. IX.

Presbytery in reality as great an enemy to Democracy and Parliaments as to monarchy. A short view of their tyrannic consistorian government over the magistracy, clergy and laity. Of the latitude and power of scandal to draw all affairs into the consistory.......The small difference betwixt a Jesuit and Geneva Presbyter. Both aim at supremacy.

"We shall find that it is absolutely inconsistent with all government (except its own oligarchic spiritual tyranny) and even that adored Democracy, which it pretends to hug and embrace with so much tenderness and affection........The real design is to dash a Parliament against a King, to break them both in pieces; and like the ape in the story to make a cat's foot of the House of Commons, to pull the nut out of the hot ashes of rebellion, into which they shall have reduced the monarchy; for when once by that assistance they shall have procured their own establishment, they will render it as absolute a slave, as they would do monarchy."—*Ibid.* 241.

" It is not the persons or names, but the superiority of the authority, against which this faction of Geneva levels all its aims."—*Ibid.*

"These saints who pretend to a power of binding Kings in chains will without scruple so claim the honour of shackling the nobles in fetters of iron."—*Ibid.* 242.

" It is the desire of sovereignty under the colour of religion at which they aim; and to which whatsoever is an obstacle, whether King, Parliament, Prelates, Lords, or Commons, shall all be declared anti-Christian and unlawful powers."—*Ibid.* 244.

" The great assembly and the moderator for the time being is the absolute and supreme sovereign power of the nation, where Presbytery bears the sway."—*Ibid.* 247.

"They [Presbytery and Jesuitry] are both inconsistent with monarchy and indeed with all government; over which they pretend a power and jurisdiction by Christ, the one for the Pope, the other for the Presbytery; from which there lies no appeal."—*Ibid.* 257.

Chapter X. *Presbytery as destructive of the People's liberty and property as it is dangerous to monarchy and all government.*

"No person whatsoever, let him pretend never so much religion, sanctity, or innocence, can possibly be a good subject, so long as he continues a true Presbyterian

or of their offspring; in regard they always carry about
with them as the main of their religion such principles,
as are directly contrary to monarchy and destructive
of loyalty; to which he can never be a firm, true and
assured friend, who owns a power superior to that of
his prince within his dominions; and that such a power
may of right depose him, and take away his crown and
life, which has been proved to be the avowed doctrine of
the consistorians of Geneva, Scotland, and England,
both in point and practice."—270.

"That Presbyterian popular consistorian supremacy,
is, and ever will be, the unchangeable, irreconcilable
enemy of monarchy, law, liberty, peace, property, and
the true Protestant Catholic religion."—279.

"Having thus taken the whole civil government
into their own hands as the Pope has done, and by
virtue of the same distinction in *ordine ad spiritualia*
they followed him likewise in that which is a natural
consequence of the other, to exempt themselves from
being accountable to the civil power even for civil
crimes."—Leslie, *The New Association*, Part II. 33.

4. *The Divine Right of Kings in reality a defence
of all secular governments against ecclesiastical agres-
sion.*

"It shall suffice to note that the Romanist makes
an unequal comparison and sets the terms of his
proposition awry, when he compares spiritual power
indefinitely taken with power royal or monarchical,
which is but a branch though the highest branch of
power civil or temporal. The question should be
betwixt authority spiritual or ecclesiastic indefinitely
taken; and between power civil or temporal alike
indefinitely taken. Power temporal or civil thus taken

is immediately from God, and government temporal
itself in some one kind or other (that is Monarchical,
Aristocratical or mixed or &c.) is *de Jure Divino*, as
well as power spiritual or ecclesiastic is."—Jackson,
Treatise of Christian Obedience. Works, III. 903.

"That this nation should be governed by a King,
another by peers and nobles, another by the people, or
by magistrates of the people's choosing, either annual
or for term of life, this is not determined *Jure Divino*
by any express or positive law of God, but is reserved
unto the guidance of his ordinary Providence, who
sometimes directs one people or nation to make choice
of this form, another to make choice of that. But the
choice of government being made by the people or imposed upon them by right of war, to yield obedience
to the form of government or power established, this is
de Jure Divino positively and peremptorily determined
and enjoined by the law of God. And whosoever
doth resist the form of government established in the
commonweal, whereof he is a member, be it of this
form or that, he doth resist the higher powers; and by
resisting them *resisteth the ordinance of God.*"—*Ibid.*
963.

5. *Inevitable conflict between temporal and spiritual powers, so long as the principle of toleration is
unrecognized.*

"It is indeed impossible that a coordination of these
powers should subsist; for each will be continually
encroaching on the other, each for its own defence and
support will continually be struggling and clambering
to get above the other; there never will be any quiet
till one come to subside and truckle under the other;
whereby the sovereignty of the one or the other will be

destroyed; each of them soon will come to claim a supremacy in all causes and the power of both swords; and one side will carry it....."—Barrow, *Treatise of the Pope's Supremacy*, 144.

The divergence of this view from that of Barclay, the representative of strict Gallicanism, is noteworthy. Barclay strongly emphasizes, that need of two coordinate authorities, which Barrow denies to be possible. "A free Church in a free State" was the ideal of the Gallican writer; the Anglican is aware, that the dream is incapable of realization.

6. *Connection of English politics with French controversies.*

"This pretence of the King's authority against his person was hatched under the Romish territories and made use of in the Holy League of France."—Falkner, *Christian Loyalty*, 356.

7. *The theory of Hobbes regarded as dangerous, notwithstanding his practical conclusions, owing to his basing it upon the original compact.*

"Though Mr Hobbs sometimes hath over-large expressions concerning the power of governors; yet he having before laid the same formation for the original of political government, doth also undermine the safety and stability of governors and government....... But as these positions are framed upon such suppositions, as look upon man in his beginning, to stand without due respect to God, and the rules and notions of good and evil; so the dangerous aspect they have on peace and government doth speak the folly of them, and they will be sufficiently in this particular confuted by asserting the divine original of sovereignty."—Falkner, *Christian Loyalty*, 409.

" I consent with him about the rights of exercising government, but I cannot agree to his means of acquiring it. It may seem strange I should praise his building, and yet mislike his foundation, but so it is, his *Jus naturae* and his *regnum institutivum* will not down with me; they appear full of contradiction and impossibilities."—Filmer, *Observations touching the original of government*, Preface.

8. *The patriarchal theory of kingship based on a belief in the state of nature and in Scripture as the only authentic testimony for it.   Natural rights are Divine rights.*

The original state of nature shewed to be a state of government and subjection not of independency.—Leslie, *The Rehearsal*, No. 55.

" The first state of nature to which all our whigs do refer, makes clearly against them, and is wholly on your side, who plead for government and the divine institution of it; against that original independent state of nature, which the whigs do suppose, but can never prove, unless they can find some other original of mankind than the holy Scriptures have told us."—*Ibid.* No. 56.

"If being born under Laws and a government whose legislative has an absolute despotic and unaccountable power over our very lives as well as our estates without staying to ask our consent, if this is to be free born, then all the world are so and ever have been so since Adam: otherwise not one, unless a King be born after his father is dead."—Leslie, *The New Association*, Part I. 15.

" ' Supposing therefore that Adam was universal

monarch or civil governor over the whole race of
mankind, during his long life this will not prove he
had a Divine right to be so?' Will it not? Then I
am very sure no after-King can claim it. If Adam had
no Divine Right, what right had he?"—Leslie, *The
Finishing Stroke*, 18.

"I go upon fact plainly recorded in Scripture."—
Ibid. 38.

"The Rehearsal had blamed those who went to
heathen authors for the original of government, because
none of their histories reached so high, and they knew
not how the world or mankind begun.......The only and
the certain account of it,......is to be found in the Holy
Scriptures."—*The Finishing Stroke*, 89.

"The Rehearsal places the original of government in
the positive institution of God, though at the same time
he shews it to be consequential, and most agreeable to
the frame of our nature, as being all deduced from
one common father. Which patriarchal or fatherly
authority is not only founded in Nature, but most
expressly and originally in the first institution of
government placed by God in Adam."—Leslie, *A Battle
Royal*, 128.

"A family is a little kingdom, but a kingdom is
nothing but a great family. Therefore such a state of
mankind, where all are upon the level and the consent
of every individual made necessary to the erection of
government, as Locke and others suppose it, because that
every man is freeborn and that no man's life and liberty or
property can be disposed of but by his own consent, I say
such a state cannot be called the state of nature because
nature implies fathers and mothers; it may be called a
state of mankind, but not of such men as we are, but of
a shower of men rained down from the clouds or new

created in multitudes, like the beasts, fish, and fowl at the beginning and no one dependent upon the other. So that even the Hottentot cannot represent this state, which yet is necessary to make the people the original of government."—Leslie, *A Battle Royal*, 128.

"But to them that believe the truth revealed in Holy Scripture, 'tis strange they should make question about it, seeing the world began in one man, that lived nigh one thousand years, at puberty the first hour; so that he could not have a less monarchy than any now extant in the world considering the vast increase there may be from one man and woman in a perfect state of health examined by the surest rules of progression. Against him should anyone in the world rise up, it had been rebellion and parricide. Nothing but the authority of God would justify the suspension of obedience to him the natural father of the world."—Leslie, *Obedience to Civil Government clearly stated*, 14.

The divergence between Leslie and the French School is shewn in the different views taken of Nimrod. To the French school he is the founder of monarchy, to Leslie he is the first instance of a successful usurper.

"If it [Self preservation] were a natural law, it would be a sin to resign it over to any......Self Preservation is only an instinct."—*Ibid.* 72.

9. *Gulf between Adamic society and modern times bridged by theory of prescriptive right.*

"Possession gives right, tho' wrongfully come by,...... [if] there is none who claims a better right than the possessor."—Leslie, *The Sham Sermon Dissected*, 2.

10. *Question of source of Law. There must be a supreme lawgiver. A sovereign needful to invest laws with binding authority.*

"Laws must be made by Kings. Therefore Kings must be before Laws."—Leslie, *Cassandra*, 22.

"Kings were kings before there were Laws......The King's Power is antecedent to Law which hath its force from him."—*The Apostate Protestant*, 41.

"He gives the prince no right but what is vested in him by law. Tho' his right is prior to the law, for he gives sanction to the law, and who gave him the right to do that? And here we are enjoined to give the prince no more than what is vested in him by law. Then he can no more give sanction to any law; unless we can find a law before there was any King, to make that King, and give him a right to give sanction to laws for the future."—Leslie, *The Sham Sermon Dissected*, 5.

"This manifests the fundamental error in politics, of those persons who make laws to have a priority, before Kings and governors; as if the laws made Kings and magistrates, when in truth God and nature vested primogeniture with the right of Kings and magistrates; and they made the first laws."—Nalson, *Common Interest of King and People*, 13.

"There can be no laws, till there be some frame of government, to establish and enact such laws; nor can anything have the force or power of a law, or oblige men to obedience, unless it does proceed from a person or persons, as have a right to command it, and authority to punish the disobedience or neglect of those who ought to be subject to it."—*Ibid.* 14.

"[The common law] follows in time after government, but cannot go before it, and be the rule to government by any original or radical constitution."—Filmer, *Anarchy of a Limited and Mixed Monarchy*, 267.

11. *There must be in every state a sovereign, not bound by positive law.*

"There must be a *dernier ressort* or there can be
no government. And where there is in an assembly
that assembly is one body, as one person."—Leslie,
Cassandra, 23.

"*Hoadly.* We are free because the government
cannot hang us on what they please but they are
bounded by law, and we must have a fair trial, and by
our peers too.

Hottentot. So you are free, because you are hanged
by a jury! But what think you of an Act of Attainder,
which can hang without any trial or giving you any
reason for it?

Hoad. This is part of our constitution, that the
Parliament should have such a power in extraordinary
case.

Hott. Yet you are free! And these cases happen,
as oft as the Parliament pleases. They are not tied to
any rule, but may make use of this power, whenever it
comes into their heads.

Hoad. Well, but the King cannot hang us at his
pleasure.

Hott. That is, you are not at the mercy of one man,
but of five hundred. O delicate freedom."—Leslie,
A Battle Royal, 142.

"After laws and society come in, all under it are
born slaves, that is under the absolute dominion of what
you call the legislature in every society. And whether
that be in the hands of one or more it is all the same
as to the destruction of liberty. For what is it to me,
whether I am hanged by the command of one or of five
hundred?"—*Ibid.* 159.

"Every government has absolute power over the
lives, as well as estates of all their subjects without
asking their leave or making any contract with them.

They are born in subjection, without conditions."—Leslie, *The Best Answer that ever was made,* 8.

"Without a last resort there can be no government. And if this be in the people, still there is no government. And if you stop short of all the people, then wherever it rests, there is 'absolute unaccountable' &c."—*Ibid.* 15.

"These men have strange notions of monarchy, and of absolute government, which, as I have often said, is the same in all sorts of governments whatsoever. All the difference is in whom this absolute power shall be placed, whether in one, in a few, or in many?"—Leslie, *The Rehearsal,* no. 59.

"All governments in the world must be arbitrary, in some hands or other; for there must be a last resort in every government, and that must be arbitrary and unaccountable, as having no superior upon earth."—*Ibid.* no. 36.

"If any man can find us out such a kind of government, wherein the supreme power can be, without being freed from human laws, they should first teach us that......a legislative power cannot be without being absolved from human laws."—Filmer, *Observations upon Mr Milton against Salmasius.*

"*A necessity to grant impunity to some in all governments to avoid confusion.*"—Dudley Diggs, *Unlawfulness of Subjects,* 43.

"If, as Mr Locke says, and says he has proved it, *No man can subject himself to the arbitrary power of another,* no man can subject himself to any government of what sort or size soever. Nor can there be such a thing as government kept up in the world."—Leslie, *The Rehearsal,* no. 38.

"In all kingdoms or commonwealths in the world, whether the prince be the supreme father of the people

or but the true heir of such a father, or whether he
come to the crown by usurpation, or by election of the
nobles or of the people, or by any other way whatsoever; or whether some few or a multitude govern the
Commonwealth; yet still the authority that is in any one
or in many or in all these is the only right and natural
authority of a supreme father."—Filmer, *Patriarcha*, I.
§ 10.

"The true debate amongst men is not whether
they shall admit of bonds......but who shall impose
them; the question is not *an servirent, sed an uni vel
pluribus*; it is commonly called liberty, to serve more
masters."—Dudley Diggs, *Unlawfulness of Subjects taking
up Arms*, 29.

12. *Sovereignty indivisible. Anarchy of a mixed
monarchy.*

"They know very well that there can be no sharing
of power, it must be one and entire; and the contest
for it is anarchy and confusion."—Leslie, *The New
Association*, Part II. 11.

"All power is one indivisible whether in the hands
of one or many."—*Cassandra*, 23.

"He lays his stress upon a constitution like ours.
And as he has dressed our constitution, we may well say
there is not a constitution like ours upon the face of the
earth. He has made it up of coordinate powers, all
opposition, nonsense, and contradiction."—Leslie, *The
Sham Sermon Dissected*, 5.

"It doth not follow, that the form of government is,
or can be in its own nature ill, because the governor
is so; it is anarchy, or want of government that can
totally destroy a nation."—Filmer, *Observations upon
Mr Milton against Salmasius*, 194.

"This mixed monarchy, just like the limited, ends in confusion and destruction of all government."— Filmer, *Anarchy of a Mixed and Limited Monarchy*, 272.

" There cannot be such a thing as *mixtum imperium* ......because if there are divers supreme powers it is no longer one state. If the supreme power be but one,......this must be placed either in one man,...... or in some nobles......or if the civil constitution of a state directs us to appeal to the people, this is an absolute and true democracy."—Dudley Diggs, *Unlawfulness*, 77.

" I have shewn before that a mixed monarchy is a contradiction."—*Ibid*. 168.

13. *Theory of Divine Right a defence of government against anarchy, far more than an apology for monarchy.*

"The endeavouring to settle sure and lasting foundations of government in opposition to these popular no principles, of sedition and eternal confusion, is all the reason I know that has stirred up the wrath of these orators of the populace."—Leslie, *Cassandra*, I. 41.

"[Government] in the largest sense is a communion of superiors and inferiors united for the safety of the whole; to disunite them is overturning it."—Leslie, *Obedience to Civil Government clearly stated*, 8.

"The reasons against Kings are as strong against all powers, for men of any titles are subject to err, and numbers more than fewer."—*Ibid*. 63.

"This doctrine may disturb the present, and threaten all future governors and governments whatsoever."— *Ibid*. 64.

" All the arguments used to justify self preservation, are grounded only on supposition that men may be wronged or oppressed by God's magistrates or rulers ; and therefore conclude as well against all civil government, as against the magistrate in being."—*Ibid.* 90.

"If the last resort be in the people, there is no end of controversy at all, but endless and unremediable confusion."—Leslie, *The Best Answer*, 14.

"It is unlawful to resist him or them in whom the supreme authority (that is all the legal power of the kingdom) is placed, and no dispensation......can excuse such resistance from the sin of rebellion. Upon this pillar not only monarchy stands firm, but all other governments are equally supported."—Dudley Diggs, *Unlawfulness of Subjects*, 10.

"*Liberty to resist those in whom the law places* jus gladii, *the right of the sword, destructive to the very nature of government.*"—*Ibid.* 8.

"This argument [of equality] doth not conclude for one form above another but equally destroys all."—*Ibid.* 29.

"*Hoadly.* He is ever representing me as maintaining such principles as are inconsistent with the safety of all government."—Leslie, *Best of All*, 8.

"Obedience is due to commonwealths by their subjects, even for conscience' sake, where the princes from whom they have revolted have given up their claim."—*Ibid.* 27.

"The power of the people which you set up is equally destructive of commonwealths as of monarchies. ......And with that it is impossible for any government to subsist."—*Ibid.* 30.

"I was the more willing to make this observation, that when I speak of sovereign princes I may not be maliciously traduced as if I spoke of them exclusively and not of other sovereigns, as if monarchy were of sole. Divine

right. For want of this distinction other writers have
had this invidious imputation laid upon them; but this
reason of not resisting the sovereign, because he is God's
vicegerent and only subject to Him, is a common reason
of passive obedience to all sovereigns, as well as unto
Kings, and unto Kings, as well as unto any other
sovereigns."—Hickes, *Jovian*, 240.

14. *Necessity of Divine institution for government.*

"Now I say that none has or can have any power
or authority, but what is given him by some other,
except God alone, who is the sole fountain of all power
and authority on earth as well as in heaven. And
therefore that God not having given man power over
his own life, nor in his natural state over the life of any
other man; consequently the power of life and death
(which is necessary in all government) could never have
come from the gift or grant of the people in their
natural state. But that the positive institution of God
is necessary to found government, and invest magistrates
with the power of life and death. And that without
this, no obligation of conscience can be laid upon any
man to submit to any government whatsoever."—Leslie,
The Best Answer, 9.

"I have you consider that there is no authority
but what is derived from God. It would be to set up
another God to suppose any other or independent authority."—*Ibid.* 18.

"What man is he who can by his own natural
authority bind the conscience of another? That would
be far more than the power of life, liberty, or property.
Therefore they saw the necessity of a divine original of
government."—Leslie, *The Rehearsal*, no. 37.

"*R.* Whatever founds government must be superior

to it, and above it. Government must derive its original and whole authority from it, and must be accountable to it, and dissolvable by it, at its pleasure whenever it thinks fit.

" Now human cannot be superior to human, therefore government among men cannot be derived from mere human authority. This is so very obvious that all governments whatever and of whatever sort, and among all nations and religions, do pretend to a divine right.......On all hands it is confessed that no government can stand without a divine original right, and authority ; for what else can give one man power over another, over his life, liberty, and property ?"— *Ibid.*, no. 53.

15. *The views of Hobbes on Passive Obedience.*

" Having thus shewn what is necessary to salvation, it is not hard to reconcile our obedience to God, with our obedience to the civil sovereign ; who is either Christian or infidel. If he be a Christian, he alloweth the belief of this article, that Jesus is the Christ ; and of all the articles that are contained in or are by evident consequence deduced from it : which is all the faith necessary to salvation. And because he is a sovereign, he requireth obedience to all his own, that is to all the civil, laws ; in which also are contained all the laws of nature, that is all the laws of God ; for besides the laws of nature and the laws of the Church, which are part of the civil law (for the Church that can make laws is the Commonwealth), there can be no other laws Divine. Whosoever therefore obeyeth his Christian sovereign, is not thereby hindered, neither from believing nor from obeying God. But suppose that a Christian King should from this foundation *Jesus is the Christ* draw some false consequences, that is to say make some superstructions of hay, or stubble, and command the teaching of the same; yet seeing S. Paul says, he shall be saved; much more shall he be saved, that teacheth them by his command and much more yet, he that teaches not, but only believes his lawful teacher. And in case a subject be forbidden by the civil sovereign to profess some of those his opinions, upon what just ground can he disobey? Christian Kings may err in deducing a consequence, but who shall judge? Shall a private man judge, when the question is of his own obedience? Or shall any man judge, but he that is appointed thereto by the Church, that is by the civil sovereign that representeth it? Or if the Pope or an Apostle judge, may he not err in deducing of a consequence? Did not one of the two, S. Peter or S. Paul, err in superstructure, when S. Paul withstood S. Peter to his face? There can therefore be no contradiction between the laws of God, and the laws of a Christian commonwealth.

"And when the civil sovereign is an infidel, every one of his own subjects that resisteth him sinneth against the laws of God (for such are the laws of nature), and rejecteth the counsel of the Apostles, that admonisheth all Christians to obey their princes, and all children and servants to obey their parents, and masters, in all things. And for their faith it is internal, and invisible; *they have the licence that Naaman had, and need not put themselves into danger for it.* But if they do, they ought to expect their reward in heaven, and not complain of their lawful sovereign, much less make war upon him. For he that is not glad of any just occasion of martyrdom, has not the faith he professeth, but pretends it only to set some colour upon his own contumacy." —*Leviathan,* III. 43.

"Whatsoever a subject, as Naaman was, is compelled to do in obedience to his sovereign, and doth it not in order to his own mind, but in order to the laws of his country, that action is not his but his sovereign's, nor is it he that in this case denieth Christ before men, but his governor and the law of his country."—*Ibid.* 42.

16.   *The views of Dudley Diggs on the Patriarchal Theory.*

"Though it be most true that paternal authority was regal, and therefore this of God's immediate constitution, and founded in nature, yet it is not much pertinent to the present decision, nor can it necessarily concern modern controversies between Rulers and people. Because it is most evident, no king at this day, (and much less other governors) holds his crown by that title, since several paternal powers in every State are given up, and united in one common father who cannot pretend a more immediate kindred to Adam, than all the rest of mankind." *The Unlawfulness of Subjects,* 16.

INDEX.

2

✗

CAMBRIDGE: PRINTED BY J. AND C. F. CLAY, AT THE UNIVERSITY PRESS.

CPSIA information can be obtained
at www.ICGtesting.com
Printed in the USA
BVHW081939220323
660941BV00004B/215